PHOENICIAN ANICONISM

Archaeology and Biblical Studies

Brian B. Schmidt, Editor

Number 21

PHOENICIAN ANICONISM IN ITS MEDITERRANEAN
AND ANCIENT NEAR EASTERN CONTEXTS

PHOENICIAN ANICONISM

IN ITS MEDITERRANEAN AND ANCIENT NEAR EASTERN CONTEXTS

by

Brian R. Doak

Atlanta, Georgia

SBL Press

PHOENICIAN ANICONISM IN ITS MEDITERRANEAN AND ANCIENT NEAR EASTERN CONTEXTS

Copyright © 2015 by SBL Press

All rights reserved. No part of this work may be reproduced or transmitted in any form or by any means, electronic or mechanical, including photocopying and recording, or by means of any information storage or retrieval system, except as may be expressly permitted by the 1976 Copyright Act or in writing from the publisher. Requests for permission should be addressed in writing to the Rights and Permissions Office, Society of Biblical Literature, 825 Houston Mill Road, Atlanta, GA 30329 USA.

Library of Congress Cataloging-in-Publication Data

Doak, Brian R.
　Phoenician aniconism in its Mediterranean and ancient Near Eastern contexts / by Brian R. Doak.
　　pages cm. — (Archaeology and biblical studies ; Number 21)
　Includes bibliographical references and index.
　ISBN 978-0-88414-097-9 (pbk. : alk. paper) — ISBN 978-0-88414-098-6 (electronic book) — ISBN 978-0-88414-099-3 (hardcover : alk. paper)
　1. Phoenicians—Religion. 2. Iconoclasm. 3. Idols and images—Worship. I. Title.
　BL1660.D63 2015
　299'.26—dc23
                                2015025646

Printed on acid-free paper

sed nulla effigies simulacraue nota deorum
maiestate locum et sacro impleuere timore

But no statues or familiar images of the gods
filled the place with solemnity and sacred awe

—Silius Italicus, *Punica* 3.30–31

Contents

List of Figures	ix
Acknowledgements	xv
Abbreviations	xvii
1. The Problem	1
2. No Statues or Familiar Images?	7
2.1. Who Were the Phoenicians?	8
2.2. Phoenician Religion	16
3. Aniconism in Theoretical and Art-Historical Perspective	21
3.1. What is an "Icon"?	22
3.2. Defining the Aniconic	27
3.3. The Critics and Proponents of Aniconism	36
4. Phoenician Iconism	41
4.1. The Phoenician Artistic Context	44
4.2. Texts Referring to Phoenician Divine Images	46
4.3. Overview of Phoenician Anthropomorphic Iconography	46
4.4. Case Studies in Iconic Phoenician Divine Representation	52
4.5. A People without Pictorial Traditions?	66
5. Phoenician Aniconism	67
5.1. Retrospective	69
5.2. Textual Accounts of Aniconism by Greek and Roman Authors	73
5.3. Stelae, Pillars, Standing Stones, Betyls	78
5.4. Shrines with Aniconic Objects and Empty Shrines	101
5.5. Thrones with Aniconic Objects and Empty Thrones	109
5.6. Divine Symbols and Body Parts	115
5.7. Comparanda: Aniconism in Mesopotamia, Egypt, Israel, and Greece	119
5.8. Phoenician Aniconism—Why?	134
6. Conclusions	141
Bibliography	145
Subject Index	175
Ancient Sources	178
Modern Authors	180

List of Figures

All drawings except 2.1 by Nora Clair, modeled after the sources listed.

CHAPTER 2

2.1	Map of the Phoenician Mediterranean world	9
2.2	Examples of Phoenician pottery; decoration patterns for Phoenician strainer-spouted jugs and example of Iron Age flask from Sarepta (Anderson 1990, 38, fig. 2; 44, fig. 4)	11
2.3	Phoenician-style sphinx plaque; Nimrud; ninth century BCE (*DCPP*, pl. X.a; Winter 2010c, 219, fig. 8)	12
2.4	Silver bowl fragment from Amathus, Cyprus; eighth–seventh century BCE; d. 18.7 cm (http://www.britishmuseum.org; ANE 123053; Room 57–59: Ancient Levant)	12

CHAPTER 3

3.1	Cylinder seal from Girsu; third millennium BCE (Dick 2005, 54, fig. 3.3; Cornelius 1997, 32, fig. 6)	25
3.2	Votive stele with "bottle idol"; Motya (Sicily); sixth century BCE; h. 36 cm (Moscati 1988a, 648.381)	30
3.3	Ovoid "cippus"; Motya (Sicily); sixth century BCE; h. 24.2 cm (Falsone 1993, 271, fig. 2)	30
3.4	Stone figure; Carthage (Bénichou-Safar 2004, pl. XLVII.5)	30
3.5	Geometrical carving on bone; Tharros (Sardinia); fifth–fourth century BCE; h. 5.4 cm (Uberti 1988, 419)	36

CHAPTER 4

4.1	Silver and gold bowl from Kourion (Cyprus); d. 16.8 cm (Markoe 1985, Cy8, 256–59; Aruz, Graff, and Rakic 2014, 159–60)	44
4.2	Terracotta shrine-stele with figure; Monte Sirai (Sardinia); fourth–third century BCE; h. 55.5 cm (Moscati 1988a, 319)	49
4.3	Terracotta shrine with figure atop lions; Sidon; fifth century BCE; h. 6 cm (Bisi 1988, 353; Gubel et al. 1986, 122)	49
4.4	Royal figure on scarab; green jasper; Persian period; Tharros (Sardinia) (Boardman 2003, pl. 16, 16.6)	50

4.5 Horus on lotus flower from Nimrud; ivory; eighth century BCE; h. 5.6 cm (Uberti 1988, 413; Gubel et al. 1986, 232) 50
4.6 Coin with figure riding winged horse, waves, and dolphin; Tyre; fourth century BCE (Elayi and Elayi 2009, pl. 34, O43, 1061) 50
4.7 Bar Hadad stele with Melqart; ninth century BCE (Dunand 1939, pl. XIII; *DCPP* 286, fig. 223; Bonnet 2007 [*IDD* illustration]) 53
4.8 The "Amrit Stele"; Tell Kazel; fifth century BCE; h. 1.78 m (Markoe 2000, 152; Gubel et al. 2002, 51) 53
4.9 Male figures on throne with incense altar; green jasper seals; sixth–fourth century BCE (Boardman 2003, 62–63, pls. 16–17; L–R 17.30, 17.7. 17.1, 17.2) 56
4.10 Yehawmilk stele with king and deity (text omitted from lower register); Byblos; h. 1.12 m (http://www.louvre.fr/en/oeuvre-notices/yehawmilk-stele; Gubel et al. 2002, 65–66) 58
4.11 Enthroned female figure; terracotta; Puig des Molins (Ibiza); fifth–fourth century BCE; h. 22 cm (Almagro Gorbea 1980, lam. XCVI, 1; Moscati 1988a, 720.800) 60
4.12 Enthroned female figure; terracotta; Es Culleram (Ibiza); third century BCE; approx. h. 10 cm (Moscati 1988a, 720.802) 60
4.13 Enthroned female figure; terracotta; Puig des Molins (Ibiza); fourth century BCE; h. 13 cm (Almagro Gorbea 1980, lam. LXXXVII, 1; Moscati 1988a, 720.801) 61
4.14 Seated figure on sphinx throne; partially reconstructed; Soluntum, Sicily; sixth–fourth century BCE (photo in Chiarenza 2013, 951, fig. 1; drawing in Gubel 1987, pl. IX.26) 62
4.15 Variety of the Tanit figure from Carthaginian stelae (Bisi 1967, fig. 7) 63
4.16 Stele with Tanit figure, hand, and caduceus; Carthage; second century BCE; h. 26.5 cm (Moscati 1988a, 615.186) 64
4.17 Stele with pillars, crescent-disc, and Tanit figure; Sousse/Hadrumetum; fourth century BCE (Bisi 1967, Tav XXII.1) 64
4.18 Stele with figures; Tyre cemetery; ninth–seventh century BCE (Aubet 2004, 385 fig. 254) 65
4.19 Stele with figures; Tyre cemetery; ninth–seventh century BCE (Aubet 2004, 386 fig. 255) 65

CHAPTER 5

5.1 Ambrosial rocks and stelae on Tyrian coins (Hill 1910, pl. 31, nos. 14–15; Bonnet 1988, fig. 2, a–c) 74
5.2 Coin depicting Paphian cone; Cyprus; second–third century CE (photo in P. Stewart 2008, fig. 2; illustration in Perrot and Chipiez 1885, 123, fig. 58) 77

5.3	Coin depicting cultic stone of Elagabalus in procession (reverse); minted at Antioch; 218–219 CE (Bardill 2012, 60, fig. 48; Abdy 2012, 509, fig. 27.23)	77
5.4	Roman bronze coin; Emesa shrine with stone of Elagabalus; ca. 215 CE (P. Stewart 2008, 299, fig. 1)	77
5.5	Stele from Ugarit with astral symbolism; Late Bronze Age; h. approx. 40 cm (Yon 1991, 330, 10.a; Bisi 1967, Tav. III, 1)	80
5.6	Hittite standing stone from Karahöyük (central Turkey); thirteenth century BCE (Collins 2005, 27, fig. 2.8)	81
5.7	Unmarked stele; Tyre al-Bass cemetery; eleventh–sixth century BCE (Sader 2005, 72, fig. 61, stele 49)	85
5.8	Inscribed stele from Tyre al-Bass cemetery; ninth–eighth century BCE (Sader 2005, 74, fig. 64, stele 51)	85
5.9	Stele with anthropomorphic head; Beirut National Museum (unclear location of find); tenth–sixth century BCE (Sader 2005, 33, fig. 12 stele 9)	87
5.10	Stele with incised object; seventh century BCE; inscribed with word *grgš* (Sader 2005, fig. 21 stele 15)	87
5.11	Stele with incised object; tenth–sixth century BCE (Sader 2005, fig. 31, stele 24)	87
5.12	Stelae from Nora and Carthage; Punic (Sader 2005, fig. 22; Bisi 1967, LII.2, XII.1)	87
5.13	Stele with incised object; tenth–sixth century BCE (Sader 2005, fig. 34, stele 27)	89
5.14	Stele with lotus bud (?); tenth–sixth century BCE (Sader 2005, fig. 15, stele 11)	89
5.15	Stele with cross, discs, and ankh; tenth–sixth century BCE (Sader 2005, fig. 33, stele 26)	89
5.16	Stele with "betyl" from Carthage; sixth century BCE; h. 50 cm (Moscati 1988a, 614.177)	90
5.17	Stele with incised twin "betyls"; Carthage; sixth century BCE; h. 55.5 cm (Moscati 1988a, 614.178)	90
5.18	Series of ovoid stones; Carthage (Bénichou-Safar 2004, pl. XVII, 1–3)	90
5.19	Two L-shaped thrones; Carthage (Bénichou-Safar 2004, pl. LII, 1–2)	91
5.20	Tiered throne; Carthage (Bénichou-Safar 2004, pl. LII, 9)	91
5.21	Bottle figure in shrine; Carthage (Bénichou-Safar 2004, pl. L, 6)	91
5.22	Razor from Carthage with standing figure; Punic; scarab from Cyprus with standing figure (both in Acquaro 1971, Tav. XXVIII [photo], fig. 40 [drawing]; fig. 75.1 [scarab])	93
5.23	Single "betyl" stele; Motya; sixth–fifth century BCE; h. 47.5 cm (Moscati 1988a, 648.380)	94

5.24	Twin "betyl" stele; Persian period; Burj esh-Shemali (Sader 2005, 77, fig. 67 stele 54)	94
5.25	Three "betyl" stele; Nora; sixth–fourth century BCE; h. 74.4 cm (Moscati 1988a, 670.509)	94
5.26	Bottle figure stele fragment; Akhziv (Patrich 1990, 176, ill. 59a; Bisi 1967, fig. 14)	96
5.27	Bottle figure stele; Nora; sixth–fourth century BCE; h. 84.3 cm (Moscati 1988d, 318)	96
5.28	Bottle figure stele; Nora; sixth–fourth century BCE; h. 79.7 cm (Moscati 1988a, 670.510)	96
5.29	Stelae with figures; Motya; sixth–fourth century BCE (Moscati 1988a, 648.380, 382, 381, 383, 384)	98
5.30	Apulian bell-krater; youth approaching Nike at altar and two youths by the stele of Nike; 380–370 BCE (Gaifman 2012, 252–53, figs. 6.7–8, faces a–b)	99
5.31	Terracotta model shrine; Akhziv; ca. seventh century BCE (Dayagi-Mendels 2002, 161, fig. 7.25)	104
5.32	Model shrine; Tyre al-Bass cemetery; seventh century BCE; h. 16.5 cm (Metzger 2004, 421, figs. 280–81)	104
5.33	Model shrine; Amathus (Cyprus); sixth century BCE (Karageorghis 2000, 60, fig. 5; Metzger 2004, 429, fig. 286.b)	106
5.34	Model shrine; Amathus (Cyprus); sixth century BCE (Karageorghis 2000, 61–62, figs. 6–7)	106
5.35	Model shrine; Nicosia (Cyprus); sixth century BCE; h. 11.5 cm (photograph in Bisi 1988, 353; drawing in Metzger 2004, 429, fig. 286.c)	106
5.36	Empty model shrine; Mount Nebo region (Jordan); ca. 900 BCE (drawing in Metzger 2004, 427, fig. 285a and Keel and Uehlinger 1998, 161, ill. 188b; photo in Brentschneider 1991a, Taf. 91, Abb. 80a–b)	107
5.37	Stele with empty niche; Tyre al-Bass cemetery; tenth–seventh century BCE; approx. h. 50 cm, w. 40 cm (Sader 2005, 64, Stele 43, fig. 50)	107
5.38	Inscribed L-shaped stele; Tyre; eighth–seventh century BCE; inscription: *grḥmn* (Sader 2005, 37, fig. 17, stele 12)	110
5.39	Astarte throne in Eshmun temple complex; Sidon; ca. fourth century BCE (Khalifeh 1997, fig. 2; Markoe 2000, 126, fig. 42)	110
5.40	Stele-shrine with sphinx throne; probably from Sidon; ninth–fifth century BCE (Sader 2005, 77, fig. 68 stele 55; Gubel 1987, pl. III)	111
5.41	Stele-shrine with throne; probably from Sidon; sixth–fifth century BCE (Sader 2005, 78, fig. 69a stele 56; Gubel 1987, pl. II)	111

5.42	Series of thrones from the Carthage tophet; ca. sixth century BCE (from left to right, Bisi 1967, Tav. V.1, XIII.1, X.2, V.2)	113
5.43	Throne with ovoid object; Sidon; second–first century BCE (?); h. 6–7 cm (photo in Seyrig 1959, pl. X.3,5; illustration in Falsone 1993, 275, fig. 6a)	114
5.44	Detail of Kulamuwa inscription; king pointing to divine symbols; Zinjirli; ninth century BCE (Ornan 2005b, 275 fig. 181)	116
5.45	Symbols on Carthaginian Punic tophet stelae (Brown 1991, 260, 18.229; 258, 16.103; 281, 39.568; 264, 22.289; 276, 34.521)	117
5.46	Reverse of two Sidonian coins with "car of Astarte" (Hill 1910, pl. 25 no. 4; pl. 24, no. 8)	118
5.47	Clay shrine plaque with figure; Sidon (Soyez 1972, pl. II.7; Sader 2005, 125 fig. 108)	118
5.48	Detail of stone tablet of Nabu-apla-iddina (text removed); ninth century BCE (Woods 2004, 26, fig. 1)	122
5.49	*Kudurru* of Meli-shipak; recovered at Susa; twelfth century BCE (photo in Seidl 1989, Taf. 15.a; illustration in Ornan 1995, 49, fig. 25)	123
5.50	Object from Karnak (left) and "omphalos" figure from Napata (Nubia) (right); Egypt; Persian or Ptolemaic period (?) (Mettinger 1995, 53, figs. 2.12–13)	125
5.51	Model shrine from Kh. Qeiyafa; tenth century BCE; h. 35 cm (Garfinkel and Mumcuoglu 2013, 140–41, figs. 4–6)	130
5.52	Taanach shrine; tenth century BCE; h. 21.2 cm (illustration in Keel and Uehlinger 1998, 159, ill. 184; photo in Hestrin 1987, 62–63, figs. 1–2 and Taylor 1993, pl. 1a–d)	131
5.53	Double rock-cut thrones of Zeus and Hekate; Chalke (near Rhodes); fourth–first century BCE (Gaifman 2012, 164, fig. 4.17)	134

Acknowledgments

This project began in a doctoral seminar on the Phoenicians in the spring of 2007 at Harvard University, taught by Peter Machinist and Lawrence Stager, and I have continued refining it as a labor of love and devotion since that time. Like almost all American scholars who study the Phoenicians, my primary training and published work has been concerned with the history and literature of ancient Israel, and yet I have maintained the study of ancient Near Eastern iconography and Phoenician iconography within that corpus as a secondary field. Thus I humbly offer the present book for the consideration of those interested in the iconography of religion in the ancient Near Eastern and Mediterranean worlds and to the lively and international group of Phoenician scholars, hoping to make a small contribution to the field of Phoenician divine representation and to the question of aniconism as an iconographic phenomenon more broadly.

I owe a debt of gratitude to the American Schools of Oriental Research, in whose meetings I presented nascent ideas from this book twice (in 2007 and 2012), and to the Dorot Foundation (in coordination with ASOR) for awarding an essay-length version of this project the Aviram Prize in archaeology in 2012. I am grateful to the Society of Biblical Literature's Ancient Near Eastern Iconography and the Bible unit as well as the Israelite Religion in its West Asian Environment unit, where I also presented and received feedback on ideas from this project in 2012, 2013, and 2015. Tammi Schneider (Claremont), then editor of the Society of Biblical Literature's Archaeology and Bible series, encouraged me to submit a proposal for the project in 2012, and I am thankful for her support. Along with his sharp editorial eye for style, grammar, and things of that nature, the current series editor, Brian B. Schmidt (University of Michigan), provided many helpful comments that made my argument much better in key places. Billie Jean Collins and Nicole Tilford of SBL Press were extremely helpful through their editing and communication, and I am grateful to both of them. The interlibrary loan staff at the Murdoch Learning and Resource Center at George Fox University, particularly Lauri Lieggi and Traci Porter, processed many requests for me from the summer of 2014 to the spring of 2015, always bearing with me in my search for hard-to-locate sources. Though she was drafted into the project at a relatively late stage, a local artist and friend, Nora Clair, produced an excellent set of illustrations and was heroic in her resolve to finish the project on time. My undergraduate teaching and research assistant (now a graduate student at Princeton Theological Seminary),

Brooke Greenburg, helped me find sources and organize the argument in various places.

My local scholarly writing group, composed of Paul Anderson, Joseph Clair, and Roger Nam (all here at George Fox University, with Nam at a distance on sabbatical in South Korea), read the entire manuscript in pieces as I wrote it and offered many excellent suggestions on the broadest level of ideas—in particular, Clair's suggestions about the larger implications of aniconism for cultural history reinvigorated me to continue with the project when my progress had stalled. Several others helped make this book far better than it would have been otherwise: Erin Darby (University of Tennessee), the first to read the manuscript in its entirety, offered many very perceptive comments, and her interest in the project several years ago inspired me to continue with it. Carolina López-Ruiz (Ohio State University) provided incisive feedback, as she has for me in the past, from her expert position in Greek classics and the Mediterranean Phoenician world. Irene Winter (Harvard University) gave me ideas for bibliography on the Mesopotamian materials that I would have missed otherwise, and I benefited from comments and encouragement from Cory Crawford (Ohio University). On two needed occasions, Tryggve Mettinger (Lund University) provided criticism and encouragement that helped me to believe this odd topic was worth pursuing. It should go without saying that none of the above-mentioned individuals are responsible for my own errors in the book, but I certainly would like to hold them responsible for things the reader finds helpful and accurate.

This book is dedicated to three of my teachers, on their recent or upcoming retirements:

My doctoral advisor, Peter Machinist (Harvard University)
James Moyer (Missouri State University)
Lawrence Stager (Harvard University)

Abbreviations

AASOR	Annual of the American Schools of Oriental Research
ASOR	American Schools of Oriental Research
ABD	Anchor Bible Dictionary. Edited by David Noel Freedman. 6 vols. New York: Doubleday, 1992
AH	De l'archéologie à l'histoire
AHL	Archaeology and History in Lebanon
AJ	Art Journal
AJBA	Australian Journal of Biblical Archaeology
AK	Antike Kunst
AN	Abr-Nahrain
ANESS	Ancient Near Eastern Studies Supplement
ANET	Ancient Near Eastern Texts Relating to the Old Testament. Edited by James B. Pritchard. 3rd ed. Princeton: Princeton University Press, 1969
Ant. Jud.	Josephus, Antiquitates Judaicae (Jewish Antiquities). Translated by Henry St. Joseph Thackeray et al. 9 vols. LCL. Cambridge: Harvard University Press, 1930–1965
AOAT	Alter Orient und Altes Testament
ASMA	Aarhus Studies in Mediterranean Antiquity
ASSM	Accordia Specialist Studies on the Mediterranean
AUSS	Andrews University Seminary Studies
AWE	Ancient West and East
BA	The Biblical Archaeologist
BAAL	Bulletin d'Archéologie et d'Architecture Libanaises
BAALHS	Bulletin d'archéologie et d'architecture libanaises, hors-série
BAI	Bulletin of the Asia Institute
BAR	Biblical Archaeology Review
BARIS	British Archaeology Review International Series
BASOR	Bulletin of the American Schools of Oriental Research
BBET	Beiträge zur biblischen Exegese und Theologie
BIS	Biblical Interpretation Series

BJS	Brown Judaic Studies
BMB	*Bulletin du Musée de Beyrouth*
BRA	Beiträge zur Religionsgeschichte des Altertums
BSRS	British School at Rome Studies
BZAW	Beihefte zur Zeitschrift für die alttestamentliche Wissenschaft
CAD	*The Assyrian Dictionary of the Oriental Institute of the University of Chicago*. Chicago: The Oriental Institute of the University of Chicago, 1956–2006
CAM	Cuadernos de Arqueología Mediterránea
CANE	*Civilizations of the Ancient Near East*. Edited by Jack M. Sasson. 4 vols. New York, 1995. Repr. in 2 vols. Peabody, MA: Hendrickson, 2006
CBOTS	Coniectanea Biblica Old Testament Series
CBQMS	Catholic Biblical Quarterly Monograph Series
CEFR	Collection de l'école française de Rome
CHANE	Culture and History of the Ancient Near East
CIDRANE	*Cult Image and Divine Representation in the Ancient Near East*. Edited by Neal H. Walls. Boston: ASOR, 2005
CMAO	*Contributi e Materiali di Archeologia Orientale*
COS	*The Context of Scripture*. Edited by William W. Hallo. 3 vols. Leiden: Brill, 1997–2002
CRJ	*Classical Receptions Journal*
CS	Classical Studies
CSF	Collezione di Studi Fenici
CTA	*Corpus des tablettes en cunéiformes alphabétiques découvertes à Ras Shamra-Ugarit de 1929 à 1939*. Edited by Andrée Herdner. Paris: Geuthner, 1963
DCPP	*Dictionnaire de la Civilisation Phénicienne et Punique*. Edited by E. Lipiński. Turnhout: Brepols, 1992
DDD	*Dictionary of Deities and Demons in the Bible*. Edited by Karel van der Toorn, Bob Becking, and Pieter W. van der Horst. Leiden: Brill, 1995
EBR	*Encyclopedia of the Bible and Its Reception*. Edited by Hans-Josef Klauck et al. Berlin: de Gruyter, 2009–
EC	Études chypriotes
EPAHA	Études de philology, d'archéologie et d'histoire anciennes
FAT	Forschungen zum Alten Testament
FRLANT	Forschungen zur Religion und Literatur des Alten und Neuen Testaments

GNES	Gorgias Near Eastern Studies
GRRS	Graeco-Roman Religion Series
GSSP	Geological Society Special Publication
HACL	History, Archaeology, and Culture of the Levant
HO	Handbuch der Orientalistik
HSM	Harvard Semitic Monographs
IAAR	Israel Antiquities Authority Reports
IDD	*Iconography of Deities and Demons in the Ancient Near East*. Edited by Christoph Uehlinger et al. OBO, Series Archaeologica. Forthcoming 2015. Electronic prepublication essays posted at http://www.religionswissenschaft.uzh.ch/idd/prepublication.php; dates cited for each author are dates on which the prepublication material was last edited.
IEJ	*Israel Exploration Journal*
IS	Ilex Series (Ilex Foundation)
ISACR	Interdisciplinary Studies in Ancient Culture and Religion
JAOS	*Journal of the American Oriental Society*
JBL	*Journal of Biblical Literature*
JCS	*Journal of Cuneiform Studies*
JMA	*Journal of Mediterranean Archaeology*
JMS	*Journal of Mediterranean Studies*
JNES	*Journal of Near Eastern Studies*
JRS	*Journal of Religion and Society* (Supplemental Series)
JRtSt	*Journal of Ritual Studies*
JSOTSup	Journal for the Old Testament Supplemental Series
KAI	*Kanaanäische und aramäische Inschriften*. Herbert Donner and Wolfgang Röllig. 2nd ed. Wiesbaden: Harrassowitz, 1966–1969. Updated vol. 1 published in 2002
Karth	*Karthago; Revue d'Archéologie Africaine*
LCL	Loeb Classical Library
LHBOTS	Library of Hebrew Bible / Old Testament Studies
LIMC	*Lexicon Iconographicum Mythologiae Classicae*. Edited by H. Christoph Ackerman and Jean-Robert Gisler. 8 vols. Zurich: Artemis, 1981–1997
MA	*Mediterraneo Antico*
MB	*Madrider Beiträge*. Deutsche Archäologisches Institut, Madrid
MS	Melammu Symposia
MUSJ	*Mélanges de l'Université Saint-Joseph*

NEA	*Near Eastern Archaeology*
OA	*Oriens Antiquus*
OAANE	*On Art in the Ancient Near East*. By I. J. Winter. 2 vols. CHANE 34.1. Leiden: Brill, 2010
OBO	Orbis Biblicus et Orientalis
Od.	Homer, *Odyssey*
OEANE	*The Oxford Encyclopedia of Archaeology in the Near East*. Edited by Eric M. Meyers. 5 vols. New York: Oxford University Press, 1997. Oxford Biblical Studies Online, http://www.oxfordbiblicalstudies.com
COIS	Chicago Oriental Institute Seminars
OLA	Orientalia Lovaniensia Analecta
PEQ	*Palestine Exploration Quarterly*
PULSEA	Publications de l'Université Libanaise, Section des Études Archéologiques
RGRW	Religions in the Graeco-Roman World
RHR	*Revue de l'Histoire des Religions*
RSF	*Revista di Studi Fenici*
RSO	Ras Shamra-Ougarit
SATI	The Stone Art Theory Institutes
SBL	Society of Biblical Literature
SBLABS	SBL Archaeology and Biblical Studies
SCL	Sather Classical Lectures
SEL	*Studi Epigrafici e Linguistici*
SJOT	*Scandinavian Journal of the Old Testament*
SM	Spal Monografías
SP	Studia Phoenicia
SP IV	*Studia Phoenica IV: Religio Phoenicia*. Edited by C. Bonnet, E. Lipiński, and P. Marchetti. Namur: Société des Études Classiques, 1986
SS	Studi Semitici
SuppTrans	Supplément à Transeuphratène
TA	*Tel Aviv*
TDOT	*Theological Dictionary of the Old Testament*. Edited by G. Johannes Botterweck and Helmer Ringgren. Translated by John T. Willis et al. 15 vols. Grand Rapids: Eerdmans, 1974–2006
TMAI	Trabajos del Museo Arqueológico de Ibiza
TT	Texts and Translations
UCOP	University of Cambridge Oriental Publications
UF	*Ugarit-Forschungen*
VO	*Vicino Oriente*

VTSup	Supplements to Vetus Testamentum
WAW	Writings from the Ancient World
WAWSup	Writings from the Ancient World Supplement
ZDPV	*Zeitschrift des Deutschen Palästina-Vereins*

1

The Problem

Divine images have long been a problem in the history of Western religious expression. Spanning many centuries, Christian authorities faced on two fronts the conundrum of which images to tolerate and which to destroy—in their clash with the polytheistic Greco-Roman and Near Eastern worlds within which the religion grew and flourished and also within Christendom, most famously in the medieval context of eighth-to-ninth-century CE Byzantine circles but also during the sixteenth-century Protestant Reformation. For emergent Islam, the strict prohibition against images of God or the prophet Mohammed—indeed, expanded to a de facto proscription of any human image or any animal in some streams of the tradition—also exerted powerful influence, as Jews, Christians, and Muslims struggled (and continue to struggle) to position themselves as true worshipers against any perceived turn toward idols. Without too much exaggeration, in fact, we might say that the problem of "idolatry" and all that it could imply is the central religious problem of the Jewish, Christian, and Islamic traditions broadly, and certainly it has been the most acute challenge at the intersection of iconography and divinity. Can God or the gods be visualized? How so? Anthropomorphically, as they are described in so many texts with a mouth, legs, hands, and eyes? What about colors? Or only as suggestive shapes or simply as nothing at all? Would an abstention from figural visualization be a more *advanced* form of spirituality? Or would that abstention signal the most *primitive* attitude, far behind on an evolutionary scale of religious development?

Such questions may seem anachronistic when applied to the ancient Mediterranean and Near Eastern worlds, where the general religious mood was straightforwardly polytheistic and divine images of many kinds abounded. Squarely within this context, though, in the Hebrew Bible, we read a potentially unexpected and sweeping notice posted at the beginning of the Ten Commandments (Exod 20:2–5a).

> I am YHWH your God, who brought you out from the land of Egypt, from the house of slavery. There shall not be any other gods before me, nor shall you make for yourself an idol [*pesel*], or any image [*tĕmûnâ*] that is in the heavens above or the earth below or

in the waters under the earth. You shall not bow down to them or worship them.¹

Explanations for this command are legion, usually focusing on the unique status of Israel's deity as one who defied the imagizing tendencies of the larger context of the ancient Near Eastern world. But, insofar as images are concerned, what was this "context," exactly, and was Israel truly alone in this severe stance against the idol?

In this book, I focus on one particular aspect of this iconographic context in Israel's Iron Age world—that of the many types of divine representations crafted by Israel's coastal neighbors, the Phoenicians. To be sure, the question of whether Phoenicians employed aniconic (as opposed to iconic) representational techniques has significance not only for the many poorly understood aspects of Phoenician religion generally but also for the question of whether aniconism can be considered a broader trend among the Semitic populations of the ancient Near East. As one might expect, past research on aniconic phenomena has often been motivated by a desire to understand the larger context of the Hebrew Bible's proscription of divine images. Does this most famous of image prohibitions cited above represent a kind of religious or intellectual parthenogenesis, or is it only one particularly vigorous form of a broader Iron Age West Semitic trend toward aniconic cultic expressions in which the Phoenicians also participated? Moreover, the very definition of "aniconism" itself is difficult and contested, and thus some of our effort here must go toward understanding what we mean when we discuss an "icon" or the avoidance of the icon.

The field of Phoenician studies has seen an explosion of publications in the past two decades, fueled by new archaeological work and the burgeoning interest of a distinctly international group of scholars exploring the effects and extent of Phoenician colonization in the Mediterranean. Previously, however, there have only been scattered and unsystematic attempts to understand whether or how Phoenicians may have employed aniconic representational strategies in their religious life. This book attempts to give a reasonably comprehensive and systematic assessment of what evidence we have—inclusive of both the material record and texts—for Phoenician aniconography. In brief, my argument is that the Phoenicians did participate in an iconographic program that moved toward divine symbols, abstract forms, and even purely aniconic expressions. This trend is not just late (during the Hellenistic period), but can be at least faintly traced much earlier into the Iron Age. The Phoenicians probably did not smash images like Christian iconoclasts, nor did they prohibit image production for ideological reasons in any text that we know of, but their artistic innovations and cultic practice in a variety of contexts moved the visual index of divine image-making in the Mediterranean and Near Eastern worlds toward increasingly abstract and nonanthropomorphic

---

1. Unless otherwise noted, all biblical translations are my own.

forms. On the other hand, some previous treatments of Phoenician iconography have inappropriately downplayed examples of native Phoenician anthropomorphic depiction, and a careful examination of what evidence we have shows hitherto unappreciated nuances of Phoenician divine imagery. As pioneering colonizers and traders, the Phoenicians exerted influence in a wide range of contexts, beginning in Egypt and the Near East and extending to Greece, Italy, and the far Western Mediterranean worlds of Iberia and Northwest Africa. This monograph is the first of its kind to explore the important question of Phoenician aniconism as a significant subject in its own right and attempts to elevate the complexity of Phoenician divine representation to its proper place alongside other iconographic movements in the ancient world.

As part of the Society of Biblical Literature's Archaeology and Bible series, this book is primarily directed to those interested in the ancient Near Eastern and Mediterranean contexts of the biblical image ban. As such, this study is intended for biblical scholars and archaeologists of Syria-Palestine studying the iconography of this region specifically as it relates to the question of the nature and extent of "aniconic" (e.g., nonfigural, nonanthropomorphic) imagery as a local and comparative phenomenon in the Levant. My hope is that a study like this one—which is synthetic and interpretive at broader levels than most stricter iconographic and archaeological studies—can serve as a bridge from the arcane, geographically segregated, and specialized world of Phoenician studies to the field of biblical studies, the archaeology of ancient Israel, and the study of iconography as it relates to the Hebrew Bible.

An outburst of work in biblical studies on textual aniconisms, on metaphor, and on the role of the "imageless image" in text as a reflection of cultic practice, as well as an archaeological focus on the lack of male divine images in ancient Israel, makes this a good time in the history of the question from a scholarly perspective to look sideways at one of Israel's neighbors; to be sure, the Bible ascribes an important role to the Phoenicians in cultic matters, that is, for the Solomonic temple. There are complex problems here, but there is also a nagging sense that this is the kind of detail that may be historically accurate. The particularly hybrid nature of Phoenician identity in the Mediterranean world requires comparisons on many fronts; the putative ancient Israelite prohibition of images has its own complications in the material record, in ancient texts, and in what has now become quite a bit of secondary literature on the topic, but Phoenician divine representation has been far less explored. Given the close geographical and historical proximity of Phoenicia and Israel and given their common background as heirs of "Canaanite" culture, the problem of divine representation shared by these two groups warrants careful scrutiny.

The Phoenician evidence is certainly rich and complex enough to be studied on its own terms, and by mentioning ancient Israel up front my study carries with it the risk of reducing this evidence to the status of mere *comparandum* to another culture. Whatever its drawbacks, my project here is a synthetic and comparative work, which attempts to make sense of some very technical historical data, difficult artistic problems, and questions of the historical development of some aspects of West Semitic religion for a people group (the Phoenicians) that are still not very well understood. I do not beg forgiveness for any missteps because of these difficulties; on the one hand, I cite and openly admit them as a limitation of the study, but on the other hand, I extol them as desiderata. Additionally, my hope is that specialists in the field of Phoenician religion and iconography will find here a useful collection and categorization of relevant images from a wide range of contexts and perhaps even an analysis of those images that helps us think about the implications of Phoenician artistic trends for religious representation in the broader Phoenician Mediterranean world.

Beyond the implications for ancient Israel, my goal is to connect this material wherever possible to discussions of aniconic trends and the larger field of comparative ancient religions in the ancient Near Eastern and Mediterranean worlds. The peculiarly diverse nature of Phoenician settlement and influence requires that we view their images through many different kinds of filters. Ancient Israel and other Mesopotamian groups farther east present one avenue for exploration here, but we must also look west, to specific geographies of Phoenician settlement and to other groups, such as the Greeks, who likewise dealt in a wide array of divine images—including aniconographic expressions. Classical Greek art historians have for some time now appreciated the comparative avenues that could exist between their topic and the Near East generally, and thus scholars interested in the aesthetics and politics of aniconism throughout the ancient world and beyond it chronologically can learn from the Phoenicians, who mediated important elements of the East-West exchange. For the Greek angle on this problem and for the most rigorous consideration of the meaning of the term "aniconism," readers should consult Milette Gaifman's excellent book *Aniconism in Greek Antiquity* (2012). For comparison with Israel, one should consult Tryggve Mettinger's groundbreaking *No Graven Image? Israelite Aniconism in Its Ancient Near Eastern Context* (1995). Both of these books have influenced my thinking on the question of Phoenician aniconism in different ways, and I have conceived of the present project as an expansion and revision of Mettinger's essay on the Phoenicians (chapter 5 of *No Graven Image?*) but following the more comprehensive and rigorous model of Gaifman's work.

Two major methodological problems appear everywhere in this study. First, a question of historical and geographical context: Although discussions of the mainland Phoenician sites (e.g., Tyre, Sidon, Byblos) tend to be considered separately from the Mediterranean colonies and indeed I discuss each piece of iconographic evidence within its geographical setting as specifically as possible, we must confront the problem of Phoenician identity in the Mediterranean as a whole to understand whether there can truly be such a phenomenon as "Phoenician aniconism." The question is obviously inseparable from another problem, namely, the extent to which we can posit a pan-Mediterranean or long-standing "Phoenician" historical identity in the Iron Age or beyond. I take up this question in the following chapter, but it must be recalled and allowed to haunt us continually as specific iconographic evidence arises. Needless to say, a study of this kind cannot pretend to provide an exhaustive presentation of the iconographic evidence for the entirety of the Iron Age Phoenician settlement in the West or the many complicating factors involved with Phoenician colonization, archaeology, or religion, but the specific focus on the putative aniconographic phenomenon narrows the potential avenues of inquiry and thus allows us to explore certain images as case studies for the religious and artistic problems of aniconism. Moreover, in many instances it was not possible to obtain clear information about the exact archaeological context of an object, for example, its specific locus information, accompanying artifacts, depositional environment, floral and faunal remains, and so on (if recovered in a professional excavation at all). Because of this fact, I mostly cite objects from their site generally, though where more specific information was available I provide it as deemed relevant for the discussion.

The comparison to ancient Israel—as well as to Mesopotamia more broadly and Greece—must be considered on specific and historically bounded terms, not simply offered typologically or by making unquestioned comparison between objects spanning many centuries. Specifically, the time horizon I would like to use as a guideline for assessing materials is the ninth–fifth centuries BCE, a nearly five-century period that saw the earliest phases of Phoenician expansion into the West and ends with the advent of classical Greece and the rise of Hellenism in the Mediterranean. Thus when I speak of the "Mediterranean and Near Eastern Contexts" of the material at hand, I do so not primarily to gesture to the strictly comparative aspects of the study, though I do explicitly compare the data here to other materials in the Mediterranean and Near Eastern environment (the Levant, Egypt, Mesopotamia, Greece), but rather to signify the many geographical contexts of Phoenician presence in the ancient world.

Second, a question of terminology and theory: Perhaps more than other disciplines, scholars of ancient history can be found complaining about the overapplication (or any application) of "theory" to their work, fearing that theory will overrun data or feeling that theory is used by dilettantes in the absence of data. In the case of the present topic, we will come to see that aniconism must be dealt with in a rigorous manner, always considering the work that art historians and philosophers have contributed toward questions of image and meaning. Obviously the Iron Age Phoenicians were not aware of these discussions, but we must at least find some terminological clarity and a scholarly pathway into the intricacy of Phoenician religious representation. Surprisingly few who invoke the language of aniconism even venture to offer a working definition of the word *aniconism*, and when they do, the term is glossed as "without images," leading to confusion. A rigorous focus on these theoretical and terminological concerns will lead to some clarity while at the same time it will enhance and sharpen the unanswered questions that persist because of the lack of data or the sheer stubbornness with which the past offers us answers. At any rate, my hope is that a proper combination of old-fashioned historical context and theoretical sophistication will give us the proper material to discuss and a clear frame within which to discuss it.

Finally, a note on the rendering of images in this book; for purposes of standardization and clarity, I decided to present all images as (relatively) simple line drawings. This has some drawbacks—short of personal examination, a range of excellent color photos for any single object is the best visual guide, and even the most detailed drawings are of course interpretations of images (on this problem, see Boardman 2000, 394–96). However, photographs are also interpretations, and it must be admitted that in many publications that utilize black and white or even color photos the images are simply not very clear (and certainly not clearer than an incisive line drawing). Given the wide range of materials analyzed in this book, necessary for any study of the Phoenicians, it was simply not practical in any sense to obtain a large amount of images by permission in photographic form. Thus I proceed with the assumption that specialists will know where to access other published examples of the iconography discussed here, and in every case I cite editions with the best photographs or images available, along with information on the physical characteristics of each object.

2

No Statues or Familiar Images?

In the first century of the Common Era, a Roman historian named Silius Italicus wrote the longest epic poem in the Latin language, the *Punica*, commemorating among other things Rome's massive victory over Hannibal at Carthage in the Second Punic War (late third century BCE). In book 3 of the poem, Hannibal makes a journey to the western colony of Gadir (Greek Gadeira, contemporary Spanish Cádiz), an old Phoenician site from at least the eighth century BCE that served as "home of a race akin to Carthage." There Hannibal worships at one of the most famous temples of the ancient world, that of Herakles (equated with the Semitic Melqart), witnessing an exotic priestly ritual. A particularly striking aspect of the Gadir cult, recorded in the *Punica* as well as other authors of the period, was the lack of a standard cult image in the inner sanctuary: "But no statues or familiar images of the gods filled the place with solemnity and sacred awe" (*Punica* 3.30–31; see edition of Delz 1987).

Modern historians attempting to learn anything about the Gadir cult of the third century BCE—or even earlier periods—through the *Punica* are faced with many layers of problems, the most obvious of which are Silius Italicus's historical distance from the events in question and the multitude of ideological distortions an author like this introduces into the study of what was to him a foreign and exotic culture. Still, the Hercules temple at Gadir was a well-known place, and a plethora of other iconographic and textual accounts from the Greek and Roman periods may suggest that Punic and earlier Phoenician cults used either nonanthropomorphic images or simply empty space to signify the presence of their deities. If such a tradition were truly early, extending back into at least the ninth–fifth centuries BCE, then historians of ancient Near Eastern religions would have to contend with a potentially aniconic Iron Age West Semitic cult, where images were avoided for some reason. But what could this reason be? And what material evidence do we have that might shed light on this allegedly aniconic representational program? Is the aniconic phenomenon prominent in the western colonies or in the eastern mainland or both? On the level of terminology, what is "aniconism"?

Before we are able to proceed with an analysis of the relevant iconography and past work on this topic, we must address some fundamental questions of Phoenician identity and religion. For other regions or nations in the ancient world, little justification may be required for simply discussing that region/nation by its accepted name; however, the category of "Phoenicia" is clearly different and requires at least some preliminary discussion. Having done this, we will then be able to turn to aniconism as a religious and art-historical problem and then analyze Phoenician divine iconography and the possibility for Phoenician aniconography.

2.1. Who Were the Phoenicians?

The term *Phoenicia* has become something of an academic catchall for several cities on the northern Levantine coast as well as an adjective (*Phoenician*) describing a complex network of settlements in the western Mediterranean, stretching from the African coast west of Egypt, including Carthage, all the way through the Strait of Gibraltar on both the Spanish and African coasts. This is not to say "Phoenicia" is purely modern or artificial; Phoenicia was a Roman province, and both Greek and Roman authors speak of Phoenicia as roughly the area of the Levant (and then including various colonies in the Mediterranean). The label Phoenician is probably best described as a flexible external ethnonym used in many periods from Homer through the Hellenistic and Roman eras and beyond.[1] On the Levantine mainland, the geographical region of Phoenicia is traditionally said to encompass a small strip of land (around 100 km north to south and 20–50 km east to west) on the coastal plain of Lebanon and northern Israel, hemmed in by the Lebanon mountains as an eastern border. Cities such as Arvad (Greek Arados) and Tell Sukas mark the northernmost reaches of the region, while Byblos, Sidon, and Tyre (Greek Tyros, Phoenician and biblical ṣur) form the core of what scholars typically identify as the Phoenician mainland, though cities such as Sarepta, Akko (Greek Akre), Dor, Akhziv, and other sites are often included (see fig. 2.1).[2]

The Greek etymology of the term "Phoenicians" (*phoinikēs*) attests to the role of these people in trade and colonization (Wathelet 1983). Most likely, the term is related to the word *phoinix*, indicating a dark hue in the red or purple range, the dye color produced by the murex snail and notable throughout the Mediterranean world (Aubet 2001, 6–25; Prag 2014). As far as we know, the Phoenicians never called themselves "Phoenicians" before Roman times—rather, they identified as residents of a particular Canaanite city, most prominently Tyre, Sidon, and Byblos. There is a reasonable amount of evidence to indicate that many of those living in the southwestern Levant during parts of the second millennium considered them-

---

1. I borrow this phrase "flexible external ethnonym" from the as yet unpublished paper of López-Ruiz (2015).

2. Tyre and Arvad were technically islands very near the coast of the mainland, though Tyre was later artificially connected to the coast during the siege of Alexander the Great in 332 BCE.

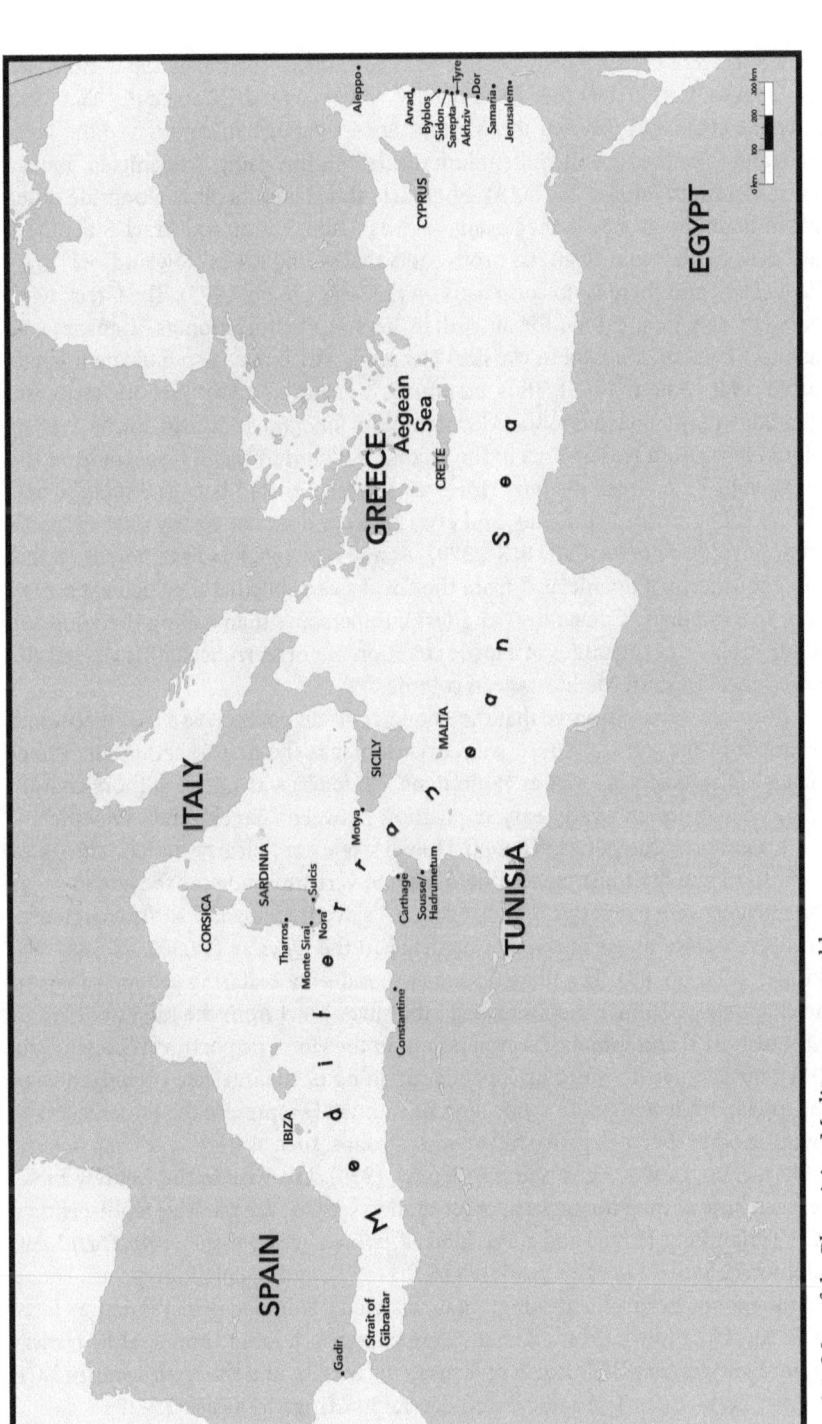

Fig. 2.1: Map of the Phoenician Mediterranean world

selves and were considered by others as "Canaanites" (Na'aman 1994, 1999; see also Lemche 1991). Thus the "Phoenicians" were essentially Canaanites that lived along the coast and traveled the Mediterranean, though many reserve the term "Canaanite" for the second-millennium residents while using "Phoenician" for the first millennium (Aubet 2001, 13). Phoenicia thus takes its place alongside other first-millennium groups in the Levant, such as Aram, Edom, and Israel. Still others have derived the term "Canaan" from roots that would mean "lowland" or "merchant class," and there is no consensus on the issue (Zobel 1995). The Greek term *phoinikēs* may be a calque for an earlier Semitic identification as "Canaan, Canaanite" (kᵊnaʿan, kᵊnaʿănî in classical Hebrew), which may also indicate the red/purple color (Astour 1965). Thus, assuming "Canaan" is a West Semitic term, the etymology may be related to the Akkadian term *kinaḫḫu*, indicating some dyed or colored fabric (attested at Nuzi in the second millennium), and if so, could be the equivalent of the Greek *phoinix*. However, the relationship between *kinaḫḫu* and *kᵊnaʿan* is linguistically dubious, and even *kinaḫḫu* does not clearly refer only to a red or purple color (see *CAD* 8[K], 379). At any rate, scholars have borrowed this ambiguous term "Phoenicians" from the Greeks as a shorthand, which is perhaps more specific than "Canaanites" and less cumbersome than calling them, as one could, "Iron I–II Canaanites of a loose coalition of northern Levantine coastal cities and their western Mediterranean colonies."

Everyone seems to agree that the Phoenicians do not receive a fair or accurate treatment in our earliest Greek sources—Homer is the first to call them "Phoenicians" (*Phoinikēs*), as well as "Sidonians" (*Sidōnēs*)—as Greek authors characteristically set up an overly easy opposition between "Greek" and "Phoenician" as ethnographic categories. Though Homer's tales are clearly fiction, stories of Phoenician activity must have exhibited some verisimilitude for the audience, as Phoenicians were stereotyped as "tricksters," slave traders, and shifty merchants, certainly capable of the abduction depicted in the *Odyssey* (14.300, 15.388–484; Skinner 2012, 86–89). The Phoenicians were indeed a seafaring group, traders in the elite objects Homer mentions (e.g., the silver bowl from the king of Sidon in *Od.* 4.614–619) and sometimes even honest in the Homeric portrayal (López-Ruiz 2011), but Homer does not understand anything of the intricate organization of Phoenician trade and politics, nor does he ultimately represent the Phoenicians as anything other than a negative foil to other groups, such as the Greeks, the fictional Phaeacians, or Odysseus himself (Winter 1995). Likewise in the Hebrew Bible, we learn little of the Phoenicians, other than to see that the putative tenth-century BCE Tyrian king Hiram had some kind of political relationship with David and Solomon (2 Sam 5:11; 1 Kgs 5:1; 7:13–14; 9:11–12), and a generation or two later a prominent northern Israelite king, Ahab, married a Sidonian princess named Jezebel (1 Kgs 16). Elsewhere, the Tyrians were known as honored and wealthy traders by the eight-century BCE Isaiah of Jerusalem (Isa 23), and the sixth-century BCE prophet Ezekiel sees Tyre's doom and decries its arrogance (Ezek 26–28).

Fig. 2.2: Examples of Phoenician pottery; decoration patterns for Phoenician strainer-spouted jugs and example of Iron Age flask from Sarepta (Anderson 1990, 38, fig. 2; 44, fig. 4)

From the perspective of material culture broadly speaking, we have some evidence toward identifying artistic productions and pottery as distinctly Phoenician (see Aubet 2013; Sader 2013). Excavation at Sarepta uncovered the first clearly stratified sequence of pottery from a mainland Phoenician site (Pritchard 1978; 1988; Bikai 1987; Anderson 1990). Though the pottery must be considered a gradual development, based on existing forms yet influenced by trade and innovation, items within the "Phoenician bichrome" category, such as globular jugs and side-spouted strainers, were prominent at Sarepta as well as other Phoenician sites such as Tyre and Tell Keisan by the eleventh century BCE (Schreiber 2003; Anderson 1990, 47–48; fig. 2.2). Francisco Jesús Núñez Calvo (2008, 69) concludes that the ceramic sequence and typology for the mainland (mostly with reference to Tyre) is "linear and clear," and hence "the diverse stages of its evolution can be recognized with a great degree of certainty."

We will address more specific questions of Phoenician art later on, but for the moment it is important to notice that Phoenician artistic work can be identified by international influences (Egyptian as well as Assyrian) and certain specialty products, such as fine ivory and metalwork, terracotta masks, and various other elite items (see overview in Markoe 1990). In some cases, even more specifically, Phoenician ivories and other pieces can be classified by their use of distinctive features, for example, specific motifs (such as a uraeus-flanked sun disc), a clear conversation with Egyptian motifs lacking in other regional examples, symmetry and a sense of spatial balance, and a type of "realism" (even for mythological animals, such as a sphinx; figs. 2.3 and 2.4; see Winter 2010c, 191–96; 2010b, 282).

From a linguistic perspective, "Phoenician" refers to a dialect range belonging to an identifiably distinct and coherent language and script (see Rollston 2014; Hackett 2004; Krahmalkov 2001; Segert 1976). The Phoenician script was

Fig. 2.3: Phoenician-style sphinx plaque; Nimrud; ninth century BCE (DCPP, pl. X.a; Winter 2010c, 219, fig. 8)

Fig. 2.4: Silver bowl fragment from Amathus, Cyprus; eighth–seventh century BCE; d. 18.7 cm (http://www.britishmuseum.org; ANE 123053; Room 57–59: Ancient Levant)

also used to write several different languages in the Levant (such as Hebrew and Aramaic, which deviated with their own scripts sometime between the tenth and eighth centuries BCE; Hackett 2004; Schniedewind 2013, 54–56; Röllig 1995a), and the Greeks adopted it to write their own language by at least the eighth century, if not earlier (see Colvin 2014, 69–78; McCarter 1975; Rollston 2014; 2010, 19–46). The case for at least a coherent Phoenician scribal identity on the basis of the script can be made, as Rollston (2010, 41) argues for "substantial continuity of the Phoenician script during any chronological horizon regardless of the region from which it hails," which he attributes to a "trans-regional Phoenician scribal apparatus." Longer inscriptions from throughout the Iron Age give us a sense of Phoenician vocabulary, grammar, and orthography and provide native historical evidence for themes of royal propaganda, building projects, and religion (COS 2.29–32:146–52; Rollston 2008; 2010; Avishur 2000; Gibson 1982). For later periods, the term "Punic" categorizes the language of Carthage and its sphere of influence from the sixth–mid-second centuries BCE, whereas "Neo-Punic" refers to the language after the fall of Carthage in 146 BCE and on into the Common Era (for a wide-ranging set of studies, see Quinn and Vella 2014, and reviews of key Mediterranean sites in Sagona 2008).

Given the concerns expressed here about the stability or meaning of Phoenician identity, the notion of a "history of Phoenicia" is bound to be misleading on various levels (but see now Peckham 2014, the subtitle for which appropriately marks the episodic nature of the enterprise). Yet a précis of what we can adduce about some general trends will help situate our discussion. Some of the Phoenician cities may have been truly ancient—Tyre in particular was probably founded in the middle of the third millennium (Katzenstein 1997; Gubel, Lipiński, and Servais-Soyez 1983). During most of the second millennium, the region was under Egyptian hegemony, with a peak in trade activity during the fourteenth century BCE, followed by a "dark age" of sorts from around 1200–1050 and then a resurgence in the tenth century (Aubet 2001, 20–25; see Stieglitz 1990 for a concise overview of early Phoenician history in the Iron Age). Still, the barrier separating the Late Bronze Age from the Iron I period in the Levant is not as meaningful for our northern coastal Canaanites as it was for other groups; the invasion of the Sea Peoples in the late thirteenth and early twelfth century seems to have left no destructive effect on the principal Phoenician cities (see Bikai 1992), although to the north, Ugarit was destroyed and the Philistines (a powerful contingent of the Sea Peoples) settled along the southern coast at the same time. Further inland, groups that came to be known as Israel and Judah occupied the central hill country, and others carved out space to the east, such as the Arameans, Moabites, and Edomites. Whether the influx of these newer populations pushed what "Canaanites" had been dwelling in the region to the coast or whether terms such as "Israel," "Moab," and so on came to characterize inland Canaanites who simply remained in their land in some transformed status through the Late Bronze Age transition crisis are difficult questions and have been the subject of an enormous amount of disagreement.

We know very little about Phoenician history from native sources, and archaeological investigation during the past several decades at the mainland sites had proved largely disappointing (with a few key exceptions). Recent excavation of key sites in the past decade, however—such as the renewed work at Sidon by the British Museum (1998–present; see Doumet-Serhal 2011–2012)—have provided a wealth of new data, and current and ongoing efforts mean that findings may be questioned at any point. Fascinating iconography continues to emerge; a life-sized partial body of what appears to be a Phoenician priest uncovered in Sidon during the spring of 2014 (as this book was being written) is the first major discovery of its kind at the site in over fifty years (Boyle 2014; for past work at Sidon, see overview in Khalifeh 1997 and the update with sources in Doumet-Serhal 2013). Excavation at Tyre in the 1970s produced limited results (Bikai 1978; Joukowsky 1992), but a large cemetery was uncovered near the site beginning in 1997, revealing rich evidence from the tenth–seventh centuries BCE (Aubet 2004; 2006; 2010). Byblos remains something of an enigma during the key Phoenician period; although clearly a powerful trading center, continuous occupation has made stratigraphic analysis difficult (Joukowsky 1997; Gubel et al. 2002, 58–59).

Phoenician history is typically discussed with reference to the major empires in the ancient Near East that exerted dominance over the region for hundreds of years; Phoenician cities (particularly Byblos) are mentioned in Egyptian sources since the early second millennium (Markoe 2000, 15–17). Assyrian kings from the eleventh–seventh centuries BCE campaigned west, often reaching the coast and taking tribute from Phoenician cities. Tiglath-Pileser I (eleventh–tenth centuries) recorded tribute from Byblos (Gubal), Sidon, and Arvad and sailed on a sea-hunting expedition in Arvadite ships; Assurnasirpal II (ninth century) likewise subdued Sidon, Byblos, Arvad, and Tyre, listing many precious objects taken in tribute; Tiglath-Pileser III (mid-eighth century) took tribute from Byblos, Arvad, and Tyre and specifically mentions "Hiram of Tyre" and "Sibitti-bi'ili of Byblos"; Sennacherib (late eighth–early seventh centuries) lists Sidon, mainland Tyre (Ushu), and Byblos among his conquered territories, forcing Luli of Sidon to flee to Cyprus (see texts in *ANET* 274–88). Something about the long-standing wealth of the Phoenician cities can be inferred from these lists, insofar as Mesopotamian kings plundered them for large amounts of tribute. Another indirect clue to indicate the wealth of the Phoenician trading industry and natural resources comes via the eleventh-century Egyptian Wenamun story, which tells of Wenamun's misadventures among the likes of various coastal peoples including the residents of Byblos, to whom he had been sent to gather precious timber (*COS* 1.41:89–93).

The first–second-century CE Byblian Philo's Phoenician History, which purports to record the writings of a certain Phoenician named Sanchouniaton (*Sakkunyatan*, "SKN has given"), tells us little that might be usable for reconstructing any early Phoenician history or religious practice in far earlier periods (López-Ruiz

2010, 94–101). Though some venture to speculate that Sanchouniaton was a real Phoenician from the Iron Age (see Baumgarten 1981, 49–50, for examples), much of the content of this Phoenician History—at least as mediated to us through other authors, in which it survives—bears the marks of a Hellenistic or Roman-era composition, such as the presentation of a theogony after cosmology (not typical of native ancient Near Eastern accounts), the Euhemeristic rendering of mythology, and the Hellenistic preoccupation with inventors (Kaldellis and López-Ruiz 2009; Baumgarten 1981; Attridge and Oden 1981; Krings 1995b, 31–38). Relevant for our purposes, Philo of Byblos does intriguingly mention the erection of potentially aniconic stelae at Tyre,[3] although such references should first be analyzed within the period of the history's authorship before they can automatically count as evidence of Iron Age Phoenician practice.

Native Phoenician sources that might shed light on major political developments are limited to a few royal inscriptions, and they are not particularly long, detailed, or revealing (see Gibson 1982 for text and translation of all of the examples summarized here). The earliest, the so-called Ahiram sarcophagus, dates to around 1000 BCE and is composed of a short warning by Ittobaal, Ahiram's son, against disturbing Ahiram's coffin. A short building foundation text on behalf of Yahimilk at Byblos (ca. 950 BCE) was recovered in a secondary context but demonstrates that this Phoenician ruler in the tenth century engaged in public projects for his city, and Shipitbaal (ca. 900 BCE) likewise left a five-line inscription for the dedication of a wall. Also at Byblos, but a half millennium later (ca. fifth–fourth centuries BCE), a ruler named Yehawmilk announced the dedication of various objects to the city's goddess, "My Lady, Mistress of Byblos" (Baalat Gubal). The Kulamuwa inscription from Zinjirli in Turkey (ancient Sam'al, ca. 830–820 BCE) falls outside of the traditional sphere of Phoenician mainland cities, yet its linguistic categorization as a type of northern Phoenician dialect (with mixed Aramaic features) could indicate some aspect of Phoenician identity. Kulamuwa tells a standard ancient Near Eastern royal tale of ascent to the throne and lists various achievements, and an image of the king accompanies the inscription on an orthostat. Also from south-central Anatolia (Karatepe) but from the early seventh century, the Azatiwada inscription is a Phoenician-Luwian bilingual in which Azatiwada tells of his royal accomplishments. Two Sidonian kings, Eshmunazor and Tabnit (fifth century), also left inscriptions warning potential grave robbers—Eshmunazor's is much longer and details his pious building projects for deities such as Astarte, Eshmun, Baal, and others.

Trade among the Levantine coastal cities and the Mediterranean world was undoubtedly as old as ships and seafaring in the region generally, but the specifically Iron Age settlements in the ninth century BCE at places like Kition in south-

---

3. See discussion below at "5.2. Textual Accounts of Aniconism by Greek and Roman Authors."

east Cyprus (J. S. Smith 2008; Reyes 1994; Aubet 2001, 51–54; Steele 2013, 173–234, on the linguistic evidence) and probably very soon thereafter at Carthage in northern Africa (Aubet 2008; Docter et al. 2008) may be the first identifiable Phoenician colonization efforts. Since the 1960s, and particularly since the 1980s, archaeological excavation has revealed a tremendous amount of information about Phoenician trading colonies in what ancient historians called "Tartessos" on the Iberian Peninsula (modern Spain) and particularly along the Andalusian coast (in southernmost Spain; see Celestino and López-Ruiz forthcoming; Dietler and López-Ruiz 2009; Bierling 2002; Aubet 2001), as well as in central Mediterranean locations such as Motya (a small island off the coast of Sicily, Italy) and Sardinia (Aubet 2001, 212–56). These colonies generally were first established in the early eighth century and flourished for around two hundred years (see Pappa 2013 for a new archaeological study of the Phoenician Mediterranean). Even after this "golden age" of Iron Age Phoenician activity, the Persian period (539–332 BCE) saw perhaps the longest period of stability, autonomy, and growth in the region for the Phoenician cities as Sidon became the capital of a province encompassing the northern Levantine coast, Egypt, and Cyprus (Elayi 1982; Elayi and Elayi 2014). Moreover, our evidence does not stop there, as the influence of these coastal cities and their colonies would continue into the Hellenistic period and on into the Common Era.

Incomplete though this sketch must be for the moment, our sources give us at least a general picture of what may be counted as "Phoenician" for purposes of religious participation and iconographic production. As we investigate Phoenician divine iconography, we must be constantly on guard against false assumptions of clear or solely "Phoenician" motifs as opposed to "Aegean" or other classifications (Knapp 2014; also Gunter 2009), and, as we will discover, the phenomenon of Phoenician aniconism participates in a hybrid system of pictorial exchange between the Phoenicians and the Aegean world, on the one hand, and the ancient Near Eastern world, on the other.

2.2. Phoenician Religion

Our knowledge of Phoenician religion is beset by the same problems that hindered our brief examination of Phoenician history and identity. Just as there was no clear or official "Phoenicia" in the Iron Age, there is no monolithic entity that can easily be summarized as "Phoenician religion" (which is not to say that others have not tried with varying degrees of success; see, e.g., Markoe 2000, 115–42; Krings 1995a; Clifford 1990; Bonnet 1988; Ribichini 1988; Harden 1963, 82–114; for the Hellenistic period, see now Bonnet 2015). Perhaps it is not any more accurate or problematic for us to speak of "Phoenician religion" as it is to speak of "Greek religion" or any other cluster of religious practice for what are inevitably nonmonolithic entities. We now have access to thousands of inscriptions, religious objects, cultic formulae, temple remains, and divine images, all of which tell particular stories about the practice of these coastal seafaring groups in a variety of different locations. Though we will be reviewing specific aspects of ritual and cult with relation to the images analyzed throughout this study, an orientation to some basic issues will help situate more specific information.

In a discussion of elements common to many expressions of Phoenician religion across the Mediterranean focusing on almost purely textual evidence, Clifford (1990, 56–58) has noticed shared features such as gods meeting in assembly; the ubiquity of the language of "Baal" as either divine title ("lord") or association with a particular locale ("Baal Labanon"); attestations spanning several centuries indicating "symposium" or *marzeach*-style celebrations in temples or for the dead; incantations against demons; and the notorious problem of child sacrifice (primarily at Carthage). Much more will need to be explored on this front, and I will have occasion to discuss divine images and religious practice in the western Mediterranean Phoenician context later on. Most now agree that the major Phoenician cities sustained a religious identification with a male-female divine pair:

Sidon: Eshmun // Astarte
Tyre: Melqart // Astarte
Byblos: Baal Shamem (?) // Baalat Gubal (= Anat?)

The fact that deities like Melqart, Astarte, and Eshmun had no dominant cult in the region in the second millennium (though Baalat Gubal did at Byblos) suggests that there was a decisive religiocultural break at the end of the Bronze Age in some areas (Aubet 2001, 152; Bloch-Smith 2014, 191).

As the principal deity of Tyre and its prominent colony of Gadir in the southern Iberian Peninsula, Melqart may be singled out as an interesting case for thinking about these deities as based in a mainland city and traveling west in the Mediterranean (see now Álvarez Martí-Aguilar forthcoming). The very word "Melqart" (*mlk* + *qrt*, "king of the city") signals much about the traditions of this deity in Tyre: by at least the second century BCE, he was considered a founding *hērōs* figure of the city, and much earlier than that had been conflated with the Greek Herakles (Aune 1995).

In a quotation from Menander of Ephesus's history of Tyre (second century BCE) in Josephus's *Ant. Jud.* (8.146-148), the putative tenth-century BCE Hiram of Tyre enacted a sweeping religious reform, building temples to Melqart-Herakles and Astarte (Ribichini 1995, 1054–55). Most assume Melqart was a "dying and rising god," a vague concept (see J. Z. Smith 1990, 97–124) but nonetheless possibly supported by a reference to an unnamed deity being buried in the sixth-century BCE Pyrgi inscription (*bym qbr 'ilm*, "on the day of the burial of the deity"; *KAI* 277; Gibson 1982, 151–59) as well as later Greek texts that specifically mention Melqart's yearly *egersis* ("awakening") ritual (Bonnet 1988, 104–12; Ribichini 1995, 1055–56). Also suggestive is the story in 1 Kgs 18, in which the prophet

Elijah battles hundreds of prophets of "Baal" (= Eshmun? Melqart?) who had been employed by Sidonian Jezebel, as Elijah mockingly suggests that the deity they attempt to invoke is sleeping and must be roused (1 Kgs 18:27; see Briquel-Chatonnet 1992, 303–13).

Greek, Roman, and biblical references do not give us a native, nuanced, or, especially in the case of the Bible, sympathetic view of the Phoenician system, so conclusions from these sources must be treated accordingly. Moreover, it should now be admitted that the evidence for the entire category of the "dying and rising god" is much more vague than many commentators on the phenomenon have assumed—at best, we have suggestions of some cyclical rituals (such as found in the Ugaritic Baal Cycle or for the Greek Persephone) but nothing like a clear account of these rituals or any dying-and-rising myth for the Phoenicians (M. S. Smith 1998, 277–82, 286–89).

The Tyrian Melqart held a striking status vis-à-vis the ruler of the city. Monarchs throughout the ancient Near Eastern world occupied a prominent place in the religious system, but at Phoenician sites the relationship between king and priesthood seems to have been particularly noteworthy (Aubet 2001, 147–48; Clifford 1990, 61; see Peckham 1987, 81–82, but see 91 n. 25). The close identification between the king and the local cult could then stand in close political-religious union with the primary deities of the city, further elevating the ruler and strengthening the local identity. Aubet (2001, 148–49) goes so far as to state that, in the case of Tyre, "the king and the god Melqart are at once the incarnation of the same institution: the state." If the Tyrian king claimed outright divinity (so Aubet, 2001, 148–49, 154; see also Lipiński 1970, 51, 53)—which would have been a rare move in the ancient Near Eastern world but with better parallels in Egypt—then the biblical prophet Ezekiel clearly directs his mockery at the institution (Ezek 28:2): "because your heart is proud, and you have said, 'I am a god ['ēl]—I sit in the seat of gods [môšab 'ĕlōhîm], in the midst of the sea.'" The founding of a new colony, such as Gadir, may have required the dedication of a temple to the appropriate deity (in this case, Melqart), thus creating a solid fusion of kingship, religion, politics, and economics between the mother city and a western colony. At such a great distance, we can imagine the psychological and political need to create this fusion; though absent in body, the king could be present through the figure of the deity, and the integration of the primary deity in the founding narrative of the colony bolstered the all-important process of legitimizing the new western colony under the aegis of the eastern sponsor (Aubet 2001, 155–57). A similar case could be made for the dynamic at Carthage.

Archaeology continues to provide clues about Phoenician religion and identity. At Sidon, a temple with Late Bronze origins existed on a seemingly continuous basis—expanded or remodeled at several points—on through the Persian period (Doumet-Serhal 2013, 108–12; 2014). The iteration of the temple during the early Iron Age (ca. 1100s BCE) is striking, for it provides evidence of ironwork connecting the temple to remains at twelfth-century Ekron, Megiddo, and the Aegean, and a rare inscription on a (now fragmentary) offering vessel from the ninth or eighth century BCE seems to reference an "altar of 'BDYH [Abadyahu?]" (Doumet-Serhal 2013, 110).

In addition to Eshmun's cult within the boundaries of Sidon proper, another temple around four kilometers north of the city yet clearly associated with it, founded in the seventh or (more likely the) sixth century BCE, gives us direct evidence of the worship of the Sidonian Eshmun, as well as Astarte (Dunand 1966; 1967; 1969; Saidah 1969; Khalifeh 1997). Eshmun was a deity of healing (the root of the name, *šmn*, means "oil," as in healing/anointing oil), a fact that facilitated the deity's conflation with Asklepios in the Hellenistic and Roman periods (Xella 1993). Astarte in particular was enshrined in a "chapel" within the larger Eshmun complex, which housed a large throne for the goddess. Strikingly, images of either Eshmun or Astarte are absent from the remains at the complex—Astarte's throne appears to have been created as an "empty throne," leaving us to wonder how these deities were represented in ritual and why worshipers avoided anthropomorphic images.

In summary, we can say that Phoenicians worshiped their deities in ways that, while distinct and unique to each city and context, make sense within the Northwest Semitic context of the mainland cities. The situation in the broader Mediterranean is more complex; in some cases colonies had clear relationships with their founding mainland cities, though we do not know to what extent we can assume this kind of relationship at every colony. In the case of Tyre-Gadir and Tyre-Carthage, at least, this dynamic will be important to recall, as some of the more intriguing textual and visual evidence for Phoenician aniconic worship comes in reference to the Melqart/Herakles sanctuary at Gadir and in the Carthage stelae. Having now given this background on some problems of Phoenician identity and religion, we turn to the question of using divine images as evidence of religious practice and the challenge of aniconography in particular.

3

Aniconism in Theoretical and Art-Historical Perspective

In what follows, I explore some philosophical and terminological problems with the language of images, icons, and aniconography. Indeed, with few exceptions, "aniconism" is not defined at all in discussions of Phoenician or Near Eastern aniconic movements, and this lacuna of method represents a major problem for studying the topic. In contemporary circles, most discussions of the image swing wildly between two poles: simplistic nonattention and bewildering theorizing. As Elkins and Naef put it (2011, vii), "Concepts like *picture, visual art,* and *realism* circulate in newspapers, galleries, and museums as if they were as obvious and natural as words like *dog, cat,* and *goldfish,*" while in the world of academic art theory these same terms "are treated like impossibly complicated machines whose workings can hardly be understood. Sometimes . . . what counts as art theory is simple and normal, and other times it seems to be the most difficult subject in visual art." In the field of art history broadly, and especially ancient art history, the approach has been very practical on the whole, allowing a wide range of material to fall under the heading "image." This is quite different from the conception of "image" in the studio, where images have been viewed as politically subversive to power and opposed to or outside of language, and different from contemporary work in "visual studies," which considers the bombardment of images we experience as part of "late capitalist first-world culture" (Elkins 2011, 1–2).

For the field of ancient Near Eastern art history, and Phoenician iconography specifically, however, discussions of the image have often become too pragmatic, to the point where we are left without the sophistication and subtlety to understand a concept as potentially sophisticated and subtle as aniconism. These problems become even more acute, to be sure, when we begin to search for a comparative context for the putative Israelite aniconism of the Iron Age. In what follows, I draw on the work of art historians, classicists, and philosophers to approach the difficult questions of representation, abstraction, and empty space in religious depiction, and I argue that aniconic representation should only be considered on a continuum, as the very notion of "aniconic representation" is something of a visual paradox. This investigation will allow us to better understand the mindset and context of "image worship" in the ancient world and thus put us in position to assess Phoenician aniconism and the motifs of aniconic expression.

3.1. What Is an "Icon"?

The genealogy of image theory in the West frequently finds its way back to Plato's *Republic* (10.601c), where in a famous discussion Socrates proposes that the "maker of an image [*eidōlon*]—an imitator [*mimētēs*]—knows nothing about that which is but only about its appearance," as well as a passage in the *Sophist* (236a–d), where a speaker offers a discourse on craftsmen who "say goodbye to truth, and produce in their images the proportions that seem to be beautiful instead of the real ones" (translation from White 1997). In the Platonic stream, an *eidōlon* is a "visible image," a "likeness (*eikōn*) or 'semblance' (*phantasma*) of the *eidos*" (i.e., Idea, Form), which is above the senses, thus rending reality and perception apart (Mitchell 1986, 5; see also Camille 2003, 36; Halliwell 2002, 183). In the *Timaeus* dialogue—perhaps the most important touchstone for Platonic thinking in the West as it was the only dialogue translated into Latin and available continuously since antiquity—Plato elaborates the major division between the pure realm of forms, that which is unchanging and not created ("that which always is"), and the realm of created things ("that which becomes"), formed by a craftsman and only ever achieving success insofar as it is a copy or reflection of the higher reality. Thus, in the Platonic stream, images never simply "are what they are" on the surface, but rather succeed or fail to the extent that they reflect the Formal qualities of being, hidden in another world inaccessible to the senses. What is at stake in all of this? On a most basic level, any distinction between a "sign" (*signum*) and a true "thing" (*res*), as with Augustine of Hippo in his theory of semiotics in *De doctrina christiana* (late fourth century CE), is supposed to help one avoid idolatry—worshiping the sign as though it were the thing.

This is an important starting point for our consideration here, since analyses of "iconic resemblance"—especially when investigating image rejection or perceived image distortion of various kinds—have tended to immediately interrogate the image in terms of the Platonic "real"-versus-"copy" duality instead of using the native understanding that an image maker or user would employ (Camille 2003, 35; Bahrani 2003, 121–22). If a given representation is to be judged as either an *eikōn* or a *phantasma*, the former being an acceptable image and the latter a false likeness not resembling the image (e.g., a "simulacrum"; see Camille 2003), we must establish some criteria by which we might judge these identities—preferably criteria not dependent on the Platonic stream within Christianity (or Judaism for that matter) already within antiquity. The history of image conception in Plato's wake is long and convoluted and cannot be reviewed here; Elkins (2011, 3–5) points to a variety of popular approaches, including the first-century BCE Roman philosopher Lucretius's view that images are "skins" of objects, physically impressed upon our eyes, and the seventh–eighth-century CE Syrian Christian iconodule John of Damascus's hope that images would act as even faint "reminders" of "divine tokens." Modern theories take up images in complex ways, as semiotics (sign systems) or as "defective sign systems," where "exemplification is syntactically and semantically dense. Neither the pictorial characteristics nor the exemplified properties are differentiated" (here quoting Goodman 1974, 234).

Even a cursory glance at this history helps us to see that it is not easy to say what an "image" is or should be, though for at least recent theorists the matter is nothing if not complicated.[4] However we come to define them, images cannot easily be separated from our ability to see or think of anything—as the influential art theorist W. J. T. Mitchell reminds us in his book *Iconology* (1986, 5), our very word *idea* is related to the verb *to see* and the term *eidōlon* ("visible image") mentioned above, thus dooming us to speak of images in terms of other images. As if constantly replaying the Platonic representational dilemma, images are now no longer seen as a "transparent window on the world" as it is, but rather they are viewed as a vehicle of "ideological mystification," bound up in the endless games of concealment and distortion as language (Mitchell 1986, 8). Moreover, images do not only function in the traditional sense in which we are used to talking about them—as tangible, graphic objects in the concrete world of visual perception. Again following Mitchell's observations (1986, 31), in another stream of thinking that harks back to antiquity and certainly to the Hebrew Bible's description of humans created in God's "image" and "likeness" (ṣelem, děmût; Gen 1:26), the "image" is a likeness of not only a material sort but also a spiritual, mystical likeness on the level of psychological identification, emotional likeness, social belonging, shared purpose, or any other host of association in realms other than the pictorial and the concrete.[5]

At this point, we arrive at a style of thought that more closely resembles the ancient visual imagination. Consider, for example, the remarks of the twentieth-century philosopher Hans-Georg Gadamer on "the religious picture": "We can see without a doubt that a picture is not a copy of a copied being, but is in ontological communion with what is copied" (quoted and discussed in Freedberg 1989, 76–78). In a similar vein, Gilles Deleuze (1990, 262, and quoted in Camille 2003, 37) considers the "simulacrum" as a phenomenon different from the Platonic form-image duality and attributes to the image the power of identity: "The simulacrum is not a degraded copy. It harbors a positive power which denies the original and the copy, the model and the reproduction. At least two divergent series are inter-

---

4. For a recent engagement with some theoretical concerns from the perspective of ancient Near Eastern art, see Crawford 2014, esp. 242–50.

5. Scholars of the Hebrew Bible have long recognized this (nonmaterial) spiritual sense of "image" in Gen 1:26; see, e.g., Garr 2003, 117–78, as well as Herring 2013, and the literature cited there. See Bahrani 2003, 121–48, on the Akkadian term ṣalmu.

nalized in the simulacrum—neither can be assigned as the original, neither the copy.... The same and the similar no longer have an essence except as simulated, that is as expressing the functioning of the simulacrum." Invoking the language of idol and icon to address some of these same concerns, Jean-Luc Marion (1991, 17–18) speaks of the icon in terms of an interplay between what is "visible" and "invisible"—the "idol" divides the invisible into a visible (the physical idol image), while the invisible remains obfuscated, whereas the "icon" draws the gaze differently, singularly, onto the invisible "as such" (e.g., assuming the theological status of the icon as *hypostasis*, by which the worshiper venerates the reality of the deity directly; see also Marion 2011).

As we turn to the ancient Near Eastern and Mediterranean world of Phoenician images, we must keep both senses of the image in mind: the pictorial, the representation, the visual, and the concrete, on one hand; and, on the other hand, what ancient worshipers considered to be nonvisible, non-"straightforward" religious identifications bound up in the notion of the image. For ancient Near Eastern audiences, images—particularly images of deities—were more than mute distortions of their subject matter or of the gods, but rather represented reality and experience with a directness that may cause a contemporary theorist to blush (notwithstanding contemporary artistic ventures that intentionally conflate an experience or medium with the artistic subject) (see Bahrani 2008, 121–22; Herring 2013, 25–26; Porter 2014; Crawford 2014).[6] Ancient Near Eastern religions were "boldly polytheistic and anthropomorphic" (Bóttero 1992, 7)—the various deities called forth a variety of representations, and the anthropomorphic conception lent itself to material representations meant to identify aspects of the human world or physical world more broadly with the divine (on this topic, see now Wagner 2014, esp. Wunn 2014; Nunn 2014; Machinist 2014; and M. S. Smith 2014).

The nature of this image identity is, however, elusive, and the variety of forms and terminology for images themselves only adds to the complexity. For example, most use the term "cult image" to mean "the main statue in a temple that represented the deity of that temple and was housed in the temple's sanctuary" (Robins 2005, 2), although smaller images were employed frequently and obviously cannot be dismissed from examination. An image may take the form of a human (*anthropomorphic*), an animal (*theriomorphic*), vegetation (*dendromorphic*), or it may even be something more abstract, such as a divine symbol (Ornan 2005b; Cornelius 1997, 21–44; A. Green 1995, 1837–55; see also Collins 2005, 15, who restricts the term "cult statue" only to anthropomorphic images). These cult images were no instrumental tokens or arrows pointing to something else. Rather, as Thorkild

---

6. E.g., Crawford (2014, 244–45) discusses the common modern division between "image" and "word"—which ranks word above image—as largely the product of the Protestant Reformer Martin Luther's "linguistic imperialism," and carried forward through such luminaries as Kant and Hegel.

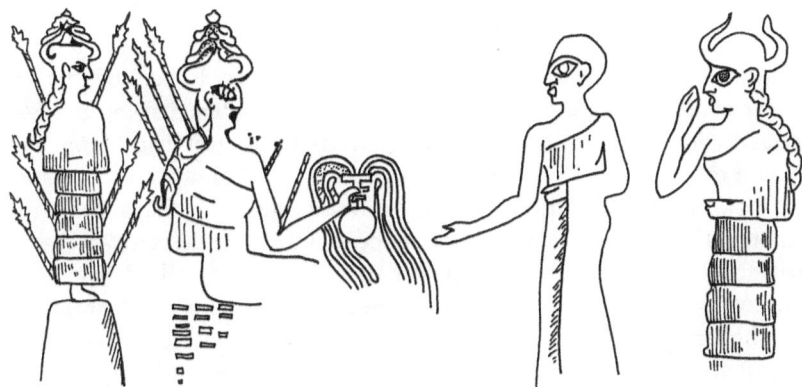

Fig. 3.1. Cylinder seal from Girsu; third millennium BCE (Dick 2005, 54, fig. 3.3; Cornelius 1997, 32, fig. 6)

Jacobsen puts it (1987, 16), ancient Near Eastern cult statues were not merely "an encouragement to pious thought"—their function must be considered in terms of "identity" with the deity (Porter 2014, 598–600). Many ancient texts simply equate the statue of a deity with the deity itself and speak plainly of the movements or processions of a particular deity, with no reference to a statue, when it is quite clear that they are speaking of a cult image (Jacobsen 1987, 16–17; Collins 2005, 34; Porter 2014, 598). Even the very materials used to make the cult statues could be considered divine, apart from ever having been fashioned into the image of the particular deity (Hurowitz 2006).

Other situations, however, demonstrate a clear differentiation of deity and image (Lambert 1990, 123; Jacobsen 1987, 17–18), and still other data seem to complicate the matter further by portraying a deity and his/her image in the same artistic scene (Dick 2005, 53–54; Collins 2005, 34–35). Consider, for example, a late third-millennium BCE cylinder seal engraved at Girsu (Dick 2005, 54; Cornelius 1997, 32–33; see fig. 3.1). The female deity (probably Ishtar) seated at left wears a many-horned helmet and exudes the *melammû* ("awe-inspiring luminosity"; Oppenheim 1977, 98) befitting the ancient Near Eastern concept of divinity, displayed through arrow-like projections from her shoulders and arm. This is, presumably, the "real" deity approached by the priest (center) on behalf of Naram-Sin (right), who dons his own horned helmet, thus displaying his own self-proclaimed divinity (although not as divine as Ishtar, whose helmet contains at least eight horns).[7]

---

7. As Bahrani (2003, 122) perceptively notices, we cannot even clearly use terms like *real* and *illusion* with regard to images or deities in the perception of ancient Near Eastern audiences.

Standing behind Ishtar, however, is a curious sight: a *statue* of the deity (far left), formed after the same pattern as the seated deity, acts as an "image within an image" and cohabits the same sacred space as the larger Ishtar. Both the deity and the sculpted image receive the supplication of Naram-Sin, drawing the viewer into reflection on the nature of the image vis-à-vis the "real deity." From some modern or Western perspectives, one might be tempted to say that the relationship between image and divine being is backward—the statue should be in front, coming between the worshiper and the goddess, obstructing the priest's access and mediating the encounter through the material. However, the relationship here is different, as powerfully suggested even in the simple two-dimensional medium of the cylinder seal: by approaching the cult image, the worshiper is approaching the deity directly. The statue does not stand between worshiper and deity to "represent" the deity, but rather the deity comes between the worshiper and the statue, animating the experience in space simultaneous with the image (cf. this with the image of worshipers approaching the sun disc, behind which sits Shamash [as the "real deity," or cult image, or both?], in a ninth-century BCE tablet of the Babylonian king Nabu-apla-iddina; Woods 2004, 50–76; Mettinger 1995, 47–48).[8]

At least one interpreter has recently discussed the identity between image and deity in terms of the transubstantiated elements in the Christian Communion celebration (Dick 2005, 43–44), a description that does not imply an exact analogy but nevertheless suggests something of the mystical world of identity from the emic perspective. So too, Jacobsen (1987, 22, 29) spoke of the Mesopotamian cult statue as a "purely mystical unity" between image and deity, composed of material that does not limit the deity but nevertheless is "transubstantiated" in the ritual encounter. Elaborate and fascinating rituals were enacted in order to bring "life" and animation to the image and even to ritually deny the earthly origin of the statue (demonstrated through the *mīs pî*, "washing of the mouth" ritual; Walker and Dick 1999, 55–122; Berlejung 1997, 45–72; see the comments on statues, symbols, and the rituals involved with them in Wiggermann 1995, 1862–63; and an overview of rituals and cult images in many traditions in Hundley 2013, 139–372).

The Hebrew Bible gives explicit attention to the status of the image, denigrating all cult statues and divine images as "idols" or "nothings." One does not find in the Bible's stinging prophetic rebukes of the idol cult the kind of sympathy that would help us understand what ancient Near Eastern audiences would have experienced when they viewed images, though in an indirect way the Bible's mockery attests to the identity between image and deity that I have been sketching out above (see Holter 1995; Dick 1999). In the two most famous passages, Jer 10:1–16 and Isa 44:9–20, the respective prophets—perhaps both writing in the same era, the sixth century BCE—contrast what they see as the limited, physical potential

---

8. On this, see also the discussion below at "5.7. Comparanda: Aniconism in Mesopotamia, Egypt, Israel, and Greece," fig. 5.48.

of the "idol" to Israel's deity. For Jeremiah, false worship is simply "the way of the nations" (Jer 10:2, *derek haggôyîm*), the common form of idolatry, and the objects of this worship repeatedly called *hebel* ("vapor, futility, mere breath," etc.). Isaiah calls the maker of the "idol" (*pesel*) a "nothing" (*tōhû*) (Isa 44:9), incredulous that anyone would make or venerate such objects.

Both Jeremiah and (Second) Isaiah fixate on the physical process of image-making, highlighting a step-by-step process of working metal, pounding nails, transporting the image, and growing tired while making the images (M. S. Smith 2001, 180–88). Such mockery clearly attempts to demythologize what we can assume—by inference from the biblical passages and by more sympathetic Mesopotamian evidence itself (Walker and Dick 1999; Berlejung 1997)—were common assumptions about the status of the divine image: its materiality was indeed divine or divinized, the deity was materialized, and the divine-image artisan was a special ritual actor, empowered to bring the deity into visible existence for the worshiper.

3.2. Defining the Aniconic

Explaining this strange term *aniconism* proves to be no easy task. If defining an "image" for the ancient world takes us into a maze of anachronistic assumptions, not to mention contemporary theoretical challenges in the field of art history, then what hope do we have of understanding a "nonimage"? As the brief discussion above has hopefully suggested, terms such as *icon*, *aniconism*, and phrases such as *"represent* a deity" or *"x is a symbol* of the deity" cannot be unleashed flippantly in a critical discussion without first understanding the methodological difficulties involved with the task at hand. The question of definition and method for this particular topic is crucial since some of the existing discussions about Phoenician aniconism are built on unquestioned assumptions about what an "image" should truly be—a problem that applies to both modern and ancient commentators on the Phoenicians. Moreover, both modern and ancient interpreters of Phoenician imagery have loaded down their interpretations with sometimes severe and dubious judgments about the religious value of certain kinds of images, further complicating the task.

The term *aniconic* could be traced back to the writings of the second–third-century CE Christian author Clement of Alexandria, who used the Greek word *aneikoniston* in an anti-idolatry polemic to describe the impossibility of representing God by an image (see discussion in Gaifman 2012, 18–20).[9] In its modern usage, the term seems to have been coined by the eminent German classical archaeologist Johannes Adolph Overbeck, who used the adjective *anikonisch* to

---

9. The most detailed and thorough investigation into the history of the term aniconic/aniconism is Gaifman 2010a, 17–45, and she gives a survey of most discussions at least as they concern aniconism as an ancient Mediterranean phenomenon.

describe a particular period of Greek image worship (*anikonische Zeit*). For Overbeck, the term had theological motivations not far from Clement's usage, since the divine was for Overbeck truly *bildlos* (imageless), and thus his "perception that the lack of images—*Bildlosigkeit*—in primordial Greece was the consequence of the impossibility of representing the divine" (Gaifman 2012, 20). In Overbeck's scheme of the progression of Greek art, divine images first came in the form of nature—for example, trees or stones—and later developed into poles and worked stones. These wrought-stone objects, often called "betyls" after the Greek term *baitylos* as used by Philo of Byblos (presumably a calque from the Semitic term *bêt 'el*, "house of God"; see Gaifman 2008),[10] were for Overbeck evidence of the primacy of unwrought stone as an original symbol of the divine along an evolutionary continuum (Gaifman 2012, 21). As a final stage in the material journey, Greeks then represented deities in human form, and the era of *Ikonismus* (as opposed to *Anikonismus*) began.

In Overbeck's trajectory, the notion of an *anikonische Zeit* became a kind of consensus among a wide variety of classicists and Orientalists, though interpreters continued to disagree about the direction of the supposed evolutionary progression—that is, were anthropomorphic or other figural forms the zenith of the development or were they a primitive fetish? As Gaifman reviews this trajectory (2012, 24–26), it seems that a bedrock assumption about the importance of aniconism for Greek religion has made its way into many standard sources and reviews in Europe and elsewhere (see, e.g., Burkert 1979, 132; Vernant 1990, 38–39; and many articles in the standard iconographic lexicon *LIMC*, as cited by Gaifman 2012, 26 n. 49).

There would seem to be advantages for not defining aniconism too closely, namely, allowing the term to cover a very wide range of representations that are not obviously figural. But there are problems here: the term could slip into very broad and thus unuseful territory, and the term could obscure variation and motivation for any particular cultural appropriation of images. Indeed, one primary and bedeviling difficulty with defining aniconism as, in some manner, "lacking images" is the fact that such a definition is inevitably and perhaps disastrously predicated on the assumption that certain kinds of images (such as anthropomorphic statuary for worship) are *natural*, that they are *normal* and *expected*. If this assumption is not correct—either for the ancient audience (emically) or from the perspective of the remote interpreter (etically)—then one may well wonder why it is that aniconism should exist at all as a category or why "iconism" should not be seen as an anomaly worthy of discussion. To be sure, any shape, pattern, or motif, no matter how mundane, can become an "image" or "icon." No religious group has ever been devoid of "images" of *any* kind, broadly defined, although several groups have been notable for a restriction on *anthropomorphic* depictions of divinity (such as Judaism, Islam, and some forms of Christianity). Empty spaces

---

10. See further discussion on this below at "5.3. Stelae, Pillars, Standing Stones, Betyls."

are presumably all around us, yet there is no quantifiable space (on earth at least) where one can look and *not* see an image of *something*—the question is whether worshipers see the divine in any particular space.

The art historian David Freedberg (1989, 54) seems annoyed that anyone would use the term *aniconism* at all: "Abstinence from figuring the deity does occasionally occur, but for the rest the notion of aniconism is wholly untenable. It is clouded in vagueness and has its roots in confusion." He goes on to make an important point regarding the identification of anthropomorphism in ancient art (Freedberg 1989, 59): "At best we may call the images of primitive or chronologically remote cultures 'schematic'; at worst we may misidentify them. We may misidentify them to such an extent that we fail to acknowledge their anthropomorphic or their more generally figurative element."

As a preview to our discussion of specific examples of alleged Phoenician aniconism, let us consider a so-called "bottle idol" figure from the sixth–fifth-century BCE Motya tophet (fig. 3.2) and an ovoid cippus (fig. 3.3) of the same location (sixth century BCE), from among other examples we will explore later in this study. Both items could be labeled "nonfigurative" or nonanthropomorphic, but in fact a careful examination reveals potentially anthropomorphic qualities in both pieces. The figure in the bottle object is not haphazard, but rather a simple (even crude) representation of the human figure, perhaps with shoulders, a body, and a head, inhabiting a miniature shrine. The two holes in the ovoid cippus may represent eyes or possibly sockets for horns or some other figurally oriented decoration (as noted by Falsone 1993, 251). Another example of potentially anthropomorphic representation that may escape notice occurs on an early type of stone monolith at Carthage (fig. 3.4); despite its grouping on a page of plates with other "ordinary" and simplistic stones, this particular item has the potentially anthropomorphic bottle-figure engraved onto its face (Bénichou-Safar 2004, 177; pl. XLVII.5; compare with Bartoloni 1976, tav. CXXXI, 480).[11] In all three examples, those who approach them from a contemporary archaeological perspective must excel as interdisciplinarians, trespassing—as archaeologists must always do—into fields of art history and religion to discern meaning. An overly quick assumption about divine images on the model of Greek, Roman, or other Mediterranean and ancient Near Eastern statuary may prevent us from asking about the meaning of these images for their creators and original audiences.

One could maintain a working definition of *aniconism* even for figural representations, if that definition included, for example, attempts to step back from more boldly anthropomorphic forms. For example, within the boundaries of "aniconism," one may posit figuralism toned down beyond what the image maker considers appropriate or necessary. So much would seem to depend on the ideological

---

11. I will return to the "bottle idol" as an aniconic or iconic form in more detail below ("5.3. Stelae, Pillars, Standing Stones, Betyls").

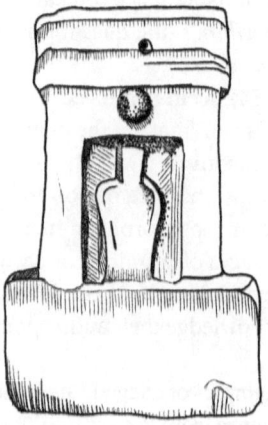 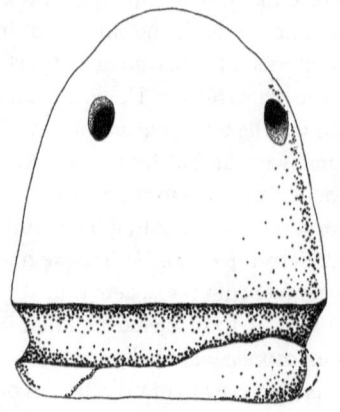

Fig. 3.2. Votive stele with "bottle idol"; Motya (Sicily); sixth century BCE; h. 36 cm (Moscati 1988a, 648.381)

Fig. 3.3. Ovoid "cippus"; Motya (Sicily); sixth century BCE; h. 24.2 cm (Falsone 1993, 271, fig. 2)

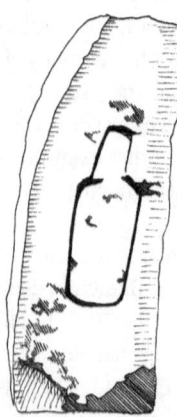

Fig. 3.4. Stone figure with bottle image; Carthage (Bénichou-Safar 2004, pl. XLVII.5)

stance of the image maker, the audience, the situation of viewing, and the interaction between (at least) these three components (not to mention the contours of the image itself). Thus one intractable problem involves the question of intentionality on the part of the worshiper: Is a particular "empty space" or "nonimage" *intentionally created* to "symbolize" or "convey" the presence of the deity in the mind of the craftsman? As Burkhard Gladigow correctly states, empty thrones, vacant inner sanctuaries, and riderless cult-wagons and horses become comprehensible *only within a specific ritual context*, where the "presence" or power of the deity appears (Gladigow 1988, 472; Metzler 1985–1986, 97, 100–101). Likewise, Fritz Blakolmer (2010, 49) draws attention to the ritual context of Bronze Age images in Minoan Crete and Mycenaean Greece to emphasize this problem: "The lack of cult images in the Aegean Bronze Age, as well as the emphasis on representations of ritual practices and cult celebrants in narrative scenes suggest that the religious focus of attention was not so much the image of the venerated deity itself, but rather the perpetuation of rituals. . . . The idea of epiphany in the context of performative rites, which should provoke the imaginary appearance of a deity . . . is a traditional one." Regarding Greek and Roman statues, Richard Gordon (1979, 11) notices how, "divested of their proper context," images "could easily be reclassified so as to be appropriate material for 'art history,'" and "such a perspective enables modern art historians to ignore a great deal of evidence about alternative ancient classifications of religions artifacts."[12]

Multiple ambiguities abound when searching for a more precise definition: How does one categorize visualizations (especially of a straightforward anthropomorphic nature) that are prompted *in the mind of a worshiper* by textual descriptions of divinity? And what about astral bodies or other natural features not created by human hands that may serve as icons of divinity (see, e.g., Schmidt 1995)? A failure to engage these questions of intentionality, form, and context can only confuse the issue. In *The HarperCollins Dictionary of Religion*, Jonathan Z. Smith (1995, 51), for example, defines *aniconic* with two words, "lacking images"; one is amazed to see such a cursory definition implicitly (or explicitly) followed for discussion of aniconic phenomena, yet even a phrase like this could serve as a bare-bones guideline as long as further explanation follows. Similarly, Victor and Edith Turner (1978, 235) gloss *aniconism* only as "indifference to icons," perhaps in order to differentiate aniconism from *iconophobia* and *iconoclasm*—the latter being defined as the destruction of images (usually anthropomorphic), although it would be inaccurate to say that the two phenomena, aniconism and iconoclasm, are not often linked (see Cancik 1988, 217; Freedberg 1989, 378–428; and various essays in Ellenbogen and Tungendhaft 2011).[13] The motivations for iconoclasm could trend toward the religious/spiritual or the political, though obviously those motivations are complicatedly intertwined in most scenarios (May 2012, sec. 2). As Troels Kristensen points out (2013, 29–32), the very term *iconoclasm* often carries with it an emphasis on the Judeo-Christian theological or scriptural stream, when in fact image "destruction" can involve more subtle types of responses—ranging from total oblitera-

---

12. This problem has been at least partly remedied for classical materials in the new studies of Gaifman 2010a; 2012; also Blakolmer 2010.

13. Though many immediately think of iconoclasm as a Christian phenomenon in antiquity (see, e.g., Kristensen 2013), iconoclastic movements are temporally, geographically, methodologically, and ideologically varied. See Besançon 2000 and May 2012 with reference to the ancient Near East.

tion on the one end but also including, on the other, strategies such as the humiliation, theft, hiding, alteration, or even "negative cultural redefinition" of images (see Kristensen's chart, 2013, 30; and May 2012, sec. 2).

Moving toward a more nuanced definition of aniconism, Gladigow provides a brief definition of an aniconic cult as one in which cult images, particularly anthropomorphic ones, are not known or permitted ("keine Bilder als Kultobjekte, insbesondere in Form von anthropomorphen Bildern kennen oder zulassen"; 1988, 472). Moreover, Gladigow proposes several categories to explain the extent and consequences of aniconic representation in a given system, such as the presence of standing stones, the centrality of a human actor rendering an image unnecessary, and the rise of idol polemics in monotheistic religions (1988, 472–73). Two additional studies stand out for their rigor in defining aniconism for their own subject matter: Tryggve Mettinger's *No Graven Image? Israelite Aniconism in Its Ancient Near Eastern Context* (1995) and Milette Gaifman's *Aniconism in Greek Antiquity* (2012). A review of each author's attempt to pin down a definition or range of definitions will give us a set of working parameters and focus our attention for consideration of the representations we will be discussing throughout this study.

For Mettinger (1995, 18), *aniconism* may be defined by "cults where there is no iconic representation of the deity (anthropomorphic or theriomorphic) serving as the dominant or central cultic symbol, that is, where we are concerned with either (a) an aniconic symbol or (b) sacred emptiness." The first of these categories (a) is termed "material aniconism" and the second (b) "empty space aniconism." (Mettinger also uses the phrase "aniconic tendencies" "where it is not clear whether the *cult* is aniconic or not," but where there are possibly indications of aniconism.) Mettinger further distinguishes between what he calls a "*de facto* tradition" and a "*programmatic* tradition" (1995, 18). De facto aniconism exhibits an "indifference" to icons, "a mere absence of images," and is "tolerant." Programmatic traditions repudiate images, are iconophobic, and thus likely to be iconoclastic. By introducing longer descriptions and more formal categories, Mettinger lays on the material a heavily etic framework, which he claims (with some justification) is necessary for cross-cultural comparisons (1995, 20). Accordingly, his discussion of aniconism is "confined to the level of the phenomenology of religion," centering "on the ritual characteristics of the cults in question." "Our definition of aniconism is not per se dependent on the type of imputed referential relation between the symbol (the theophoric object) and its referent (the worshippers' notion of God)" (1995, 20).[14] The implications of Mettinger's theoretical moves are many and complicate our task in several respects. For the moment, two examples will have to suffice.

---

14. See Mettinger 1995, 38 n. 114, where Mettinger distinguishes between *Gottesvorstellung* (a mental concept) and *Gottesbild* (reflected by language, ritual, image).

First, for some analogous materials in the Hittite sphere, Billie Jean Collins (2005, 21–22) has demonstrated that various "symbolic representations" (categorized under Mettinger's "material aniconism") received the same ritual/cultic attention as anthropomorphic images, thus blurring the line between "material aniconism" and straightforward iconism in some cases—at least with respect to the phenomenology of ritual. (The same case can be made for iconic versus aniconic images in the Greco-Roman world; see P. Stewart 2008, 303.) Moreover, as Angelika Berlejung rightly asserts, "aniconism can be just one of the religious practices in a cultural system which can interchange with iconic cults according to different temporal/local needs or traditions" (2009, 1211). Thus we must be on guard against creating an anachronistic "rivalry between aniconic and iconic cults" as a "retrojection of modern debates which are already deeply influenced by the biblical and/or philosophical controversy about idols" (Berlejung 2009, 1211).

Second, the boundary between Mettinger's de facto aniconism and simply having *no aniconic phenomena at all* could be very difficult (if not impossible) to discern in light of the inability to consider "the imputed referential relation between the symbol... and its referent." Without this imputed relationship, what exactly differentiates an architectural feature of a temple, such as a plain pillar, from a pillar created as an abstract form of the deity and thus an *intentional abstention from anthropomorphic representation*?

Having raised this question, it is fair to notice that in his definition and assessment Mettinger seeks to avoid an impossible analysis of the "mental concepts" of a worshiper in an idiosyncratic fashion, and his focus on "religious practice, with cultic behavior" is thus contrasted to the "mental concepts" of the worshiper insofar as such mental concepts are inaccessible (1995, 20). Furthermore, he affirms the "user's perspective" and does not advocate abandoning Peircian semiotics with its emphasis on the sign user in favor of the Saussurian perspective (which does not treat the sign user in the same way; Mettinger 1995, 21; Sheriff 1989). Whatever its drawbacks, Mettinger's system is helpful for thinking about ritual and image in an ancient context, where so much is unknown, and for thinking about how we might engage with text in the search for the aniconic.

In Gaifman's view (2012, 28), *aniconism*, considered in the abstract, "is a kind of highly malleable play-dough that can be transformed according to a field's traits and axioms." For the Greek materials, she asks us to give up the notion that aniconism should only be "limited to the veneration of non-figural material," thus opening the door to expressions similar to what Mettinger calls "material aniconism" (Gaifman 2012, 28). Moreover, when we engage in comparative work, Gaifman encourages us to consider that "the aniconism of one tradition is not necessarily compatible with that of another. For instance, aniconic Buddhist art could have elaborate narrative scenes that we would not normally find in Islamic aniconic art" (2012, 27). This "grey-area" style of definition (Gaifman 2012, 17), relative to specific contexts, is a strength of Gaifman's approach, though comparison among different groups' aniconisms must then proceed very carefully, as the interpreter clarifies in each case what kind of visual abstention is employed. Though she uses the definitions of Mettinger (1995) and Gladigow (1988) reviewed above as a starting point, Gaifman questions Mettinger's categories for some of the same reasons I do: "material" and "empty space" aniconism may not have been separate categories for the ancient worshiper, and in the case of the empty throne, the aniconism is not exactly an "empty space"—since the throne shapes and constrains the appearance of the deity on it—and even the throne itself could be an object of veneration in its own right. Moreover, we may be forced to interpret images from a heavily emic perspective, requiring us to engage beyond the "phenomenology of religion" as viewed by the detached scholar (Gaifman 2012, 35).

For the Greek aniconism(s) that are the focus of her study, Gaifman focuses on the question of divine representation (as opposed to many other types of non-figural art) and draws attention to the problem of a "focal point" of ritual: "An aniconic focal point in ritual could be defined as something that does not make a visual reference to a particular divinity through its form, as an object that without an accompanying text or identifying inscription is not indicative of the identity of a particular divinity" (Gaifman 2012, 39, see also 40–41). Even if attention to the focal point cannot answer every question or erase ambiguity, consideration of the concept "nurtures our sensitivity" as we look for alternate meanings and as we question why a particular type of representation was chosen vis-à-vis other possibilities (Gaifman 2012, 39). Ultimately, for Gaifman, aniconism manifests itself multiply, not rigidly or singly, and just as we must recognize iconic expression along a spectrum so too we should be dealing with a *spectrum* of aniconism (Gaifman 2012, 44).

My own working definition, then, proceeds from the helpful discussions of Mettinger, Gladigow, Gaifman, and others: for our purposes here, *aniconism* may be defined as a representational style that systematically (i.e., not inadvertently) avoids specific kinds of figural representation, most specifically anthropomorphic images of the deity or deities. Rather than using longer phrases throughout this study such as "anthropomorphic aniconism" or "nonanthropomorphic iconism," both of which could accurately describe the iconographic variety we find in the material record, I prefer the multivalence of the bare word *aniconism* as qualified by Gaifman through her focus on ambiguity, gray areas, and multiplicity. By making anthropomorphism—or indeed, any kind of clear "figurism" (images that clearly point back to an identifiable form, whether that be human, divine, animal, plant, astral, etc.)—a prominent part of the meaning of aniconism, I am still allowing for the use of some symbols, marks, and images to take part in aniconic phenomena. Moreover, a nuanced discussion of "aniconic" depictions may even *include* anthropomorphic or other images of a certain kind that avoid or "tone down" other existing figural representations for some explicit purpose (a purpose that may remain unknown to us)—and we may only be able to discern this avoidance through comparisons with surrounding cultures or images from the broader historical-cultural context of the alleged aniconic phenomenon. Though artistic,

Fig. 3.5. Geometrical carving on bone; Tharros (Sardinia); fifth–fourth century BCE; h. 5.4 cm (Uberti 1988, 419)

religious, or authorial "intention" of all kinds has justifiably come under great scrutiny in the past several decades, I confess that I remain haunted by this question of intentionality insofar as we must, for any historically or archaeologically oriented analysis, come to terms with ancient ritual practice and the particular stance toward and use of images in specific cultic contexts.

The problem at hand may be sharpened by reference to an actual image—a small Phoenician geometrical bone carving of a mere five centimeters in height from the colony at Tharros (Sardinia), dating to the fifth or fourth century BCE (fig. 3.5). Is this image "aniconic"? Perhaps it is in the sense that it does not portray an anthropomorphic or figural image, though it is an image *of some kind*—it is a series of rectangles within one another. That is not *nothing*; it is not purely "empty space" (at best it might be described as "abstracted space"). It is not zero representation. It is an image of something, and it is identifiable as an image. All of this is fair enough. However, without knowing whether in some ritual or other religious or personal context we are to fixate on, say, the inmost rectangle as some point of meditative focus or some place where a deity dwells or puts his or her face, how are *we* to know whether this is any kind of deviation from or variation on the notion of a "proper" iconic image? The answer of course is that we would not know. With enough context or other indicators, we could know (or claim to know), but there would seem to be little we could say about an object presented like this, isolated as an image on a page. In my conception, then, the iconic and the aniconic are *distinctly religious phenomena*, and religion—again presuming a particular definition for my purposes here—does not happen by accident or in a state of complete unawareness. Thus it seems inevitable that we must link the notions of the iconic and the aniconic in terms of not just a phenomenologistic art history but rather a religious representation of deities for some exact purpose in a particular context. Having said that, it seems clear that someone could take up the term *aniconism* for purposes of classifying images without any intent on making thick interpretations of an image's religious purpose; everything depends on what we are looking for.

In many cases, as we will see, interpreters will simply not be able to come to satisfying conclusions about the ritual contexts of certain images (whether iconic or aniconic), and yet in other cases a consideration of such contexts will lead to plausible ideas about the meaning of aniconism. As the situation stands, we must remain content to use the term *aniconism* broadly, taking care in each instance to consider whether anthropomorphic form is in fact being employed and to what extent aniconic forms are used alongside iconic ones.

3.3. The Critics and Proponents of Aniconism

Scholarly literature on forms typically deemed aniconic in some way—such as unmarked stones, pillars, or stelae—has sometimes exhibited a curious tendency to judge these expressions in a polarized manner, often trending toward either denigrating them as evidence of the extreme stupidity of their venerators or vaunting them as sublime examples of highly evolved spiritual sensibilities. We may trace the origins of many of these judgments to assumptions about the normative stance of images—that icons or anthropomorphic images were or were not the default mode of cultic expression (as discussed above).[15] Each in their own ways, three influential late nineteenth- and early twentieth-century studies helped disseminate the idea that "crude" (nonfigural) objects of worship, such as aniconic pillars, were "fetishes" predominant among "primitive" groups: Edward B. Tylor's *Primitive Culture* (1871; 1920), James G. Frazer's *The Golden Bough* (1890), and William Robertson Smith's *Religion of the Semites* (1894) (on Tylor and Frazer regarding this topic, see Gaifman 2010b, 277–80; 2012, 23).

Smith (1894, 166–67, 186–90), for example, saw rudimentary "natural symbols" such as streams and trees as sites for particularly "superstitious reverence," connected with the "Canaanite" Baal religions in particular. Nonnatural objects,

---

15. Compare Gaifman's comments on Greek aniconism in this respect (2012, 3): "The subject of aniconism requires us to set aside one of the central suppositions predominant in the field—albeit not to the same degree in all schools of thought—namely, the view of 'iconism' as essentially a normative default of Greek image-making." See also Mettinger 1995, 19–20, who explicitly rejects making any value judgments about whether "an aniconic divine symbol should imply a more spiritual notion of deity than an iconic one."

such as standing stones, were for Smith only rude precursors to the altar, which Smith calls the "real meeting-place between man and his god" (1894, 200). Despite acknowledging that many would consider sacred-stone-worship to be a "fetish" and disparaging such objects from an artistic point of view, Smith does admit that "from a purely religious point of view its inferiority to image worship is not so evident" (1894, 209). Remarking on the Phoenicians specifically, Smith views certain votive objects as at least marking an advancement—in terms of religious meaning and human relatability—above a "mere pillar," since such objects would presumably need explanation whereas a votive with an inscription would make clear sense for personal use. Smith assumed that the Phoenicians (along with the Israelites and the "Arabs at the time of Mohammed") preferred "small gods for private use," whereas central sanctuaries needed only a pillar or some other presumably aniconic symbol (1894, 209).

The putative movement from nature worship to idols to something more sublime (and probably aniconic)—usually in this evolutionary order—could be interpreted as a religious problem or as evidence of some other religious dynamic related to aniconism. In his analysis of "fetishism" and the "rhetoric of iconoclasm" by Marx and others in the modern period, Mitchell traces a complex genealogy of ideas regarding the image and the value of the icon (1986, 190–99). Discussing Ludwig Feuerbach (citing the famous *The Essence of Christianity*, 1841), Mitchell shows how Feuerbach recognized a progression in Judaism from "idol" worship to monotheism, but this move was for Feuerbach a negative one, since polytheism represents a positive connection with nature and its symbols—whereas Judaism simply transformed the idol into an "idol of the egoistic will" in the figure of the Lord. Deeply influenced by Feuerbach, Marx seized on this logic to posit the Jew as the "arch-iconoclast who wants to smash all the traditional fetishes and replace them with commodities" (in Mitchell's words; Mitchell 1986, 199). For at least early Second Temple, Hellenistic, and Roman Judaism, often considered offhandedly as the aniconic religion of antiquity par excellence, past assumptions about rigorous antifigural trends ran afoul of archaeological discovery of a great variety of iconography, such as lavish human depictions and even God's own hands in the Dura-Europos synagogue (third century CE; see Fine 2005, 165–209; and the overview in Katz 2009). As Maya Balakirsky Katz points out (2009, 1216), alleged aspects of Jewish aniconism could provide either a helpful congener for the post-Reformation Protestant rejection of Catholic imagery (so Immanuel Kant) or a point of disparagement against Jews in Europe (so Hegel).

These types of discussions were obviously not limited to Jews in this context of modernist scholarship. In her study of Greek aniconism, Gaifman (2010, 1–2) notices that the seminal work of the German archaeologist and art historian Johannes Joachim Winckelmann, *Geschichte der Kunst des Altertums* (published in 1764), presents natural images and nonanthropomorphic stones as the historically primary form of Greek image worship. This recognition apparently allowed Winckelmann to assert the superior nature of Greek expression, since these "unwrought stones" give us "pivotal proof that art was inherent to the Greeks and had not been imported" (Gaifman 2012, 1–2). In Winkelmann's own words, the Greeks "already visibly honored thirty deities before they gave them human form," and thus "among the Greeks, art began much later than in the Eastern lands but with the same simplicity, such that the Greeks appear, as they themselves report, not to have gathered the first seeds for their art from other people but rather to have been its original inventors" (quoted in Gaifman 2012, 2 n. 6).

I offer these selective examples not in order to heap abuse on what contemporary theorists of religion can only view with grave and legitimate suspicion, but rather to show that the tendency to discuss the iconic and aniconic in a value-loaded way was a stock part of eighteenth-to-twentieth-century analysis, and indeed such trends continue—even specifically in the case of the Phoenicians and their images. In an article comparing Israelite and Phoenician religion, for example, Brian Peckham (1987, 80) follows up a brief discussion of the "standing stone" phenomenon by calling Tyrian religion "effete" (?) and later declares the Carthage stelae to be "tiresome and unimaginative" (88). Eugene Stockton speaks of Semitic aniconism as opposed to Egyptian "animal worship and preoccupation with death," which could only be a "bizarre" aberration vis-à-vis the "more theological, abstract religious thought of the Semite" (1974–1975, 2). Though a nontechnical and now somewhat dated source, Aldo Massa's *The Phoenicians* (1977) exhibits an ongoing tendency to view Phoenician religion and material representation as "primitive" on an evolutionary scale: "Phoenician religion . . . had a distinct air of fetishism . . . sacrifices and prayers were offered to the rocks, caves, springs and rivers" (Massa 1977, 85–86). In this context, the author claims, "we must seek the origin of the worship of the *betyl*," with betyl worship dating

> back to the very birth of religious sentiment, and its first manifestations, though the homage paid to these crude symbols was never so intense as during the decadent period of the ancient world. In fact, their very strangeness, with its capacity to arouse curiosity, had a strong appeal for the jaded imagination of the decadent. It was particularly at this time that a crude stone could be regarded as the highest incarnation of the divinity. What happened was a regression on the part of society, towards the tastes of childhood, not unlike the corresponding phenomenon in individuals. (Massa 1977, 85–86)

The reason for this stunted artistic tradition, according to Massa, is geographical and political: the identification of various gods with different cities and locales "could not fail to slow down the development of religious thinking, and was not likely to arouse and inspire the artistic imagination" (this, as opposed to the Greeks, whose deities allegedly transcended the specific and united all Greece with corresponding lofty images; Massa 1977, 96–97).

Later in this study, we will turn to analyze various aniconic religious movements in the ancient world of the Phoenicians generally,[16] but for the moment I would like to make some brief comments on the perceived political, religious, and ideological value of image abstentions of various kinds for those who employ and value these abstentions. Figural, anthropomorphic iconography held (and holds) the attention of worshipers for perhaps obvious reasons: the correspondence between deity-as-figural-image and worshiper-as-figure draws a meaningful relationship between the world of the worshiper and the deity—just as a strong human arm may cultivate crops, so too a visibly obvious, strong divine arm may aid such a process. Just as a king sits on a throne, wears a crown, and receives obeisance and taxes, the divine figure wears a divine crown, sits on a thrown, and receives obeisance and offerings. These corresponding visual indices reinforce the permanence, power, and divine nature of the symbolic universe of the monarchy within the political, economic, and social spheres of the image-viewer.

In light of these advantages for figural divine representation, where the "concrete" and the "spiritual" overlap as they do for the audience, what value might aniconic representations offer? Some interpreters have made outright theological judgments on the value of the image vis-à-vis its avoidance or transcendence; as one relatively recent reviewer of the iconic-aniconic continuum in ancient Near Eastern religions asserts, "The true essence of the gods will always transcend the image" (Cornelius 1997, 43), and another avers that what is "concretized" cannot "instill the feeling of the numinous" (Lewis 2005, 106–7). In his study of blank spaces in theologically and legally loaded print pages and paintings in the sixteenth and seventeenth centuries CE, Peter Goodrich rightly argues that "blank space is neither innocent nor indifferent," despite frequent suspicions (in the context Goodrich addresses, but also for many different materials and periods) that blank space signals an "unfinished quality" (Goodrich 1999, 89, 97). Opposed to these suspicions of artistic bungling, Goodrich (1999, 91) argues that emptiness signals "a future or external power that irrupts within the frame of the painting"; in specific circumstances, this emptiness may even become an argument of sorts, even polemical, especially when juxtaposed with images in the immediate cultic context or in a broader context of "images" of all kinds (e.g., see Welten and Goud 2009 on aniconism and its relation to the philosophical and ethical program of Emmanuel Levinas).

Even when the image creator does not intend an aniconic piece polemically— most aniconic forms from the ancient world were undoubtedly not intentionally subversive—aniconism automatically evokes questions of presence and absence for the viewer. A striking contemporary example might be the Rothko Chapel in Houston, Texas, where the famed twentieth-century artist Mark Rothko installed a series of dark, imageless paintings as a point of religious contemplation. Art his-

---

16. See below "5. Phoenician Aniconism."

torians continue to debate the success of these images, but many come away with the sense that Rothko's "'imageless' art" in this context can "place each person in contact with a tragic idea" (Novak and O'Doherty 1998, 273), perhaps death or something solemn, while at the same time the chapel provides a standing argument at the end of modernist art on the varied effects of abstract painting, evoking emotions of tranquility or a brooding, buzzing presence beneath the void or the enormous complexity of any experience (Novak and O'Doherty 1998, 273–75). Scholarship on Buddhist art presents a long genealogy of explanations for aniconic references to the Buddha, with spiritual motivations and explanations not so unlike those given for the Rothko Chapel pieces (see a review in Huntington 1990, but with challenges to the entire concept of Buddhist aniconism; see also Swearer 2003).

Obviously one could adduce many more examples on this front. Needless to say, then, the notion that simple or nonfigural representations are "simplistic" or "childish" fetishes would not stand before a scrutiny of imageless art and worship through many centuries and in varied contexts. Indeed, we will see that, for the Phoenicians, the long-standing appearance of aniconic cultic objects, such as the distinctly Phoenician petaled incense stands found in multiple contexts were, for around a thousand years (tenth century BCE–first century CE), reproduced not out of a slavish, simplistic, or conservative material tradition but rather because of religious *meaning*: incense burning was a central act in Phoenician religion, and even unadorned stands may have served as a focus of veneration as synechdotal indicators of the temple as cosmos (see Culican 1980, 99–101).

4

Phoenician Iconism

Amid the many ambiguities about Phoenician identity and the problems of locating aniconism in the material record, we can be sure of one thing: Phoenicians produced anthropomorphic images of their deities. Indeed, they did so in a variety of ways that often reflect well-known conventions in ancient Near Eastern and Mediterranean art, and it is important for us to establish this base so as to more accurately and sensitively see deviations from iconicity in the realm of the aniconic. In this section of the study, then, I provide a geographically and chronologically broad review of Phoenician religious iconography, with a particular focus on the presentation of deities and other figures in anthropomorphic form. Given the diversity of Phoenician identity and influence in the Mediterranean world, this review will of course be highly selective, and specific environments involving potentially aniconic objects are treated in the following chapter.

4.1. The Phoenician Artistic Context

Phoenician religious representation cannot be divorced from Phoenician material production generally; the very term *religion*, as a reified modern concept, could unhelpfully obscure the vital connection between religious and art-historical concerns, and thus we begin here with a brief review of Phoenician art. Already in one of the first attempts at a comprehensive treatment of the topic, Georges Perrot and Charles Chipiez bemoaned the lack of clear boundaries for defining any distinctly Phoenician style, concluding that interpreters simply had to rely on "tact and appreciation" for making decisions about inclusion in the Phoenician corpus (1885, 102). Henri Frankfort characterized the "hallmark" of Phoenician art as the "lavish use of bungled Egyptian themes" (1970, 310) and found both Phoenician ivorywork and metal bowls to be "garish" (1970, 331). More specifically, and reflecting criticisms of Phoenician art leveled by others, Frankfort saw the Phoenicians as a people "without pictorial traditions," forced to adopt symbols from others (i.e., the Egyptians) that were used willy-nilly or at least in ways for which the original Egyptian context of the image was misunderstood or misconstrued entirely (1970, 321–22). Even so, Frankfort was able to recognize that the wide distribution of

Phoenician craftsmanship in the Near East and Mediterranean would ensure that these bungled motifs could be grasped by a wide variety of users and, as apparently for the Phoenicians themselves, the iconographic mismatch or void could be filled in with concepts native to the user of the image (1970, 322).

More recent interpreters, however, have moved toward an increasingly nuanced appreciation of what the Phoenicians could accomplish with their images (e.g., Gubel 2000; Brown 1992, 21; Markoe 1990).[17] This appreciation does not constitute a clear or simplistic assumption about what "Phoenician art" is to begin with—as Marian Feldman points out (2014, 36–37), when we say "Phoenician art" it is often not clear whether we mean a particular style, material culture produced by individuals with "Phoenician" parents, people (regardless of blood lineage) who live in "Phoenician" cities or colonies, and so on.[18] Moreover, the incomplete nature of archaeological investigation means our views of Phoenician art must remain more provisional than for other groups, given that two of the most prized Phoenician artistic traditions—textiles and woodwork—have been lost due to environmental factors (disintegration) (Markoe 2000, 143). What has emerged from the materials we do possess demonstrates a relatively clear continuity of material tradition along the northern Levantine coast from the Late Bronze Age through the Iron Age (Markoe 1990, 13–14), signaling long-standing traditions that cannot be dismissed as ad hoc or unorganized borrowings from other groups. Indeed, the influence of the Phoenician tradition farther east into Syria-Palestine generally shows that Phoenician style was perceived as distinct and valuable (Markoe 2000, 143, 145; Moscati 1988b, 246).

Furthermore, what some had labeled as "unimaginative" borrowing has been reassessed more positively as a "unique and often unprecedented combination of contrasting styles and motifs" (Markoe 2000, 145). The notable amount of variation we find among different periods of Egyptian "borrowing" shows that artistic adap-

---

17. The most lavishly illustrated and coherent visual presentation of Phoenician images of all kinds to date is Moscati 1988a, with summary interpretation (as well as some more detailed forays) of divine images in particular by Acquaro 1988; Bisi 1988; Ciasca 1988; Moscati 1988b; 1988c; 1988d; 1988e; Uberti 1988. In the catalog style, see also Gubel et al. 1986; 2002; various portions of Aruz, Graff, and Rakic 2014. See the review of materials by many authors in Krings 1995, 426–552, especially Ciafaloni 1995 on iconography. Markoe 2000, 143–69, is a systematic single review of Phoenician material culture focusing on art and iconography; see also Brown 1992 for a shorter summary, in addition to the other works cited below.

18. Feldman (2014, 37) goes on to state that these complications regarding the meaning of the individual, geography, and culture are alleviated when we eschew very particular assumptions about identity, viz., that it is "inherent and completely prior to material expression." Identity is also social, involving communities and the fullest engagements those communities provide. Similarly, consider Boardman's comments (2003, 3) on the phrase "Greco-Phoenician" with regard to either Greek or Phoenician craftsman.

tation was not the product of a single utilitarian moment nor a uniform chronological phenomenon (Gubel 1983, 45) but rather an ongoing conversation of exchange (also Gubel 2000, 209–12; Markoe 2000, 146; Moscati 1988b, 247; Brown 1992, 7–8). Even for those who continue to characterize Phoenician art in terms of motifs and symbols that were reduced to meaningless decoration through time (such as Moscati 1988b, 247; "representation is neglected in favor of decoration"; Gubel 1993, 121–22, on the use of decorative hieroglyphics; Brown 1992, 7–8), there is still recognition that this "decorative reduction" (supposing such a reduction exists) is not the primary goal but rather the result of a longer process. Commenting on the Phoenician bowl tradition in terms of its elite status, design constraints, and iconographic strategy, Francesca Onnis concludes that these objects are marked by a "strong sensitivity for composition," not a mere "decorative impulse," to the point that "the iconographic motifs were entirely linked to the object that constituted the physical medium, from the point of view of its material use [for elite eating/drinking activities], symbolism, or evocative potential" (2014, 180).

As far as more specific identifying features of Phoenician representation, we have already briefly discussed the style of the Phoenician ivory corpus from ninth-century Nimrud and elsewhere, which utilized a particular artistic flair. Such a distinctive type of "realism" in the presentation of human, divine, and animal figures (even sphinxes and other mythological animals) involved the repeated use of specific motifs (e.g., uraeus-flanked sun disc) and the pervasive adaption of Egyptian motifs (Winter 2010c, 191–96; 2010b, 282; Barnett 1957; compare with Gunter 2009, 95–101). In his still authoritative study of the Phoenician metal bowl tradition, Glenn Markoe affirms the inimitable and boldly eclectic nature of the designs generally—but more specifically, Markoe contends, what we find as distinctive of the Phoenician style is the combination of Egyptian, Aegean, and Mesopotamian features in "unprecedented" and unique stylistic expression (but cf. Onnis 2014 on the identity of these bowls as clearly or only "Phoenician," as well as some remarks in Feldman 2014, 31–32, and the rigorous methodological outline set out in Winter 2005, 36–38).[19]

As a particular example of this creative hybridizing, an artistic process about which we will have more to say later in this study, consider a gold-plated silver bowl, originally from Kourion (Cyprus) and probably dating to the late eighth–early seventh centuries BCE (fig. 4.1; image and discussion in Markoe 1985, 177–78, 256–59). The Greek Cypriote inscriptions on the piece (not visible in the rendering here and only noticed recently on the piece itself) attest to the linguistic associations of the bowl with the Aegean world, and the iconographic register of the bowl attests to the "melting pot" of cultures and influences from Iron Age

---

19. More specifically, Onnis (2014, 160) considers the appellative "Phoenician" to be a conventional if not misleading label for the "Iron Age stage" of the "evolution" of a broadly Mediterranean artistic style from the mid–late second millennium BCE.

Fig. 4.1. Silver and gold bowl from Kourion (Cyprus); d. 16.8 cm (Markoe 1985, Cy8, 256–59; Aruz, Graff, and Rakic 2014, 159–60)

Cyprus (see Steele 2013 on the linguistic situation, and Markoe 1985, 177–78, on the imagery). The figures offer a "greatest hits" set of popular Near Eastern images: at center, an Assyrian-style "genius" figure enacts the great Assyrian lion hunt, shielded by Egyptian Horus falcons as well as many other Egyptian motifs (the smiting-Pharaoh scene with the Egyptian falcon deity Re-Harakhte, as well as the Egyptian winged goddess on the model of Isis). To the left of the central scene, on the outer rim, a heroic figure fights a lion—the leonine appearance of the figure as well as the activity may suggest the deity is Melqart (Markoe 1985, 177, calls it a "'Melqart' figure"), the primary Phoenician god at Tyre. The stylized palmettes are ubiquitous in ancient Near Eastern and Syro-Palestinian art generally. Even given these multinational influences, Eric Gubel still believes some bowls of this kind can "inform us about long lost key monuments of Phoenician architecture," even shedding light on the biblical description of the Solomonic temple (2000, 195, esp. fig. 16a–b).

4.2. Texts Referring to Phoenician Divine Images

Before returning to further direct examples of Phoenician images, we should acknowledge the few native Phoenician textual/inscriptional materials that speak of divine iconography we do possess (see parallel discussion in Mettinger 1995, 83-84). Such references are scarce and allow for only an indirect observation of the Phoenicians's own view of their images. Let us consider three examples from the Iron Age, right at the heart of Phoenician expansion in the eighth-sixth centuries BCE.

The sixth-century BCE Phoenician inscription from Pyrgi (modern Santa Severa, Italy) gives us two tantalizing references to an image (*KAI* 227; Fitzmyer 1966; Gibson 1982, 151-59). The author (*TBRY' WLNŠ*) informs us of Astarte's request to build a temple or shrine, which the individual receives in a particular month "on the day of the burial of the deity" (*bym qbr 'lm*). The concluding wish for blessing in the inscription asks for "the years (granted) to the statue of the deity in her temple [*wsnt lm'š 'lm bbty*]" to be "years like the stars above!" (Gibson 1982, 154). In the phrase *lm'š 'lm*, the aleph is probably not an internal *mater lectionis* at this early date; *m'š* can mean "gift," but both *m'š* and *mš* can mean "sacred object" or "statue" (see Hoftijzer and Jongeling 1995, 589-90; Gibson 1982, 158). The terms *mš* and *sml*, indicating a divine statue as a gift or simply a divine image (respectively), can also be found in one of the Lapethos inscriptions (Cyprus, early third century BCE) (*KAI* 46; see the translation and commentary in Gibson 1982).

The reference to the "burial of the deity" is enigmatic but may refer to a process wherein a statue of a deity is buried and then ritually "revived" (Hallo 1983, 8, 15-16; Lewis 2005, 102; Mettinger 2001; cf. with Gen 35:4). The prayer for a long life for the statue of the deity (*lm'š 'lm*) is especially interesting for our purposes and, recalling our discussion of the ancient Near Eastern perspectives on the image, implicitly reveals something about the image and its perceived relationship to divinity—deities have a "life," albeit of their own kind, and the ruination of a divine statue can be disastrous for the well-being of the deity. As an analogy for this close association between the life of the statue and the deity, we may consider Marduk's close relationship with his cult image (and/or symbolic paraphernalia) in the Erra Poem (eighth century BCE), where Marduk's very position of authority at the head of the divine assembly is threatened when his cult image falls into disrepair and needs cleaning (see translation and comments in Cagni 1977; Machinist 1984, 222).

The bilingual (Phoenician and Hieroglyphic Hittite) inscription from Karatepe (late eighth-early seventh century BCE) also provides a reference to the presence and treatment of images (*KAI* 26; *ANET* 653-54; Gibson 1982, 41-64; Younger 2003, 148-50; Röllig 1995b, 206-8). The rendering of the key text here is disputed; however, the "traditional" translation (as in *ANET* and Gibson 1982) reads as follows: "I made Baal KRNTRYŠ dwell in it. Now let people bring a sacrifice for all the images [*hmskt*], the yearly sacrifice of one ox, and at plowing [time] one sheep, and at harvest time one sheep!" (Aii.18-19-Aiii.1-2) (Gibson 1982, 51). Newer analyses, on the other hand, have questioned the translation of *hmskt* as "images" and pointed to the appearance of another common term for images, *sml*, in another line as being the only term used for a divine image in the inscription (c.iv.15–16, *bsml ʾln*, "the statue of his deity"; Röllig 1995b, 206–8; Hoftijzer and Jongeling 1995, 792–93). Younger translates *hmskt* as "riverland," apparently taking *mskt* as a *maqtal* noun of *nsk*, designating localities (*massakot*, river plains; Younger 2003, 150; see also Röllig 1995b, 208). This translation is not entirely convincing, however. Jacob Hoftijzer and Karel Jongeling retain "molten image" as a definition for *mskh* (1995, 664–65); although the term is admittedly rare (or possibly a *hapax* in the Northwest Semitic inscriptional corpus), it is equally a stretch to take *mskh* as a variant of *mšqh* ("riverland"), which is itself a very rare designation (see Hoftijzer and Jongeling 1995, 665). We may also point to the Punic *nskh* (*KAI* 122,1.2), which clearly does indicate a statue cast in metal (Hoftijzer and Jongeling 1995, 736).

One annalistic reference from the Assyrian king Ashurbanipal (668–633 BCE) is also worth noting. On his return from a battle against Uateʾ, king of Arabia, Ashurbanipal claims to have conquered the town of Ushu (i.e., mainland Tyre) as punishment for a failed tribute payment. "Their images and the (surviving) people I led as booty to Assyria" (*ANET* 300; see also the reference to Tiglath-Pileser III's campaign in Syro-Palestine, *ANET* 283). Some would claim that this particular boast should be seen as merely formulaic and thus reveals little about the role of images in Tyre (Mettinger 1995, 194–95; but see also Hallo 1983, 13–14). However, the statement might also be a straightforward indication of images in a central position within Tyrian temples, and thus the capture of such items was ideologically noteworthy for the Assyrians.

4.3. Overview of Phoenician Anthropomorphic Iconography

Turning now more specifically to the range of Phoenician divine anthropomorphic iconography, my strategy will be to sketch out the range of materials we have on this front at the broadest possible level, then focus on some particular "case studies" of anthropomorphic divine representation—both from mainland Phoenician sites and the Mediterranean colonies. As noted earlier, on the whole, much of the available textual and inscriptional evidence suggests that the Phoenicians conceived of their deities in a manner fully congruent with the rest of the ancient Near East: gods and goddesses met in assemblies, decided the important affairs of humanity, and were often connected to a particular city or natural phenomenon (Clifford 1990, 56–57; Ribichini 1990). As we might expect, then, ample evidence for anthropomorphic representations of Phoenician deities is easily documented, and no one has argued (or should argue) for any kind of sweeping, programmatic Phoenician aniconism.

Nevertheless, clear examples of Phoenician divine iconography should be established upfront in order to show that the Phoenicians apparently felt free to represent in anthropomorphic form both male and female deities for a long period of time. This recognition is important, because in the most detailed attempt to discuss Phoenician aniconism to date (Mettinger 1995), the treatment somewhat downplays the significance of Phoenician anthropomorphic representation, and examples are chosen from dubious textual sources or materials that are very late (Mettinger 1995, 82–83). The bronze image of Kronos (Phoenician Baal Hammon), for example, described by Diodorus in his *World History* (ca. 60–30 BCE) is often paraded as an example of Phoenician divine statuary (see the edition of Veh and Wirth 2005, 220, XX, 14.6; Mettinger 1995, 82), but there is no reason to tout such a polemical source as primary information for Phoenician iconism.[20] Even though we are able to document some examples of anthropomorphic imagery, the amount of material vis-à-vis Mesopotamia and Egypt is admittedly underwhelming—though this gap in evidence could be attributed to a lack of thorough excavation at key sites (most specifically Tyre or Sidon on the mainland, though more work on these fronts has been done since at least Mettinger's study).

Perhaps the most traditional, "official" form of the divine image in the ancient Near Eastern world would be the statue of the deity—Phoenician examples range in media from bronze statuettes, coroplastic (terracotta) figures, and other statuary (e.g., in stone; see Gubel 2000). Most agree that the Phoenicians did not nurture a large-scale tradition of freestanding-stone-statue making (Moscati 1988c, 284; Markoe 2000, 152–53). Having said that, we do have scattered examples of stone torsos and male figures of various kinds from Tyre, Sarepta, and Sidon, with analogies and comparable objects in colonial settings. Obviously it is not always possible to tell if the anthropomorphic figures are humans or deities (or of some other nature), a problem that exists for many aspects of ancient art (see, e.g., Suter 2014). If we include stelae in this category, the dataset could expand considerably, especially considering the Carthage tophet images (on which see below). The term *stele* traditionally describes flat-faced stone objects on which texts and/or images are inscribed, yet many Phoenician examples straddle the borderline between flat stelae and more three dimensional examples with figures deeply carved into the stone. Many of these feature an anthropomorphic form of some kind in a shrine or temple-in-miniature setting (sometimes on the *naiskos* model)—of the shrine-stelae of this type, the vast majority that we now possess are from nonmainland sites such as Carthage, Motya (western Sicily), Selinus (Selinunte; southern Sicily), Sulcis (southwestern Sardinia), and Nora (far southern Sardinia), dating as early as the sixth century BCE in some cases but usually later (in the fourth–second centuries; see the overview in Moscati 1988d, esp. 313–26, on this category of images; fig. 4.2).

A different production process—nevertheless with similar visual results—generated terracotta *naiskoi* ("temples") with clear Aegean influences, a motif that circulated from east to west and west to east and back again through Cyprus (fig. 4.3; see Bisi 1988; for variations from Cyprus, see, e.g., Karageorghis 1993, 86–88,

---

20. See below at "5.1 Retrospective."

pl. XXXVIII). In the figures pictured here (figs. 4.2, 4.3), the anthropomorphic figures are not necessarily both deities—indeed, in figure 4.2, the figure carries an offering cup and a textile of some sort over the shoulder, possibly suggesting a priest or supplicant in the shrine, whereas the figure striding the lions (quite eroded in the piece itself but still visible) in the example from Sidon (fig. 4.3) more clearly displays a deity. As we will see, these shrine scenes are particularly important for thinking about aniconic strategies, since we must provide some analysis of the meaning for shrines that feature "betyl"-style pillars at the center instead of the anthropomorphic figure or even no figure whatsoever.

For small bronze and other freestanding terracotta figures, examples abound. From mainland Phoenician sites, we have many examples of clay female "pillar figurines" exhibiting stylistic parallels of varying degrees with the numerous Israelite and Judahite examples from the Iron Age. Presumably, all of the problems relating to the identity of these figures in the debate over the ancient Israelite pillar figurines—most assume they are goddesses—would pertain to the Phoenician data as well (see the earlier major study of Kletter 1996, and the now authoritative treatment of Darby 2014, esp. 312–13, 322–33, 343–50, and 358–60).

Though the metal statuette tradition was more limited in scope, many in the "smiting god" stance are reminiscent of Baal images from Late Bronze Age Ugarit, with ample parallels in Egypt. (See the review in Acquaro 1988 and also Bisi 1986 on the smiting god motif in the western colonies as evidence of the complex artistic interaction between colonizer and native peoples who are willing to incorporate Phoenician religious iconography; compare with other examples in Negbi 1976.) Here too many of the best-preserved examples are from the western Mediterranean, particularly Gadir and Huelva; a shipwreck discovered in 1955 near Sicily featured a bronze statuette of a deity in a striking pose (possibly Resheph) with clear Canaanite origins (Aubet 2001, 201–2), and such figures were very traditional ("preserving all [of their] archaizing features," according to Aubet 2001, 203–4) in their production through the seventh century BCE. The goddess also strikes a smiting pose in bronze, as demonstrated in an eighth–ninth-century piece from Syria-Lebanon, which Gioacchino Falsone (1986, 76) claims is "a syncretistic figure of the ancient Oriental goddess of love and warfare, in which Anath, Astarte, Ishtar, the Baalat Gebal and Hathor are all assimilated into a single deity."

Smaller images played a very important role and come in the form of scarabs, coins (after the fifth century BCE), bone carving, ivories, masks, and various other kinds of metalwork and inscribed objects (see figs. 4.4, 4.5 [cf. the Horus figure with images in Boardman 2003, pl. 52]; for an overview of Phoenician glyptic art, see Gubel 1993, and for other Persian-period anthropomorphic examples, Nunn 2008). For example, John Boardman (2003, 30–36) has cataloged hundreds of green jasper scarabs, produced from Phoenician workshops during the Persian period (sixth–fourth centuries BCE; see also Culican 1960–1961; 1968; e.g., fig. 4.4). Egyptian-style deities and divine motifs appear on dozens of these seals (Boardman 2003, pls. 4–13); scarabs from Ibiza depict several figures—probably

Fig. 4.2. Terracotta shrine-stele with figure; Monte Sirai (Sardinia); fourth–third century BCE; h. 55.5 cm (Moscati 1988a, 319)

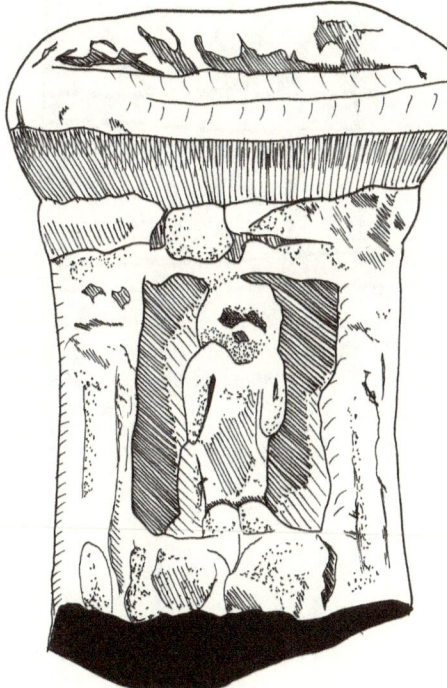

Fig. 4.3. Terracotta shrine with figure atop lions; Sidon; fifth century BCE; h. 6 cm (Bisi 1988, 353; Gubel et al. 1986, 122)

Fig. 4.4 (left). Royal figure on scarab; green jasper; Persian period; Tharros (Sardinia) (Boardman 2003, pl. 16, 16.6)

Fig. 4.5 (center). Horus on lotus flower from Nimrud; ivory; eighth century BCE; h. 5.6 cm (Uberti 1988, 413; Gubel et al. 1986, 232)

Fig. 4.6 (right). Coin with figure riding winged horse, waves, and dolphin; Tyre; fourth century BCE (Elayi and Elayi 2009, pl. 34, O43, 1061)

deities—with canonical headdress seated on sphinx thrones nearly always with a raised hand and incense burner before them. (On the incense burner as a particularly Phoenician image in this context, see Culican 1960–1961, 45.) On coins, the figure or half figure of a male figure—some possibly Melqart—appears from the late fifth–early fourth century BCE (examples in Hill 1910: xvii–xxi, pls. I.1–10; cf. Betlyon 1982, 79–80, esp. pls. 1.1, 1.4, 6.7–9, 7.1–9, and review in Alexandropoulos 1992, 319–27), and other coins from Sidon portray a goddess, possibly in the Astarte/Ishtar tradition, who rides a lion (though the historical context is unclear; see Hill 1910; cxii, pl. XXV.8).

A particularly unique example—not paralleled in any other iconography of the period or earlier—from fourth-century BCE Tyrian coinage depicts a male figure riding a winged horse, holding a bow, soaring above a horizontal set of waves under which a dolphin swims (see Elayi and Elayi 2009, 265–71 and accompanying plates; fig. 4.6).[21] Some have analyzed the Tyrian figure as a "wave-rider" deity on parallel with the Baal "cloud-rider" (textual) image from Late Bronze Age Ugarit, while others see Taras, a dolphin-riding hero parallel to the figure on the Tarentine didrachms (on the dolphin, which is sometimes associated with the Tyrian Astarte, see Gubel 1993, 114); Josette and Alain Gérard Elayi think it is Melqart or some other syncretized figure (2009, 271; cf. with the bow-and-club wielding Herakles/Melqart figures in Boardman 2003, pls. 33–35).

Regarding these chronologically, geographically, and materially disparate examples as a whole, it is obviously difficult to come to any meaningful, singular conclusion about what exactly is "Phoenician" about these images. Indeed, this is why there currently exists no comprehensive treatment of the manner in which Phoenicians represented their own deities. For the Iron Age, we are able to document a number of images that likely qualify as "Phoenician," based on the location of the find (at a Phoenician mainland city or established Phoenician colony) or an accompanying Phoenician inscription. No single uniting iconographic feature distinguishes Phoenician divine imagery from that of another Levantine or Mediterranean group; if anything, however, the Phoenician images are distinctive for their bold mixture of native styles and borrowed iconography, though there is no a priori sense in which we know that items exhibiting "mixed styles" or hybrid features are the product of any particular kind of hybridizing or conscious mix of influences. A more specific analysis for some discrete objects will give us some sense of the iconographic strategies against which the allegedly aniconographic examples may deviate.

---

21. The Sidonian coins from the same time period also frequently depict the male archer figure, but not in concert with the dolphin and waves (at least not in the same scene—though the waves are ubiquitous on the reverse side of the archer on the Sidonian coins); see plates in Elayi and Elayi 2004, vol. 2, and a discussion of the archer figure at 1:524–31.

4.4. Case Studies in Iconic Phoenician Divine Representation

In the first four cases below—dealing with depictions of Melqart and various goddess figures that are harder to identify with precision—my strategy is to show a clearly anthropomorphic image that can be discussed within the orbit or intersection of Phoenician style, geography, and historical horizon, though as noted at various points so far in this study these criteria are not as precise as one may want. Nevertheless, the comparison of Melqart's image in the East versus the West and of the female deities between Byblos and the more western-Mediterranean examples provide an iconographic register to demonstrate some coherence of divine imagery for the Phoenicians in the Iron Age Mediterranean world. Moreover, the examples I have chosen here display iconographic intersection of some kind (shared imagery, symbolism, context, function) with the examples of aniconic representation taken up in the next chapter.

Bar Hadad Stele of Melqart

The anthropomorphic depiction of Melqart on the mid-ninth-century BCE Bar Hadad stele (fig. 4.7) is one of the older recovered anthropomorphic divine images to be associated with the Phoenicians—and in particular, probably the oldest for the primary god of Tyre, Melqart.[22] Melqart's association with Tyre, combined with the Tyrian political and religious influence as far away as Gadir, makes the object a potentially quite important early example of Phoenician representation and could offer some early sense (isolated though it is) of Melqart's image that seemed to have been avoided in the West at Gadir centuries later (if not sooner). Gubel claims that this piece "is at most an Aramaean version of a Phoenician theme," and accordingly does not analyze it at length in his important treatment of Iron Age art in Tyre (1983, 25); nevertheless, Melqart's representation here is significant for our purposes since it may bear on the question of Phoenician aniconism, particularly regarding the question of whether the Tyrian Melqart temple had a central cult image of the deity. To this end, Culican ventures to guess that the figure here is a replica of the Melqart cult statue at Tyre (Culican 1960–1961, 41; see also Bonnet 1988), and it is quite possible that aspects of this same image were reflected in later seals from the western Mediterranean as well as other potential Melqart images on bowls from Cyprus (Culican 1968).

To be sure, it is not entirely clear on what grounds the image is to be identified as "Phoenician"—the object was recovered near Aleppo, which is some eighty

---

22. The *editio princeps* is Dunand 1939. For the imagery on the stele, see Culican 1960–1961; Reinhold 1986, 123–24; Bonnet 1988, 132–36. On the language and references of the stele, see *KAI* 201; Albright 1942; Lipiński 1975, 15–19; Shea 1979; Dearman and Miller 1983; Pitard 1988.

 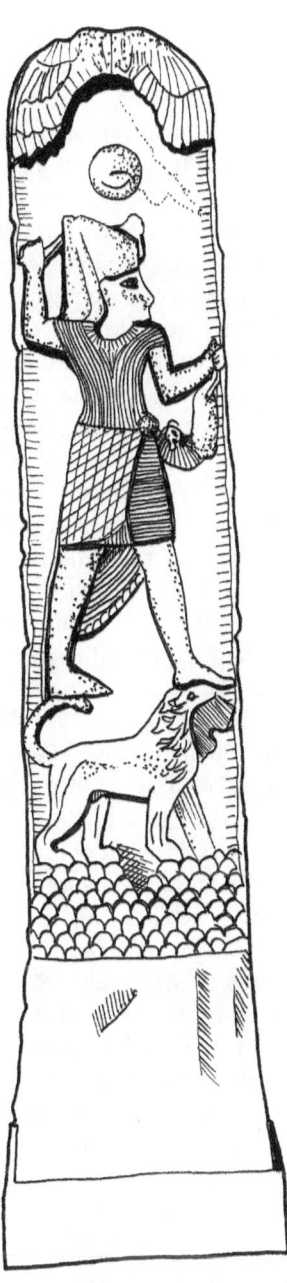

Fig. 4.7. Bar Hadad stele with Melqart; ninth century BCE (Dunand 1939, pl. XIII; DCPP 286, fig. 223; Bonnet 2007 [IDD illustration])

Fig. 4.8. The "Amrit Stele"; Tell Kazel; fifth century BCE; h. 1.78 m (Markoe 2000, 152; Gubel et al. 2002, 51)

kilometers inland from Ugarit and Alalakh on the northern Levantine coast, not especially near to the cities of the Phoenician heartland. Still, most have assumed a basically Phoenician artistic influence for the region, an influence that obviously made its way in ivory and other media to Assyria (e.g., the Nimrud ivories) and beyond in the East (see Winter 2010b, 279–81; 2010c; overview in Aruz, Graff, and Rakic 2014, 141–56). Aram is traditionally left out of this orbit of influence in the standard categorization of "Phoenician" and "Northern Syrian" groups (Winter 2010b, 279), leaving us to wonder where the region's products fit into the schema.

In one sense, we might say that the stele participates more closely in what has often been called the "northern style," lacking great technical acumen, detail, and the heavy Egyptianizing characteristics of Phoenician production and instead featuring a broad, frontal figure dominating the space of the stele (Winter 2010b, 282). This is not to say that the Melqart figure here—identified in the inscription itself by the dedicatory phrase *lmlqrt* ("for Melqart") and the accompanying vow (*nzr*) by Bar Hadad—lacks the Egyptianizing and other mixed/international features of Phoenician art as we have already characterized them. The item in Melqart's right hand, the *ankh*, is clearly Egyptian, as are possibly the cobras that stand erect before the torso at the waist. The fenestrated ax is something of an oddity here, with parallels in Middle Bronze Age examples (Bonnet 1988, 135), thus potentially representing an archaizing element or some unknown connotation, and the headdress and beard are similar to Melqart representations in other, later iconography (Culican 1960–1961, 41–42; see two examples below at "5.3. Stelae, Pillars, Standing Stones, Betyls," fig. 5.22). Gubel considers the ax in particular as potential evidence of "a strong sense of traditionalism in the art of Tyre," since it seems to be related to nineteenth-century BCE examples from Byblos (1983, 25).[23]

The skirt itself does intersect with other Phoenician attributes, particularly the style found on statues from Cyprus in the sixth–fifth centuries, but also with Egyptian parallels (the "royal *shenti*"; see Culican 1960–1961, 41). Though William Albright identified the lines behind the right leg as a bow (1942, 29; see also Dunand 1939; Culican 1960–1961, 41), which would indeed be fitting for Melqart as a hunter, the intent here is to display the back of the skirt, as indicated by the hem (parallel strips of cloth) across the obverse of the left leg, which then continues behind the left leg and across the figure. Whatever the case, what we have here, as William Culican suggests (1960–1961, 43), is not a hapless mélange of iconography for decorative purposes, but rather the presentation of Melqart as a striding hero-deity with an ax evokes the mythology of this particular deity—tellingly identified with the Aegean Herakles on this front—as a hero and a hunter, just as in other instances the adaption of the Egyptian smiting-Pharaoh scene by the Phoenicians for Melqart identifies the deity with tropes of hunting and heroism.

---

23. See now also Yasur-Landau 2015, who argues for the great antiquity of this ax type, with origins in the Levant between the twentieth–eighteenth centuries BCE.

In stele format, some similarities appear in the roughly contemporaneous (ninth–eighth century BCE) "Amrit Stele" (fig. 4.8) from the coastal region of Amrit, Syria (probably from Tell Kazel; see Gubel 2000, 186–87; Gubel et al. 2002, 51; Cecchini 1997; Markoe 2000, 150–52). In this stele, Gubel finds "the hallmarks of Phoenician sculpture," which includes continuity with the regional Late Bronze Age iconography as well as the Egyptianizing smiting-Baal motif (2000, 186–87). Overall the scene is much more elaborate than the Bar Hadad Melqart stele, but the stance of the figure, hairstyle, beard, and helmet all cohere—even as the smiting pose as opposed to the relaxed stance on the Bar Hadad stele obviously portray the central figure in a different type of activity. The identity of the Amrit stele deity is not obvious, however—the figure striding the bull suggests the "storm god" type known from Anatolian and Levantine religions generally in the period, and it is not clear whether Melqart was worshiped in this capacity.

Male Figures on "Classical Phoenician" Seals

Moving some distance from the Bar Hadad stele discussed above, the depictions of Melqart, Baal, or other male "hero deities" on a series of seals—most on a type of green jasper—from the sixth-fourth centuries BCE as well as early coinage from Arvad and Byblos give us some sense of the iconographic range between the earlier images of the male deities and later examples in different media. The sheer amount of material and its diversity is one of the more vexing problems for trying to make systematic statements for this category (the scarabs come from Ibiza [Puig des Molins] and various other sites in Spain, Sardinia [Tharros], Carthage, and scattered locations in the Levant), as is the problem of identifying the anthropomorphic figures. A brief look at some examples from the group Boardman has labeled as "classical Phoenician" (2003, 3)—to distinguish the green jasper group from earlier examples (usually not cut on green jasper)—helps narrow the focus. About twenty of these scarabs give us possible depictions of a "Herakles-Melqart" figure, and in all of these the hero raises his signature club in the right hand (Boardman 2003, 101–3, pls. 33–35),[24] and other prominent motifs include a seated figure with raised hand before an incense altar (fig. 4.9; see further discussion in Bonnet 1988, 239–40; Culican 1960–1961; 1968; 1976a).

These examples of the seated deity or royal figure are particularly relevant since the petaled incense altar may be identified as a long-standing Phoenician tradition, spanning a millennium and indicating a central act of Phoenician religious devotion (Culican 1980, 99–101). Moreover, the sphinx throne was a staple feature in Levantine art (Gubel 1987; Culican 1968, 58; Keel and Uehlinger 1998,

---

24. Cf. with one or two possible anthropomorphic images of Herakles/Melqart and a number of other male figures on Tyrian coins; see Hill 1910, pl. XXXII.13, which Hill had identified as Herakles/Melqart, and other unidentified "heroic" male figures in pls. XXXIII.12, XXXIV.11, 17, 18.

Fig. 4.9. Male figures on throne with incense altar; green jasper seals; sixth–fourth century BCE (Boardman 2003, 62–63, pls. 16–17; L–R 17.30, 17.7, 17.1, 17.2)

234–35; and on the specifically Phoenician characteristics of these seals, Culican 1968, 54–56) and appears in the depiction of some of the seated female figures discussed below. Regarding the identity of the seated male in the seals, it is difficult to say whether it is a deity or a human king (see Betlyon 1982, 79–80, for this problem in the coinage); it is quite possible that the depiction intentionally conflates king and deity in such a way as to suggest the divinity through the enthroned king or vice versa, a phenomenon that can be observed in other places and periods in Near Eastern royal-divine imagery (see Ornan 2004, 113; 2014). Culican (1960–1961, 43) refers to a "Melqart-Baal figure" and notices that the vegetative associations and fertility functions of Melqart could easily lead to conflations with Baal (1960–1961, 48). Whatever the case, Culican certainly thinks the seated figures are deities (1960–1961, 44), perhaps even more specifically the supreme deity of the Phoenician pantheon writ large, a sky god of the type found seated on thrones in other ancient Near Eastern contexts and even venerated aniconographically "seated" on or above an empty throne (1968, 81–82).

Yehawmilk Stele

The so-called Yehawmilk (*yḥwmlk*) stele from Byblos (not to be confused with the much early Yehimilk inscription from the tenth century BCE) contains a picture of a certain "Lady of Gubal (Byblos)" (*bʿlt gbl*) in the setting of an offering scene (fig. 4.10; Gubel et al. 2002, 64–66; cf. with the terracotta plaque with a similar scene from Byblos, also fifth century, in Markoe 2000, 128, fig. 43).[25] The dating of the image and accompanying inscription seems secure in the fifth century BCE (but possibly as late as the early fourth century). Relatively little analysis has been devoted to this stele compared to the tenth-century Byblian corpus, but the image itself is simple enough: a seated female figure at left receives an offering bowl and sign of veneration from the male figure at right. The seated stance of the female deity, the Baalat Gubal, clearly follows standard Egyptian conventions for Hathor (e.g., the horns with sun disc and staff), which, in this peaceful seated posture, could be the Semitic Phoenician goddess Anat or Astarte (Cornelius 2004, 29–30; Bloch-Smith 2014). Byblos remained a long-standing partner of trade and other exchange with Egypt, and the strongly Egyptian flavor here—notwithstanding the Persian garb of Yehawmilk (see examples in Llewellyn-Jones 2013, 61–66)—was common in Phoenician art generally (Markoe 1990, 16–23).

The text of the inscription mentions various cultic items devoted to the goddess along with the stele: a bronze altar (*hmzbḥ nḥšt*) and a gold object of some kind, which presumably fit inside the socket at the center of the winged sun disc crowning the entire scene as it follows the curve of the top of the stele. Moreover, Yehawmilk describes repairs or additions to a temple complex or shrine area,

---

25. For text and translation, see *KAI* 10; *COS* 2:151–52; Gibson 1982, 93–99; for other comments, see, e.g., Vance 1994, 9–10; Ciafaloni 1995, 536–37; Bonnet 1996, 25–26.

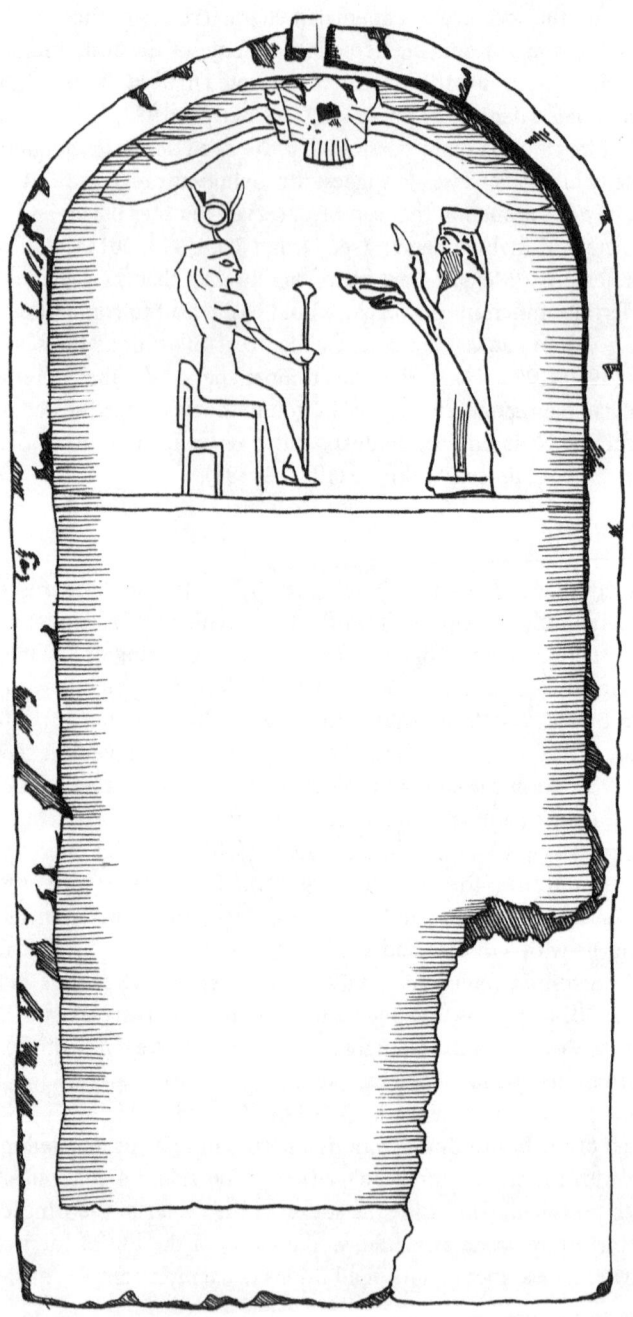

Fig. 4.10. Yehawmilk stele with king and deity (text omitted from lower register); Byblos; h. 1.12 m (http://www.louvre.fr/en/oeuvre-notices/yehawmilk-stele; Gubel et al. 2002, 65–66)

which included not only the bronze altar but also a portico column ('*md*) and roof for the structure. Whether the image of the Baalat Gubal on the stele corresponds to any other figure inside of this shrine or in the larger temple complex is not at all clear.

Enthroned Deities in Terracotta

The image of the enthroned goddess appears sporadically in the available published iconography of the Phoenician settlements, such as a series of terracotta figures from Ibiza (figs. 4.11, 4.12, 4.13). In particular, a sanctuary cave at Es Culleram in use from the fourth–second centuries BCE at the remote northeast corner of the island yielded a large collection of small terracotta statues, all presumably offered as gifts to the deities worshiped there (van Dommelen and López-Bertran 2013, 282–86). María Eugenia Aubet suggests that one of these deities was a "local version of the effigy of Tanit" (the primary goddess of Carthage also in the fifth century and beyond; 1982, 53, 45), though others speak of her in terms of a Demeter type or a combination of forms for Demeter or Tanit. (The latter is identified as a recipient of devotion along with Resheph-Melqart in an inscription within the cave; see van Dommelen and López-Bertran 2013, 274–75, 280–81, and literature cited there; see also Almagro Gorbea 1980, esp. 151–67, and accompanying plates; San Nicolas 2000; Marín Ceballos 2004; Marín Ceballos; and Horn 2007.) The hairstyle, facial structure, seated posture (including the hand grasping a dove [as in fig. 4.11] or circular object), and "winged" throne style can be found in terracotta female figures at the Demeter and Kore sanctuary at Corinth, Greece, during roughly the same chronological horizon as the pieces discussed here (Merker 2000, 42–47, 157, and images C77–93B in particular; cf. also with Almagro Gorbea 1980, lam. LXXXVII, 1-2; LXXXIX).

The most common style from the site is a bell-shaped terracotta statuette, though enthroned figures of the type shown here (fig. 4.13) were a distinct subgroup (Aubet 1982, lam. XX).[26] The bell-shaped divine figures themselves display a range of intricacy and style, from very simple and indistinct anthropomorphic forms all the way to ornate styles (e.g., very clear face, dress) that interact with the Hellenistic imagery of deities like Demeter and Kore as known from Sicily during the same time period. (For a typology, see Aubet 1982, 15–27, lam. XXX; on the complexity of the interchange between Aegean, Phoenician, and Punic identities and features, see van Dommelen and López-Bertran 2013 and other literature cited there.) Similar goddess figures as votive offerings—in a range of styles, including the enthroned figure—were also recovered at another Phoenician-Punic

---

26. Almagro Gorbea 1980, 151, thinks this particular enthroned figure in fig. 4.13 is "una deidad oriental, casi con seguridad Baal Hamon," but this identification seems less clear to me. The sphinx throne would be better associated with the goddess, but the canonical headdress could suggest a male deity.

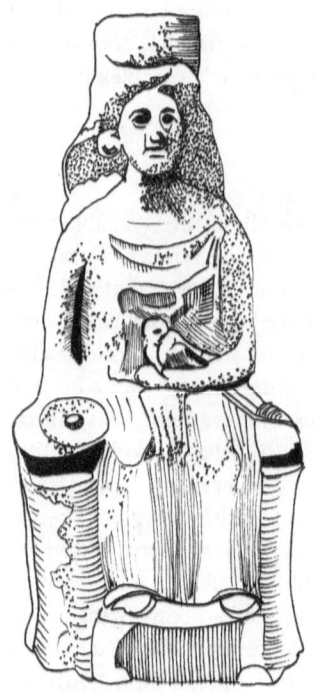

Fig. 4.11. Enthroned female figure; terracotta; Puig des Molins (Ibiza); fifth–fourth century BCE; h. 22 cm (Almagro Gorbea 1980, lam. XCVI, 1; Moscati 1988a, 720.800)

Fig. 4.12. Enthroned female figure; terracotta; Es Culleram (Ibiza); third century BCE; approx. h. 10 cm (Moscati 1988a, 720.802)

settlement, Puig des Molins (figs. 4.11, 4.13), on the southern coast of the island (Gubel et al. 1986, 132–33).

Another notable image of an enthroned female deity, also exhibiting a similar mix of styles and an equally complicated position among east and west in the Phoenician-Punic world comes from the settlement of Soluntum, on the northern coast of Sicily (fig. 4.14). The most recent interpreter of the piece (Chiarenza 2013) dates the statue to the fourth or third century BCE, though the consensus seems to rest closer to the sixth century (see brief discussion and image in Gubel 1987, 46, and pl. IX.26). Nicola Chiarenza finds the style of striding-sphinx arms to the throne to be evidence of an "archaizing" style, meant to remind worshipers of the Phoenician mainland (2013, 948); to this end, the sphinx-throne style may be compared to the notable sphinx throne from Sidon at the Eshmun sanctuary

Fig. 4.13. Enthroned female figure; terracotta; Puig des Molins (Ibiza); fourth century BCE; h. 13 cm (Almagro Gorbea 1980, lam. LXXXVII, 1; Moscati 1988a, 720.801)

(compare with fig. 4.13).[27] Many parts of the image are now lost, including the face, arms, and part of the back of the goddess, though most associate her with Astarte (perhaps based on the parallel with Sidon; see Chiarenza 2013, 948, and literature cited there).

Tanit Figures

Perhaps the greatest treasure trove of Phoenician divine representation comes from tophet monuments of Carthage (founded as a trade colony of Tyre in the late ninth century BCE), spanning a period from the late seventh century through the Punic period (deposited in several phases; see Quinn 2011; Bénichou-Safar 2004; Brown 1991; Bartoloni 1976).[28] The sheer amount of iconographic data from Carthage defies easy categorization, and some of the artistic motifs approach abstraction

---

27. Analyzed below at "5.5. Thrones with Aniconic Objects and Empty Thrones."
28. For a detailed discussion of Punic religion and material culture, see González Blanco, Matilla Séiquer, and Egea Vivancos 2004; Stavrakopoulou 2004, 215–39 has a very thorough review of the literature through 2003 on the key evidence regarding the child sacrifice/burials at Carthage and elsewhere, including a discussion of the Tanit imagery. D'Andrea 2014a (to which I have not yet had full access) appears to be the most recent and comprehensive study of the Carthage tophets.

Fig. 4.14. Seated figure on sphinx throne; partially reconstructed; Soluntum, Sicily; sixth–fourth century BCE (photo in Chiarenza 2013, 951, fig. 1; drawing in Gubel 1987, pl. IX.26)

(to modern eyes, at least) or display astrological symbols or an isolated anthropomorphic hand.[29] The earlier stelae (beginning in the seventh century) feature the "cippus throne" motif, that is, plain stone monuments with an empty throne at the top at one piece with the cippus, or geometric shapes (various kinds of pillars) enshrined within the stelae. Beginning in the fifth century, we find mostly rectangular stelae featuring a stylized female figure (see overview in Moscati 1988d, 304–5; Bisi 1967; Brown 1991, 77–117). The inscriptions related to the imagery from the Punic tophet garnered the lion's share of the attention, with interpreters lining up on either side to debate the question of whether children were sacrificed as a vow (*ndr*) to deities such as Tanit (*ltnt*) or Baal Hammon (*lbʿl ḥmn*) or merely buried in the tophet (see the recent round by Smith, Avishai, Greene, and Stager 2011; Schwartz, Houghton, Bondioli, and Macchiarelli 2012; Smith, Stager, Greene, and Avishai 2013; Xella, Quinn, Mechiorri, and van Dommelen 2013; Stager 2014 [following earlier publications in Stager 1980; 1982]; on the inscriptions, first studied in depth by Eissfeldt 1935, see Amadasi Guzzo and Zamora López 2012–2013).

---

29. The tradition of divine symbols has deep roots in earlier Levantine cultures and is well attested in the Late Bronze Age. See, e.g., some examples and references in López-Ruiz 2010, 205–10.

Fig. 4.15. Variety of the Tanit figure from Carthaginian stelae (Bisi 1967, fig. 7)

For the moment, let us say that there seems to be a consensus that children were indeed sacrificed, though perhaps there were other purposes for the monuments and other ways some of the children died besides sacrifice.

The most common anthropomorphic figure from Carthage (among other prominent locations, such as nearby Sousse [Roman Hadrumetum], the so-called Tanit symbol, for all of its variation is composed of a triangular base, pointed at the top, on which sits a circular shape (sometimes shaded by a crescent) and upraised "arms" (see figs. 4.15, 4.16, 4.17). The simplicity of the figure, the relatively enigmatic status of Tanit, and her relationship to other deities are all beguiling topics; the etymology of *tnt* remains unclear, and speculations about the origin of the triangle base, circular head, and upraised arms have ranged from combinations involving a primal female symbol (the pubic triangle), the Egyptian *ankh*, astral imagery, altars, scales, to many other things (see Hvidberg-Hansen 1979; Brown 1991, 123–31; Culican 1970; Bertrandy 1992b; Sader 2005, 123–31). What seems clear at least is the anthropomorphic nature of the depiction—the symbol is a humanoid figure, with a body, head, and arms. Tanit was worshiped outside of Carthage (Linder 1973; Stern 2006), and could easily be conflated with other goddesses or their symbolism (see Rich 2012). Often the Tanit image appears with an open hand, often assumed to be the hand of Baal Hammon or less commonly

Fig. 4.16. Stele with Tanit figure, hand, and caduceus; Carthage; second century BCE; h. 26.5 cm (Moscati 1988a, 615.186)

Fig. 4.17. Stele with pillars, crescent-disc, and Tanit figure; Sousse/Hadrumetum; fourth century BCE (Bisi 1967, Tav XXII.1)

that of a worshiper in veneration, as well as the caduceus, a sacrificial animal, or *masseboth* pillars (as in figs. 4.16–17).

The ambiguity of the image may leave some to wonder who the figure represents—in the dedicatory inscriptions, other deities are mentioned along with Tanit.[30] In what is still the most comprehensive and authoritative treatment of the figure, Shelby Brown concludes that the figure is indeed the goddess Tanit (1991, 123-31, 144-45; see, e.g., the images on 270.383, 276.521, 282.572, 298b; also Stager and Wolf 1984, 36-38, 45-46). Brown views the pervasive crescent-disk imagery "in a general way as having an astral and probably divine symbolism," while the presence of single, uplifted hand on several stelae represents the

---

30. The standard dedicatory formula on the stelae reads: *lrbt ltnt pn bʿl wlʾdn lbʿl ḥmn*, "To the Lady, to Tanit, face of Baal, and to the Lord Baal Hammon" (see Amadasi Guzzo and Zamora López 2012-2013, 171-72).

 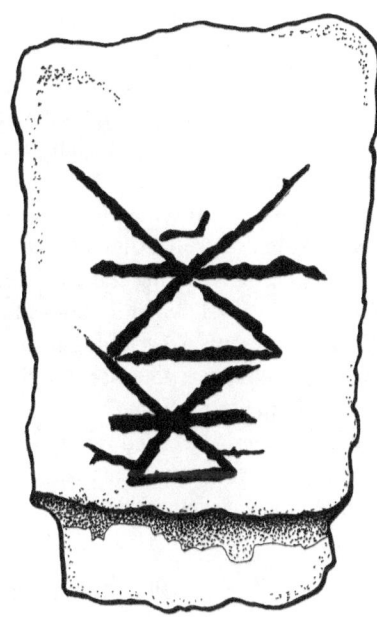

Fig. 4.18 . Stele with figures; Tyre cemetery; ninth–seventh century BCE (Aubet 2004, 385 fig. 254)

Fig. 4.19 . Stele with figures; Tyre cemetery; ninth–seventh century BCE (Aubet 2004, 386 fig. 255)

worshiper fulfilling the vow and the "Tanit symbol" with uplifted arms represents the goddess Tanit. Brown characterizes this imagery as "entirely Phoenician, not influenced by the religious iconography of other peoples" (1991, 144–45), though the presence of the caduceus wand, associated with underworld passage through the Greek Hermes, as well as other features (such as the *ankh* imagery) suggest, again, the varied iconographic influences of the broader Mediterranean world on the Phoenician artisans.

Excavations at the Iron Age Tyre cemetery (conducted between 1997–2002; see Aubet 2004, 2006, 2010) have now revealed additional Tanit-type imagery, though in this case we can be less certain that the figure is indeed Tanit. Nevertheless, there are some similarities in form, possibly suggesting that a Tanit-like symbol was used in mortuary contexts from an earlier period in the Phoenician mainland—the Tyre cemetery in question (in the Al-Bass district) was apparently used from the tenth–seventh centuries BCE, making the imagery now published from this site the first anthropomorphic examples from a Phoenician mortuary context and some of the earliest of any kind from a controlled, scientific excavation in the Phoenician mainland (see Sader 2004, 384). Of the seven stelae, two small examples bear anthropomorphic incisions worth noting (figs. 4.18 and 4.19; both under 50 cm in height; see analysis in Sader 2004). The clearer example features a round face hovering over an *ankh* figure that resembles the later Tanit images from Carthage with respect to the head, outstretched arms, and general proportion of the body (4.19; cf. with examples in Cross 2002, 171–72, 1.4 and 1.6).

On the other, a series of triangles and crossed lines form potentially two discrete figures, one atop the other (comparable to Tanit figures with regard to the triangle as well as the outstretched "arms"; 4.19); if indeed this is the case, then it is interesting to notice that both of these stelae depict exactly two figures in this way, perhaps one representing the deceased, the individual, [?] and the other, deity. Hélène Sader (2004, 387) mentions the possibility that the triangle with intersecting lines represents a "weighing measure," comparable with similar forms across the Levant. Whatever the case, the simpler images on these stelae from Tyre and even the Tanit figures from Carthage and elsewhere begin to push the boundary of what can properly be called "iconic" imagery, as the anthropomorphic qualities of the images move toward schematic shapes and symbols that many not be readily identified for their figural qualities.

4.5. A People without Pictorial Traditions?

In summary, we have now seen that the Phoenicians were far from being a people "without pictorial traditions," and indeed we can already begin to see that this notion of the Phoenicians as slavish iconographic copiers could lead one into inappropriate assessments of the creativity with which Phoenicians borrowed motifs and the religious meanings they could create in new contexts with borrowed imagery. Thus we cannot find an avenue into the alleged aniconic phenomena among the Phoenicians by downplaying the number and types of iconic (figural, anthropomorphic) examples, nor can we allow older statements about the inadequacy or paucity of Phoenician art generally to lead us into examining objects with a de facto suspicion about their iconographic potential or native status.

Obviously the Phoenicians did not systematically or clearly avoid representing deities in anthropomorphic form, but their proclivity for vacant thrones, empty model-shrines, and many other varieties of nonfigural imagery in ritual space do call for an explanation. What were the ritual strategies, religious beliefs, material considerations, artistic preferences, and political relationships that informed Phoenician images in the cases of these nonfigural objects and empty spaces? When does iconism move into aniconism—and why?

5

Phoenician Aniconism

Here I attempt a categorization of Phoenician materials that might be accurately considered under the rubric of the aniconic, examining these items in light of the theoretical considerations already raised concerning the definition of aniconism as well as Phoenician artistic style and religious practice. Given the prominence of stelae in the Phoenician and Punic material record—Tryggve Mettinger had wryly noted that the Phoenicians loved stelae so much that they took to inscribing stelae on other stelae—my consideration of these objects will be most robust, followed by considerations of aniconism by category for several other types of objects, such as empty shrines of various kinds, empty thrones and thrones holding nonanthropomorphic items, as well as divine symbols.

A brief review of our discussion so far is in order along with some additional comments on the nature of the colonial sites in relation to the Phoenician mainland (Tyre in particular). The incomplete and at times unsystematic excavation of key Phoenician mainland sites (Tyre, Sidon, Byblos) has left the material culture of the Phoenicians under a vague cloud, and the complexity of specifically "Phoenician" expansion into the western Mediterranean beginning in the ninth and eighth centuries BCE (first in Cyprus and Carthage, and then farther west) has created, on the one hand, a very rich, emerging picture of Phoenician identity and presence in the Mediterranean while, on the other hand, creating new problems for the study of religion and material culture (see reflection on this problem in van Dommelen 2014; Quinn and Vella 2014; Álvarez Martí-Aguilar forthcoming). At what point do ritual objects in a colony, for example, cease being "Phoenician" and start being considered "native," with "Phoenician characteristics"? At what point do we take up or abandon labels such as "Greco-Phoenician," "Cypro-Phoenician," "hybridizing forms," and so on? The notion that any identity can be strictly considered under naive essentialist categories has now been (rightly) abandoned in most fields of study, not just for the Phoenicians, though for many important purposes—histories of all kinds (social, economic, political), comparative religion, myth, and material culture—we remain in need of larger frameworks that can be acknowledged as heuristic and yet applied with rigor to what evidence we do have.

Indeed, there are some promising signs that suggest the relationship between mother city on the mainland and the colonies was in many respects conservative and strong, suggesting that it is not a complete derogation of historical duty to speak of distinctly Phoenician characteristics that pertain between distant areas. In a compelling new study, Manuel Álvarez Martí-Aguilar (forthcoming) takes up the question of the "colony network based on Tyrian identity" and goes on to show how elements of the founding narratives of Gadir (historically founded in the ninth century BCE by his dating) can be linked with the founding Tyre;[1] though these correspondences come to us through later Greek and Roman historians, there is striking continuity in areas of visual imagery between the two sites (pairs of stelae, the ambrosial rocks, olive trees) and foundations accounts (involving dream revelations, Melqart's involvement, bird sacrifice, etc.; see also Bonnet 1988, 213–5l; and Marín Ceballos 2011b). Also on the iconographic front, Hélène Sader (2004, 384–85) has noticed that the only clear parallels to a particular Iron Age stele from Tyre (fig. 4.18 in the previous chapter) come from the first century BCE–second century CE (e.g., from Sassari, Sardinia; cf. also with a similar face and upraised arm motif on a stele from the Punic Monte Sirai tophet in southern Sardinia; image in Bisi 1967, tav. LXV, 1). True, simple forms may persist over long periods of time and in diverse places without a rigorous or direct model of visual solidarity or historical genealogy between locations, but then again the discovery of what turns out to be very specific iconographic motifs in an early context that "reappear" in much later contexts—with the early example coming from the colonial headquarters for major Mediterranean settlements—is suggestive of a long chain of visual use (with its foundation in Tyre in this case).

This identity between Tyre and colony can be observed "in process," long before the comments of Roman historians, in settlements at Malta, Sardinia, and Ibiza, where we find inscriptions from the fourth–second century BCE referring to Melqart (sometimes by name as *mlqrt ʿl ḥṣr*, "Melqart upon the Rock," with reference to *ṣr*, Tyre, or as *bʿl ṣr*, "Lord of Tyre"; see Amadasi Guzzo 2005). At other sites, such as Carthage, the relationship with Tyre is far less clear, and Álvarez Martí-Aguilar warns against taking the specificity of the cultic and political solidarity too far, but it was nevertheless the case that "the worship of Melqart in the new community required the purity or legitimacy which can only be granted by the sanctuary of the god in Tyre," and the inscriptional references to Melqart in the western Mediterranean may be evidence of colonial re-creation of a truly "Tyrian identity, highlighting the existence of an element of 'fiction,' of adaptive

---

1. The following information is from the forthcoming work of Álvarez Martí-Aguilar (forthcoming), who graciously provided me a prepublication copy of the paper. On the Phoenician Gadir cult, see also the essays in Marín Ceballos 2011a, to which I have not yet had access.

construction in local contexts" (Álvarez Martí-Aguilar forthcoming; on this, see also Garbati 2012; on the local adaptation, see, e.g., Marín Ceballos 2011b, 220).

In the area of Phoenician divine representation, our study so far has sketched out a wide range of techniques and examples for anthropomorphic forms. For images of Melqart specifically, we do not have much clear evidence, though the Bar Hadad/Melqart stele may reflect native Phoenician traditions. In the sphere of glyptic representation, many male enthroned figures on seals, for example, probably portray a seated deity of the Melqart type, though obviously we cannot rule out associations with male warrior, hunter, or fertility deities of various kinds. It seems that the vast majority of enthroned figures in terracotta are goddesses, and we will have occasion here in this chapter to explore the iconography of Astarte at Sidon in the form of empty thrones. The Tanit figures from Carthage indicate a clear figural program for the goddess there, with some potential connections to imagery from Tyre in earlier periods, though the Tanit figures—viewed alongside the stele tradition from Carthage—begin to gesture toward simplified forms, divine symbols, or even pure abstraction.

5.1. Retrospective

As we turn to the aniconographic record, then, we notice that no one has yet attempted a relatively comprehensive view of nonfigural and nonanthropomorphic Phoenician imagery within the broader context of Phoenician identity, religion, and iconic representation, though there have been some inroads to the topic and scattered recognitions that aniconographic techniques were prevalent among Phoenicians. In the modern period, as early as 1862 the prolific German theologian J. J. I. Döllinger declared that "Baal had been worshipped without an image in Tyre and its colonies." Characteristically of the study of religion in the nineteenth century, Döllinger adopted an evolutionary perspective that viewed aniconic worship as a kind of pristine, early form of religion in Tyre, after which the cult "had grown into an idolatry of the most wanton character" (1862, 425). Indeed, these kinds of assessments are sometimes still made regarding divine representation, even if in a more subtle form.[2] Though laden with moralizing, Döllinger's assertions could only have been extracted from the classical texts, as vital archaeological evidence had not yet come to light during his time. In his classic study of the Phoenicians, first published in 1889, George Rawlinson seemed to accept Döllinger's generic characterization of the Iron Age aniconism related to Baal (as had other sources of the period) and quotes Döllinger on that point and others for six pages without comment (1889, 112–17).

---

2. See above at "3.3. The Critics and Proponents of Aniconism," and note the critiques of bias in favor of aniconism in Freedberg 1989, 54.

The twentieth century saw more or less scattered comments devoted to our question. Sabatino Moscati (1969) devoted an essay to the interchange between iconic and aniconic Punic stelae from Mozia, Sicily; if I have understood his analysis correctly, Moscati concludes that we cannot trace a clear evolutionary direction from iconic to aniconic or vice versa, and various material factors—such as the training of local craftsmen, the availability of materials, and other economic concerns—could determine the preference for one form over the other. Moreover, Moscati points out that not all "aniconic" materials may have been properly finished in the form that they were recovered,[3] and some aniconic symbols may have been merely suggestions of much more elaborate iconic imagery with which a given piece was to be associated (1969, 66). It should be pointed out, however, that even if aniconic symbols are meant to refer the viewer to another, iconic image, those aniconic images are still visually aniconic and thus suggestive of all that the aniconic may imply, visually or otherwise. In the end, for Moscati, we are looking at an artistic tradition and not religious meaning ("che debbano distinguersi i fattori realmente artistici da quelli religiosi o altri ancora"; 1969, 67).

Focusing on the tradition of cultic stones in particular, Eugene Stockton (1974–1975) argued for a cultic continuity across space in the Phoenician Mediterranean, seeing items such as sacred pillars, stones, stelae, and various empty temple or shrine spaces as the primary evidence of the "more theological, abstract religious thought of the Semite" (1974–1975, 2). For Stockton, both Byblos and Tyre supported originally aniconic worship (1974–1975, 10–11), and the tophet monuments communicate a spiritual interchange between the votive offerer ("the simple faithful") and the deity in aniconic form (1974–1975, 18). In a more focused and technical study, Gioacchino Falsone (1993) reviews the broader context of the "betyl" and various other stone and stele-like objects—of particular notice is the sensitivity Falsone shows to potentially anthropomorphic features on even very plain objects, such as "eyes" in an otherwise unadorned stone (1993, 253). Other isolated studies have identified particular motifs as "aniconic" without giving definition to the term or without attempting to explain the phenomenon as something particularly Phoenician (see, e.g., Culican 1960–1961, 48–49; 1968,

---

3. E.g., Moscati 1969, 66: "Non che il caso sia diffuso o frequente ["Not that the case is widespread or frequent"]: ma ad esempio la stele 164 di Mozia (tav. XIX, 1), contenente una figura costituita da tre trapezi sovrapposti con la base maggiore in alto e senza linea di separazione (la descrizione è convenzionale ma indicative), incise ma con inizio di escavazione, può far supporre che essa fosse destinata a una successive elaborazione in immagine umana, per esempio del genere di quella che si realizza nella stele 191 (tav. XX, 2)" ("the trapezoidal images on a particular piece were quite possibly intended for further elaboration into a human image, as can be seen in other models of the same type, etc."). See, e.g., Bisi 1967, tav. XXXIX, 1–2; and Moscati 1970, tav. XV, 30, for some aniconic figures on Punic stelae from Mozia (Sicily) and Nora (Sardinia), respectively, that may reflect "in process" compositions.

81–82; 1970, 34–45; 1976, 47, 49–50; Lipiński 1995, 66; Karageorghis 2000; and a range of examples scattered in Markoe 2000, 120–56; but for a more rigorous framework see Nunn 2008, 113–15; 2010, 142–45).

The most sustained analysis to date of Phoenician aniconism has been carried out by the Swedish biblical scholar Tryggve Mettinger in his book *No Graven Image?* (1995; see also a follow up in Mettinger 2006, 284–89, in which Mettinger doubles down on the importance of the Phoenician evidence for his case). Mettinger's work in this area is careful and balanced, and he offers definitive yet cautious and reasonable conclusions about a wide range of Phoenician-Punic materials; my own analysis tracks to some extent with Mettinger's work, though I differ in several important respects with his confident categorizations of aniconism in some cases. As we will recall from earlier in this study,[4] Mettinger had defined "aniconism" within a range of categories, differentiating between aniconism as a de facto tradition (indifference toward images even as images may be absent, and "tolerant" toward other visual systems) versus a programmatic tradition (images are banned, feared, or even destroyed). "Material aniconism" features symbols or material signs as "the central cultic symbol," whereas "empty-space aniconism" utilizes "sacred emptiness," a lack of any image. Though he is cautions not to completely "ignore the user's perspective," he demurs from making this question central, instead preferring to confine his definition "to the level of the phenomenology of religion," and *"not . . . on the type of imputed referential relation between the symbol (the theophoric object) and its referent (the worshippers' notion of God)"* (Mettinger 1995, 18–21 [emphasis original]).

Mettinger begins by affirming the basic continuity between mainland sites such as Tyre and Sidon with their "daughter cults" throughout the Mediterranean and acknowledges the existence of anthropomorphic imagery throughout the Phoenician period (1995, 81–82). Still, the examples he chooses to highlight this anthropomorphic iconism are curious in that they skew toward very late materials (even as late as the fourth century CE) and at times fixate on questionable examples—for example, Mettinger highlights the "bronze image of Kronos" supposedly used in child sacrifice rituals at Carthage as "the best-known example" of this anthropomorphism (1995, 82), but in fact, as Mettinger knows, this is a textual description (not an object we now possess) mentioned in the polemical context of Diodorus Siculus's account of a lurid Punic sacrifice scene in the first century BCE.[5]

---

4. See above at "3.2. Defining the Aniconic."

5. Diodorus Siculus, *Library of History*, 20.14.5–7 (see Geer 1954): "When they had given thought to these things and saw their enemy encamped before their walls, they were filled with superstitious dread, for they believed that they had neglected the honours of the gods that had been established by their fathers. In their zeal to make amends for their omission, they selected two hundred of the noblest children and sacrificed them publicly; and others who were under suspicion sacrificed themselves voluntarily, in number not less than three

The cult at Gadir, the image (or lack of images) of Melqart from Tyre, and sphinx thrones from Sidon form the heart of Mettinger's presentation. For the Gadir cult, he posits aniconism as an "actual, essential feature of that cult, at least in its older, traditional form," based on textual descriptions of the site by Greek and Roman authors (1995, 84–88). Regarding Tyre, Mettinger sees a dearth of native Melqart imagery, finding what William Culican (1962) had called a "Melqart-Baal" figure in the glyptic record to be actually Baal Hammon (Mettinger 1995, 91).[6] I will take up Mettinger's view on the Bar Hadad stele below, but for the moment suffice it to say that Mettinger tends to disqualify what anthropomorphic imagery we do have because of its "borrowed" iconography or its affinity with older motifs as opposed to a supposedly native (= "genuine") Phoenician religious style. Nevertheless, Mettinger is correct to notice that we have fewer and more uncertain images of Melqart than we might wish to see for a group that treasured his depiction in anthropomorphic form and perhaps fewer clear depictions of specifically "Phoenician deities" than we find in Egypt or Mesopotamia (Mettinger 1995, 94, 82). For the Sidonian sphinx thrones, even those that are not empty but rather bear inscribed stelae, Mettinger proposes that we see these stelae as the equivalent of "empty space," and the whole lot of the empty-throne items helps demonstrate an aniconic cult "representing a special, Phoenician subtype" among other Northwest Semitic aniconisms (1995, 106).

In the end, Mettinger concludes that in many areas we find the coexistence of aniconic and anthropomorphic images, perhaps nowhere more numerously on display than in the Punic stelae and Tanit symbolism from Carthage. For "material aniconism," the various sacred stones and stelae form the main body of evidence, while the empty Sidonian thrones are "empty space." Mettinger is rightly careful to point out that we have no evidence of a de facto aniconographic tradition, and certainly no iconoclasm (1995, 111–13). Mettinger's analysis for the Phoenicians specifically does not address the question of *why* these types of images/nonimages were distinct to the Phoenicians and profuse in certain contexts—a topic to which we will return below—except to eventually conclude that the Phoenician evidence provides striking examples of that broader West Semitic aniconic context for which Israel's own image prohibition forms one part (1995, 193–97).

---

hundred. There was in their city a bronze image of Cronus, extending its hands, palms up and sloping toward the ground, so that each of the children when placed thereon rolled down and fell into a sort of gaping pit filled with fire. It is probable that it was from this that Euripides has drawn the mythical story found in his works about the sacrifice in Tauris, in which he presents Iphigeneia being asked by Orestes: But what tomb shall receive me when I die? A sacred fire within, and earth's broad rift. Also the story passed down among the Greeks from ancient myth that Cronus did away with his own children appears to have been kept in mind among the Carthaginians through this observance."

6. See, e.g., the seals discussed above at "4.3. Overview of Phoenician Anthropomorphic Iconography."

We now turn to the ancient textual and material evidence at hand. Given the widely varying geographical and chronological contexts under consideration, after reviewing some descriptions of allegedly Phoenician aniconography in the Hellenistic and Roman textual record, I organize the material by object type, moving from stelae and stones to empty shrines and thrones to other types of divine symbols. Though our chronological aim here remains to peer back as far as possible into the Iron Age context, we can hardly ignore later materials as potential developments of what is older, and thus we will seek a more inclusive range of examples in some cases.

5.2. Textual Accounts of Aniconism by Greek and Roman Authors

A number of Greek and Roman historians described what they saw as notable, odd, or deviant visual phenomena in cultic settings that could be evidence of aniconographic trends in Phoenician temples (see some references in Aubet 2001, 275–76; Mettinger 1995, 82–89; Bunnens 1979; and texts relating to Gadir specifically in Álvarez Martí-Aguilar forthcoming).[7] Although the descriptions provided by these post-Phoenician historians should not be taken as primary evidence of aniconic cults for earlier periods, the astonishment and even condescension evident in a wide range of classical sources regarding Phoenician cultic representation cannot be a coincidence and may indeed have its roots in earlier periods. While our sampling of these sources is not comprehensive, a few examples will be enough to give us the sense of how these authors dealt with their material.

The earliest of these authors, Herodotus (fifth century BCE), will be treated below, since his comments are nearer to the time period in question we wish to investigate (ninth–fifth centuries BCE). For now, we begin by starting nearly a millennium after Herodotus: perhaps the most famous account of Tyre in specifically cultic terms comes from the fifth century CE (but probably drawing on sources at least two centuries earlier) in the form of Nonnus of Panopolis's *Dionysiaca* (40.311–505; for summary and comment, see Bijovsky 2005; Naster 1986; Mettinger 1995, 95–96; and Hirt 2015, most specifically with a connection to the coins). In this account, Melqart himself narrates the founding of his resident city, which occurred when two rocks—the "Ambrosial Rocks," clearly physical indicators of Tyre's two-island geography—settled in Tyre's current location. This "twin motif" appears in other Phoenician-related myth and iconography repeatedly; Philo of Byblos (first–second century CE) describes the founding of Tyre by Hypsouranios, whose brother, Ousōos, dedicated two stelae to celebrate his invention of sea travel (two brothers, two elements, two stelae). Philo reports that these stelae, one for fire and one for wind, were then worshiped by successive generations

---

7. On Phoenician religion in the Greek period, see now Bonnet 2015 (to which I have not yet had access).

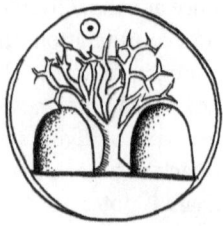  

Fig. 5.1. Ambrosial rocks and stelae on Tyrian coins (Hill 1910, pl. 31, nos. 14–15; Bonnet 1988, fig. 2, a–c)

in the city (Attridge and Oden 1981, 42–43). Motifs common in coinage of the second–fourth centuries CE depict elements of these founding myths, either as the Ambrosial Rocks themselves (marked *AMBROSIE PAITRE*) or a pair of stelae that could represent the stelae in Philo's account or the stelae as substitutes for, or identifications with, the rocks as narrated in the *Dionysiaca* (see examples of wider rock figures flanking an olive tree as well as the taller/thinner twin-stelae motif in fig. 5.1; cf. with the stelae on a coin possibly depicting Melqart/Herakles in Bonnet 1988, pl. 1, fig. 3.d).

In his Latin epic poem dealing with the Second Punic War (218–201 BCE), the *Punica*, Silius Italicus (first century CE) has this to say regarding the Gadir temple complex (3.30–31; Delz 1987; Mettinger 1995, 87; Marín Ceballos and Jiménez Flores 2005): "But no statues or familiar images of the gods filled the place with solemnity and sacred awe." The residents of Gadir, Silius Italicus notes, were "a race akin to Carthage," and the general Hannibal witnessed at Gadir an exotic ritual as well as the imageless worship space. Describing his own travels to Spain, the orator Philostratus II (170–ca. 250 CE) recounts some of the religious aspects of Gadir, including a sanctuary of Herakles.

> The island on which the sanctuary stands is as large as the temple itself, and is in no way like a rock, but resembles a polished platform. Both the Heracleses are said to be honored in the sanctuary, but there are no statues of them. Instead there are two altars of plain bronze for the Egyptian Heracles, and one for the Theban. (Jones 2005, 5.5)

In his *Against Apion* (1.117–118), Josephus (first century CE) quotes a "pillar tradition" regarding the Tyre temple that he claims to have received from Menander the Ephesian, author of a lost history of Tyre from the second century BCE,[8] which,

---

8. See Van Seters 1997, 195–99 for a historiographical assessment of the Menander source.

if it were accurate, would provide a base for the Gadir tradition in the colonial home (translation and commentary in Barclay 2007, 72–74).

> So, writing about those who reigned in Tyre and coming to the time of Eiromos, he [Menander] says this: When Abibalos died, his son Eiromos inherited the kingdom; he lived for 53 years and reigned for 34. He created the embankment for the Broad Place and dedicated the golden pillar in the sanctuary of Zeus; he also went in quest of timber and felled cedar trees from the mountain called Libanos for the roofs of temples. He demolished ancient temples and built new ones, both to Heracles and to Astarte. He initiated the "Awakening" of Heracles, in the month of Peritios.

From Cyprus, Tacitus (first–second century CE) tells of the journeys of Titus Vespasianus, who stops to see the temple of Venus at Paphos. He claims the image of the goddess is "unparalleled elsewhere." "The goddess is not represented in human form; the idol is cone-shaped, rising from a broad circular base to a narrow circumference at the top. The reason for this is unknown" (Levene 1997, 3.1–3).[9] A late-second–early-third-century CE coin from Cyprus depicts what interpreters have often viewed as this very cone (fig. 5.2; see discussion in P. Stewart 2008, 304–8); a similar image from the third century appears on a coin from Emesa depicting the stone of the Roman priest "Elagabalus" (Varius Avitus Bassianus//Marcus Aurelius Antoninus; see Turcan 1985; on both images, see most extensively P. Stewart 2008, but also Mettinger 1995, 85; D'Orazio 2007, 220–21; Bardill 2012, 59–61; Abdy 2012, 509–10; see D'Orazio 2007, fig. 2, for a range of other examples like this as well as P. Stewart 2008, figs. 1–6). In his Roman history (written in Greek in the second–third centuries CE), Herodian describes the temple at Emesa.

> There was a huge temple built there, richly ornamented with gold and silver and valuable stones. . . . There was no actual man-made statue [*agalma*] of the god, the sort the Greeks and Romans put up; but there was an enormous stone, rounded at the base and coming to a point on the top, conical in shape and black. This stone is worshipped as though it were sent from heaven; on it there are some small projecting pieces and markings that are pointed out, which the people would like to believe are rough pictures of the sun, because this is how they see them. (Whittaker 1969, 3.4–5)

This temple was dedicated to Elagabalus (El-Gabal, "God of Byblos"), a ruler who appointed himself priest of the local sun god by the same name, El-Gabal. Elaga-

---

9. P. Stewart notes that although the Paphian sanctuary has been excavated, the small fragment of a black conical stone discovered there is "rather disappointing." Even so, it may be a cult image of some kind (P. Stewart 2008, 306).

balus apparently brought a black rock from Rome—possibly a meteorite (D'Orazio 2007)—which functioned as a central, aniconic object within the temple (depicted here in procession on a horse-drawn cart on the reverse of a coin in fig. 5.3, and enshrined in a temple in fig. 5.4). Notice, in the literary account quoted above, how Herodian is careful to point out the images on the stone that are taken as symbolizing the sun; not just any rock can function as a divine image—it is a specific kind of rock, namely, one with unusual natural markings that were accepted as a deity's self-revelation. Here, the worshiper is not *avoiding* the image of the deity, but rather *searching for it* in the representational markings on the rock. Herodian's condescension is characteristic of this type of primitive ethnography; there is an explicit dichotomy drawn between images of "the sort the Greeks and Romans" find appropriate and "Oriental" expressions (see an analysis of the narrative strategy here in M. Sommer 2008). For these classical authors, as for some modern art historians (Gaifman 2012, 3), it seems that a "proper" image will be clearly anthropomorphic, and anything short of this is cause for wonder. Thus, even though this particular example may not represent a genuine "Phoenician" tradition as opposed to other local Arabian roots (as Mettinger 1995, 86, suspects), Herodian's account still gives us insight into the (at least the perceived) mentality of worshipers of such unadorned objects.

In Lucian of Samosata's *De Dea Syria* (second century CE), two passages describing divine images in the Syrian "Hierapolis" (holy city) deserve mention (both passages below from Attridge and Oden 1976; some vigorously debate Lucian's authorship of the piece, e.g., Dirven 1997). Paragraph 33 describes an image situated between the Zeus and Hera statues, which

> does not have its own particular character, but it bears the qualities of the other gods. It is called "Sign" [*sēmion*] by the Assyrians themselves, and they have not given it any particular name, nor do they speak of its origin or form . . . on its head stands a golden dove.

The nature of this "sign" or "symbol" has generated much discussion (Oden 1977, 109–55). The *sēmion* can be plausibly identified with the nonanthropomorphic figure depicted on a third-century CE Hierapolis coin issued under Caracalla and contains "objects which probably symbolize the traits of some deity" (Oden 1977, 110–11, 114). In addition to this well-known reference, in the following paragraph Lucian describes a

> throne of Helios, but his image is not on it. For only of Helios and Selene do they not display statues. The reason for this custom I also discovered. They say it is right to make images for the other gods, for their forms are not visible to everyone, but Helios and Selene are completely visible and all see them. So, what reason is there to make statues of those gods who appear in the open air?

Fig. 5.2. Coin depicting Paphian cone; Cyprus; second or third century CE (photo in P. Stewart 2008, fig. 2; illustration in Perrot and Chipiez 1885, 123, fig. 58)

Fig. 5.3. Coin depicting cultic stone of Elagabalus in procession (reverse); minted at Antioch; 218–219 CE (Bardill 2012, 60, fig. 48; Abdy 2012, 509, fig. 27.23)

Fig. 5.4. Roman bronze coin; Emesa shrine with stone of Elagabalus; ca. 215 CE (P. Stewart 2008, 299, fig. 1)

Moreover, in the following section, even when Lucian describes an anthropomorphic image of Apollo (positioned behind the throne mentioned here), the Apollo statue is "not as it is usually made"—rather, it is bearded, as opposed to youthful, the reason being that the worshipers think it "utter stupidity to make the forms of the gods imperfect, and they consider youth an imperfect state. They make yet another innovation in their Apollo, for they alone adorn Apollo with clothing" (Attridge and Oden 1976, 46–47, para. 35).

It is unclear whether the reasons given here for the empty throne or the deviant Apollo image are truly native Phoenician interpretations or simply Lucian's attempt at rationalization (see discussion in Gaifman 2012, 108–10). With this example and the others we have offered here from the classical world, one is immediately presented with the problem of how to assess such descriptions, most of which come embedded in accounts fraught with historical difficulties, exaggerations, and unreliable polemics. Still, the confluence of similar descriptions in several different authors is enough to show that some perceived aniconographic phenomenon was in play at several first–fourth-century CE locations. The difficult question is how much earlier this aniconism can be traced. In at least the case of the solar imagery, Joseph Azize (2005) has attempted to make the case that sun worship was a non-Greek Phoenician religious focus, connected to solar veneration in the ancient Near East and perhaps with origins as early as the sixth century BCE.

Having reviewed these textual accounts, we now turn to some possible instances of aniconism from the earlier Phoenician material record. For these examples, I proceed through categories of representation that are sometimes thought to reflect aniconism or aniconic tendencies, in that they are ways to avoid representing a deity (anthropomorphically or otherwise); they include betyls, stelae, cultic stones, empty thrones, empty spaces, and emblems. In some cases (e.g., the empty shrines or thrones), we may have more to say about the ritual function of the object, while for others, we must be content to notice the nonfigural qualities in a piece and document the range of examples.

5.3. Stelae, Pillars, Standing Stones, Betyls

Writing in his *Histories* in the middle of the fifth century BCE, Herodotus claims to have sailed up to Tyre on a quest to understand the origins of the Herakles cult; there in Tyre he finds

> a sanctuary sacred to Heracles . . . and I found that the sanctuary there was very lavishly appointed with a large number of dedicatory offerings. In it were two pillars [*stēlai*], one of pure gold, the other of emerald which gleamed brightly at night. (Waterfield 2008, 2.66)

Pushing back even a century or more earlier, we may see some dim reflection of the Tyre-sanctuary tradition in the prophet Ezekiel, writing (or speaking) probably between the 590s–570s BCE, who mentions "pillars" and "stones" within speeches denouncing Tyre.

> Ezek 26:11: With the hooves of his horses he will trample down all of your streets; he will slay your people with the sword, and your strong columns [*maṣṣĕbôt ʿuzzēk*] will go down to the earth.

> Ezek 28:16: In the great abundance of your commerce you were filled with violence, and you sinned—therefore I cast you down as a profane thing from the divine mountain, and the guardian cherub drove you out from the midst of the stones of fire [*ʾabnê-ʾēš*].

Though Herodotus does not function as a straightforward historian in the modern sense, and Ezekiel's references are cryptic (see Bonnet 1988, 42–50; Mettinger 1995, 97–98; Saur 2010, 217–18), Tyre's famed sanctuary certainly drew attention from these authors and both seem to refer to pillar-like objects, "stones of fire" (possibly with some cultic association), or freestanding stelae as prominent objects of worship. Our first foray into Phoenician aniconic material culture thus involves Tyre and the tradition of cultic stones of various kinds there. To what extent was the cult of Melqart at Tyre actually aniconic, focused on the worship of pillars or stones instead of anthropomorphic statuary? To what extent is a "standing stone"—or indeed any nonfigural stone or natural object—aniconic, and what was the cultic function of these objects?

Terminology and Past Interpretations

Though I cannot review the complete genealogy of the scholarly discussion regarding the standing-stone tradition in the ancient Near Eastern and Mediterranean worlds, a few prefatory comments are in order.[10] First, a note on terminology. Perhaps the most formal designation for intentionally wrought, flat-faced monuments is "stele/stelae" (Greek *stele/stēlai*), usually made of stone and vertical in structure; some stelae are triangularly pointed at the top (gabled), though many are flat or conical, and they may bear markings or inscriptions of various kinds (even iconic images). "Pillars" should technically describe architectural elements in a temple, though it is not always clear whether ancient or modern interpreters differentiate pillars from "stelae" in any rigorous sense (e.g., Herodotus's term for the "pillars" in the translation provided above is *stēlai*).

Terms such as "standing stone" and "betyl" are decidedly less formal—a "standing stone" could encompass any object, whether wrought or natural, that exists in a particular place—whether in nature or a constructed cult site—for a ritual purpose; the term *cippus/cippi* (Latin "stake, post, marker") could also describe a small pillar-like or ovoid item. Many have used the term "betyl" for items covering the same range as "stele," "standing stone," or "cippus," but "betyl" is presumably derived from a generic Semitic designation or even more specifically from the Bible's description of Bethel (*bêt 'el*, "house of god") in Gen 28, in which Jacob anoints a stone "pillar" (*maṣṣēbâ*) at a place he proclaims to be the "house of God" (see B. Sommer 2009, 28–29; Gaifman 2008, 47–48) and then later used in Greek to refer to divine stones with a heavenly origin (Gaifman 2008; P. Stewart 2008, 297–98).[11] Though "betyl" could etymologically describe any number of stelae or

---

10. For helpful reviews of this topic from various perspectives see, e.g., Sader 2005 (Phoenician-Punic world); Patrich 1990, 167–84 (Nabateans and Phoenicians); Gaifman 2012, 181–241 (Greece); Collins 2005, 26–28; and Michel 2014, 2015 (Hittites); Mettinger 1995, passim (ancient Israel, compared with the Nabateans, Phoenicians, and others); Zevit 2001, 142–46, 191–96, 256–63, 348–49 (focusing on ancient Israel and Edom); B. Sommer 2009, 28–29, 48–57 (ancient Israel within the broader Mesopotamian context); de Hulster 2009b, 154–63 (on ancient Israel, with comparisons).

11. The etymology of the Hebrew *maṣṣēbâ* does not reveal much: *nṣb*, "stand up, erect" (thus a *maṣṣēbâ* is a "thing made to stand up"). Philo of Byblos recounts that it was "the god

Fig. 5.5. Stele from Ugarit with astral symbolism; Late Bronze Age; h. approx. 40 cm (Yon 1991, 330, 10.a; Bisi 1967, tav. III, 1)

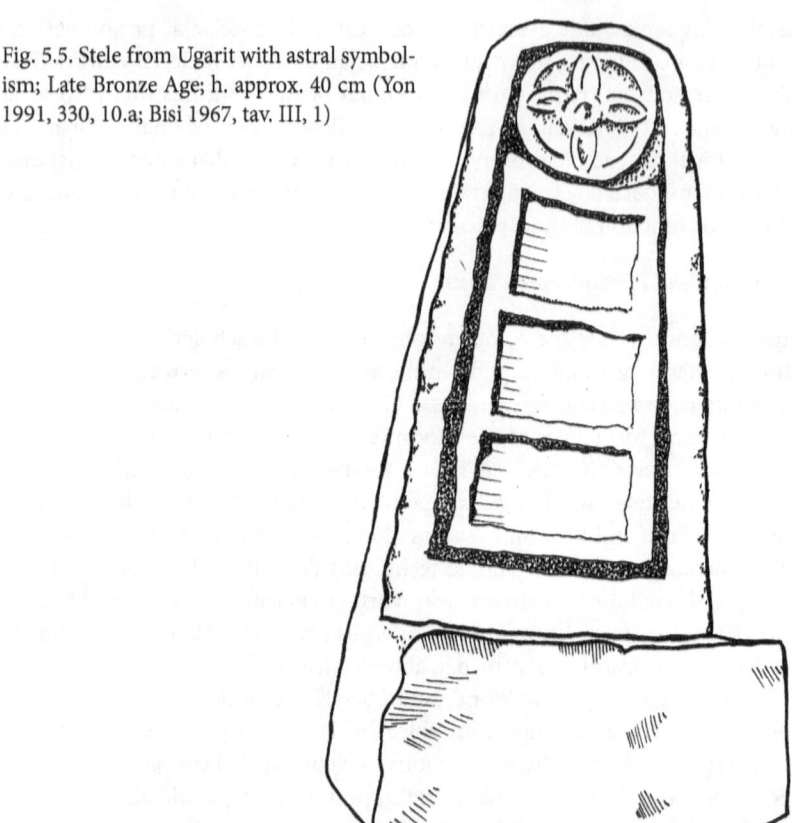

pillars that house a deity, in the field of Phoenician studies the term is often used for (relatively) small ovoid or conical objects, such as the egg-shaped stones enshrined in various thrones, cult stands, and on other two-dimensional surfaces (e.g., coins and stelae; see Soyez 1972; Falsone 1993; and discussion below). One sometimes sees references to stelae and a wide range of other objects come under the "betyl" label, and, as Gaifman points out (2008, 42–44), archaeologists of Greek religion have used the term *baitylos* to cover a similarly wide range of objects. Biblical scholars will be familiar with the "standing-stone" tradition from the Bible itself, where various authors pillory the practice of erecting *maṣṣēbôt* as a deviant form of Yahwism or outright polytheism. One can obviously see that some of the terms, such as *maṣṣēbâ*, come preloaded with the biblical polemic, while

---

Ouranos" who "further invented baetyls [*baitylia*], by devising stones endowed with life" (Attridge and Oden 1981, 52–53).

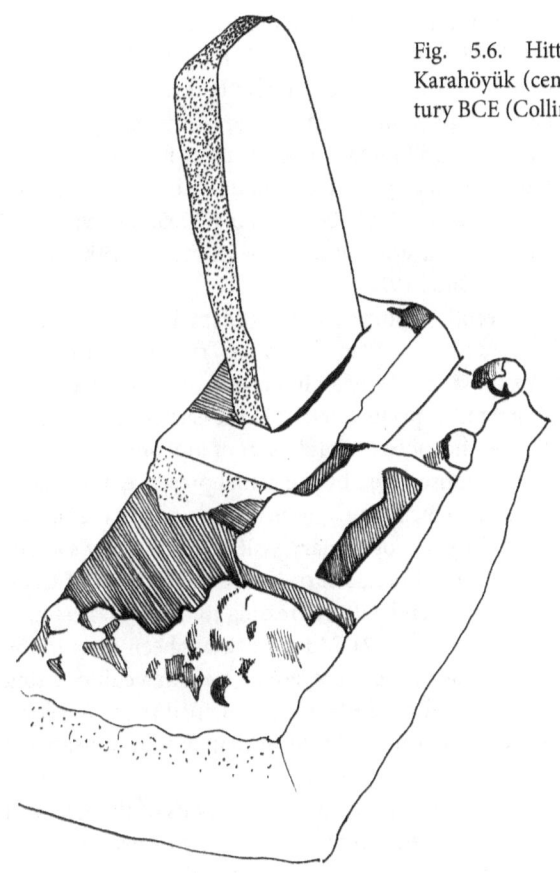

Fig. 5.6. Hittite standing stone from Karahöyük (central Turkey); thirteenth century BCE (Collins 2005, 27, fig. 2.8)

"betyl" would already seem to provide an interpretation of the object as a place where a deity dwells (thus prejudging the question of aniconism in an inappropriate manner; on this, see Quinn 2011, 408, n. 43).

Seemingly all cultures in the ancient Near Eastern and Mediterranean world used stele-like objects for some purpose. For example, from Late Bronze Age Ugarit funerary ritual text ("Duties of the Ideal Son," CTA 17:1.26–34) mentions a son who "sets up the stele of his divine ancestor in the sanctuary, the marker of his clansman" (nṣb skn ilibh bqdš ztr ʿmh), presumably a reference to a funerary marker for the dead in a context of veneration. (See fig. 5.5 for what some have claimed to be an example of just such a stele from Ugarit; see text, interpretation, and debate about key terms here in Lewis 1989, 53–63, esp. 59–60, on the term ztr and the astral imagery on the stele.) The famous Late Bronze Age "stele shrine" at Hazor featured a set of stelae including an inscribed example, central to a set of stelae, with upward-gesturing hands and a crescent disc (Area C, shrine 6136; fourteenth–thirteenth centuries BCE); here iconic figures, perhaps ancestral representations, as well as completely unmarked stelae, all functioned together in the same cultic setting (Mettinger 1995, 178–81, and fig. 7.26). In roughly the same historical context the Hittites used "*ḫuwaši*-stones," a term that refers to stele-like objects or even the open-air sanctuaries in which they are situated; apparently these stones embodied a deity and could function as a substitute for a formal temple structure with the usual anthropomorphic divine statuary that such a temple would contain (see Michel 2015; Bonatz 2007, 8–9; Collins 2005, 26–29; Popko 1993, 324–6; fig. 5.6 is an example of a stone of this type in situ; cf. with the use of nonanthropomorphic figures in Bittel 1976, 191.214).[12]

In his influential late nineteenth-century study, William Robertson Smith (1894, 200) had considered the "sacrificial pillar," "cairn," or "rude altar" to be the center of the Semitic sanctuary, making it quite an important piece for analysis of the development of the religion. Smith speculated that in the earliest narratives of the biblical ancestors (Gen 12–50) the *maṣṣēbâ* was "a sort of idol or embodiment of the divine presence," an object "consecrated by the actual presence of the godhead," whereas the physical space on which such a stone item stood was the "house of god," the betyl (1894, 204–5). In his evolutionary vision,[13] Smith saw sacred-stone worship as originating from the veneration of nature in the form of trees, found objects like stones, and so on, then later progressing to using these simple objects in more formal settings (1894, 206–12). Much work has been done in the past 120 years, though the notion that a prominent stone object in a cultic setting is somehow an embodiment or home for the deity has remained popular. (For a contemporary review of tree and stone worship in the ancient Mediterranean, see López-Ruiz 2010, 205–10.)

Let us recall at this point the earlier discussion on the status of the image in the ancient Near Eastern world more generally[14]—the modern or even Platonic concept of an "image" as disassociated from the "thing itself" does not apply as a blanket concept to the objects in question here, and the "ontological communion" between object and deity may extend not only to three-dimensional metal "cult statues" of the classic type but also to inscribed objects or stelae. In a discussion of some third-millennium BCE Mesopotamian materials, for example, Anne Porter notes that both "statues and stelae were equally the material embodiment of [the] person. That Mesopotamians did not necessarily conceptualize stelae and statues as ontologically different is evident in the fact that an Akkadian-period stele is designated as alan, the Sumerian word for statue, in its own inscription" (2014, 612).

---

12. Note also a newer study addressing the situation of standing stones among the Hittites and at Emar by Michel 2015 and the longer version in Michel 2014 (to which I have not yet had access).
13. See discussion above at "3.2. Defining the Aniconic."
14. See discussion above at "3.1. What Is an 'Icon'?"

There is no ideal form under which all figures of this type must be subsumed, and no single interpretation of the various nonfigural stone-object traditions that can be cast over all of the evidence—even within the Phoenician world. Sader has provided a recent analysis of stelae from Iron Age and Punic Tyre and the surrounding environs, which can serve as a helpful starting point for our investigation of their aniconic potential (2005, 20–22).[15] She notes that some of the classically "Phoenician" stelae from the mainland are marked with the term *mnṣbt/ mṣbt* (2005, 13) so the identification on that front with the *maṣṣĕbôt* tradition (by name) for the funerary items she considers seems beyond question (cf. warnings on the identification of *maṣṣĕbôt* in Israel by Bloch-Smith 2005, 2006, and LaRocca-Pitts 2001, 205–28, for caution against overgeneralizing the function of standing stones). This does not mean that biblical notions of the *maṣṣēbâ* can be automatically imported to the Phoenician data, but we do have this correlation of philological data linking the phenomena. From Sader's review of the literature on the Phoenician-Punic materials specifically (2005, 20–22), we may single out three common interpretations:

(1) The stelae function as a tomb marker. Sader herself finds this to be the "primary and original function" of the pieces she analyzes (2005, 20), though of course if there is no body buried beneath/near the object then this interpretation cannot represent the primary or original function of the stelae.

(2) The stelae represent or commemorate the dead in some manner—this could range from a hope for memory of the deceased to some kind of "house" for the "soul." In favor of some interpretation within this range is the fact that many of the tenth–sixth-century BCE stelae mention the name of the dead, as do indeed all of the later examples from the coastal sites in Lebanon. The most recent study on this topic, by Matthew Suriano (2014), explores this function for some analogous materials, as the soul interpretation was recently revived with the discovery of the so-called Katumuwa stele from Zincirli (eighth century BCE; on this, see also Pardee 2009; Struble and Herrmann 2009; Sanders 2013), in which the stele dedicant, Katumuwa, comments on the food and support that must be offered for his "soul" (*nbš*), which is "in the stele" (*bnṣb*).

(3) The stelae play a cultic function, serving in a larger ritual setting at the site. Some stelae contain a niche that would seem to be a place where something was meant to be placed—perhaps a divine image, or food for

---

15. For two other reviews of Phoenician and Punic stelae, see Uberti 1992; Moscati 1988d; Bisi 1967. None of these three sources, however, were able to address the important newly discovered/obtained material from the Tyre cemeteries or surrounding coastal areas from the Iron Age.

the dead?—suggesting a ritual purpose. Moreover, symbols of various kinds on the stelae may represent deities, perhaps to guard the stele and what it represents or as a site of direct veneration. The anthropomorphic images on the stelae in particular could have had differing functions, from portraits of a remembered human to the "personification of a force enjoying apotropaic powers" to a deity (Sader 2005, 134–35).

There are interpretations of stelae that could disqualify them from a discussion of a certain kind of cultic aniconism under the terms that we have defined them here. For example, if a stele in a given context was a memorial signal for a burial or a "house" for a human postmortem existence, then the object is not ritually "aniconic" *as a nonfigural way of representing a deity*. Having said that, the modern distinction between the human and divine could slant the discussion in unadvisable ways. From the ancient Northwest Semitic world one thinks of the famous example of Samuel's ghost in 1 Sam 28 being called an ʾĕlōhîm ("divine being," "god") or the Late Bronze Age Ugaritic rapiʾuma rituals in which deceased kings were venerated not merely as memorialized humans but as transformed beings, capable of receiving offerings and influencing affairs on earth in a manner not unlike deities (Doak 2012, 153–99; see also Schmidt 1996). Many more examples like this could be offered, but the basic point is that stelae functioning in roles (1) and (2) above cannot be immediately dismissed from a discussion of cultic aniconism based only on the fact that they may signify or portray deceased humans.

Iron Age Stelae from Khalde, Sidon, Tell el-Burak, and Tyre

We now turn to examples of Phoenician stelae and particularly their employment of aniconic techniques. Through the 1980s, a mere handful of legitimately "Phoenician" stelae from the earlier-period coastal mainland had been identified (see Bisi 1967; Moscati 1988d). Today, however, a small but rich corpus of over fifty pieces now in museums from the sites of Khalde, Sidon, Tell el-Burak, and Tyre (from north to south, respectively, spanning a stretch of around 30 km of the contemporary Lebanese coast) and dating to the tenth–sixth centuries BCE may be examined, pending further excavation, as a new and authoritative starting point for the understanding of Phoenician stelae (now collected and discussed in Sader 2005; see also Sader 1991; 1992). The group of stelae in focus here from this time period Sader calls "the common stelae" due to their widespread use and function in cemeteries. The group shares many characteristics in common (Sader 2005, 18): all were hewn from local sandstone; they are "crudely made," with ample tool marks; they are small (at maximum, h. 76 cm, w. 40 cm); most have inscriptions or images; all came from cemeteries; and all can be tentatively but confidently dated to the tenth–sixth-century horizon.

There is a question as to whether these stelae might represent, in their very existence, a type of aniconism, regardless of their shape or markings. Only one

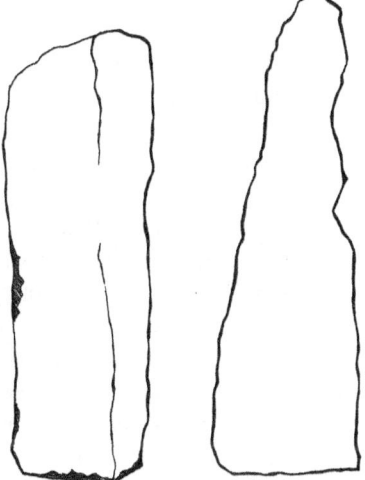 

Fig. 5.7. Unmarked stele; Tyre al-Bass cemetery; eleventh–sixth century BCE (Sader 2005, 72, fig. 61, stele 49)

Fig. 5.8. Inscribed stele from Tyre al-Bass cemetery; ninth–eighth century BCE (Sader 2005, 74, fig. 64, stele 51)

of Sader's examples is an intentionally worked stone monument with no inscription or markings (fig. 5.7), so clearly this was not the preferred type—although, if indeed there were no images on the stele that have faded, the piece attests to the acceptability of this type. The earliest stele from Tyre discovered in situ (fig. 5.8), which may be more specifically dated to the ninth or eighth century,[16] bears the inscription 'bd pʿm bn ʿn', "Servant of PʿM, son of 'N.'" PʿM is a recognized Phoenician deity (see Lipiński 1995, 215), whereas 'n' is more ambiguous, perhaps a shorthand description for another deity or some other element of a name (Sader 2005, 74–75). This stele also has no clear figural markings, but the association of the deceased with at least one deity (PʿM) does draw the stone into a "conversation" with the presence of the deity. In this category, we must also include stelae with a cut niche (whether inscribed or not), which were possibly meant to hold a divine image or serve as a space for a deity or venerated ancestor to become present (see Sader 2005, 30–31, 64, and images there). This category will be discussed below with the "empty-shrine" phenomenon, but for the moment we can say that stelae of this type are potentially aniconic.

---

16. I tentatively follow Sader's epigraphic dating schema for the stelae of this type cited here; see her analysis in Sader 2005, 84–109.

The most blatantly figural stelae of this type would include examples where the stele itself is forged into a rough anthropomorphic shape (Sader 2005, 68–73, figs. 56–59, 62) or stelae with clear figural images (Sader 2005, 33, fig. 12; 66, fig. 53; figs. 4.18, 5.9). In addition to the completely nonfigural stelae, of special interest for our consideration of aniconic motifs are stelae that bear more abstract representations of the "Tanit" or *ankh*-like sign and others with symbols of unclear meaning.[17]

Two points here are worth noting. First, several of the stelae with an ovoid object inscribed on them (figs. 5.10 and 5.11) may already prefigure the much later betyls that we find enshrined as what most have assumed are a symbol of Astarte on sphinx thrones, coins, and other objects—from Tyre in the east and also from Carthage and other sites farther west (Soyez 1972; Falsone 1993; for a comparison with fig. 5.11 from Motya, consider D'Andrea 2014b, 139–40, figs. 6–7). Indeed, the most helpful parallels Sader adduces in her own study are from Nora and Carthage (respectively, in fig. 5.12; date unknown, but presumably much later than the example from Tyre in figs. 5.10–11), suggesting that, on at least the typological level, but at most a level of direct cultic influence, we have an origin (i.e., an earlier origin than we had previously) in the mainland at an early date of some aniconic objects that appear much later in the west. Sader mentions the possibility that the mounds on these stelae could be some form of the Ambrosial Rocks mentioned in Nonnus's founding myth and depicted on later Tyrian coins (fig. 5.1), but she also finds it "highly plausible" that the object is a betyl-style representation of some deity with important cultic significance in Phoenician religion. Having said that, the feature could be some type of architecture or furniture, and the clumsiness of the carving leaves ample room for doubt (as Sader also notes; 2005, 120–21).

Second, the Tanit, *ankh*, or "pseudo-*ankh*" symbols can become abstract, and/or elements could become detached and used pars pro toto in a manner that takes what was once figural (iconic) and transforms it into the aniconic. Elements such as the isosceles triangles, cross symbols, "outstretched arms" motifs, circles and ovoids of various kinds, and borrowed (and possibly misunderstood) hieroglyphics that we find on the stelae from the Lebanese Iron Age sites probably belonged to a constellation of referents that included the sun, a female deity (or several), and various cultic objects. Though it is impossible to elaborate on the meaning of all of the motifs represented on these stelae—Sader gives an excellent review, with ample sources (2005, 115–40)—several examples demonstrate the aniconic possibilities at hand.

---

17. For the Tanit or *ankh* types, see Sader 2005, 29, fig. 8; 43, fig. 24; 58, fig. 39; 63, fig. 49; 66, fig. 53; 67, fig. 55 (fig. 4.18 above); for other symbols, see 34, fig. 14 (a phallic image?); 35, fig. 15 (lotus bud or other vegetation?); 37, fig. 17, and 40, fig. 20 (crescent discs); 41, fig. 21; and 50, fig. 31 (ovoid shape); 53, figs. 33–34 (cross, disc, ovoid); 54, fig. 35 (U-shape, vertical line, inverted T-shape); 61, fig. 45 (cross); 75, fig. 65 (*nfr* sign, meaning "good, perfect").

Fig. 5.9. Stele with anthropomorphic head; Beirut National Museum (unclear location of find); tenth–sixth century BCE (Sader 2005 33, fig. 12 stele 9)

Fig. 5.10. Stele with incised object; seventh century BCE; inscribed with word grgš (Sader 2005, fig. 21 stele 15)

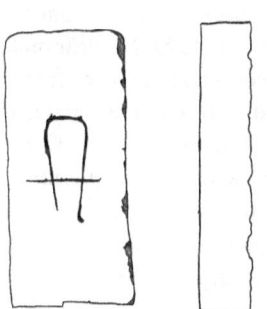

Fig. 5.11. Stele with incised object; tenth–sixth century BCE (Sader 2005, fig. 31, stele 24)

Fig. 5.12. Stelae from Nora and Carthage; Punic (Sader 2005, fig. 22; Bisi 1967, LII.2, XII.1)

The ovoid/betyl marker may find more and less elaborate expression from what we examined above in several other pieces, for example, a figure on a stand (?) of some kind (fig. 5.13),[18] a lotus bud (fig. 5.14; cf. with Berthier and Charlier 1952, XVII.A), and in the upper left- and right-hand quadrants of a cross symbol (fig. 5.15). Moreover, it is possible that the cross symbol in fact represents the sun, known as a major focus of worship in the later religion, as the isolated cross symbol was known in much earlier Mesopotamian seals and other regional examples in the East as solar imagery (Sader 2005, 132, with examples and literature cited there). On figure 5.13, the vertical line above the betyl shape may also be the top vertical stroke of a cross, amid which the betyl (as solar disc?) is embedded. On figure 5.15, we see in close proximity the fact that the "head" of the *ankh*—and perhaps by extension the head of the more distinct Tanit figure—is the same sort of disc as the solo disc, the cross the same cross as the "body" of the *ankh*, the body of the *ankh* the same body as the Tanit development (assuming the Tanit and *ankh* represent a "development"). The images suggest one another within a reasonably contained range of motifs.

What then do we make of these items in terms of their categorization as aniconic? There is admittedly little we can say with great confidence about the shapes and signs—the fully figural images are probably visages of the human to be remembered or venerated or housed in some sense that we cannot recover in particular for each piece, but the range of visual strategies is striking: from boldly (if crudely) anthropomorphic to Tanit-type figures, to discs and crosses that may represent body parts, plants, the sun, or other independent items. No clear preference or reason for using one over the other emerges; there is no preference for figurism yet no denial of it. The differences may have been due to economic factors involving those who commissioned the stelae (recall Moscati 1969) or simply personal inclinations now lost to us. After all, in the cemetery setting we are presumably not dealing with tightly controlled, "official" religious displays, but rather with those of individuals and their families (cf. with the analysis of funerary iconography in Birney and Doak 2011).

The Earlier Carthaginian Stelae

The most famous stelae from Carthage are from the fifth century (discussed below), featuring the prominent Tanit symbol combined with the epigraphic evidence regarding the sacrifice or dedication of children at the tophet.[19] Though not as iconographically intricate, the earlier period at Carthage—from the early eighth

---

18. The visual effect may be a coincidence, but a stele from Constantine (Algeria) in Berthier and Charlier 1952, XXIX, shows a Tanit figure with upraised arms whose body and head take on a similar shape to this stele, which could suggest that fig. 5.13 is possibly a crude or symbolic form of the Tanit figure.

19. For a helpful overview, see Moscati 1988d, esp. 304, 306 on Carthage, as well as more

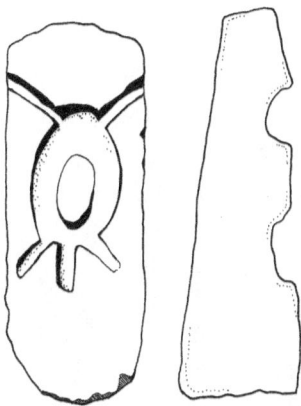

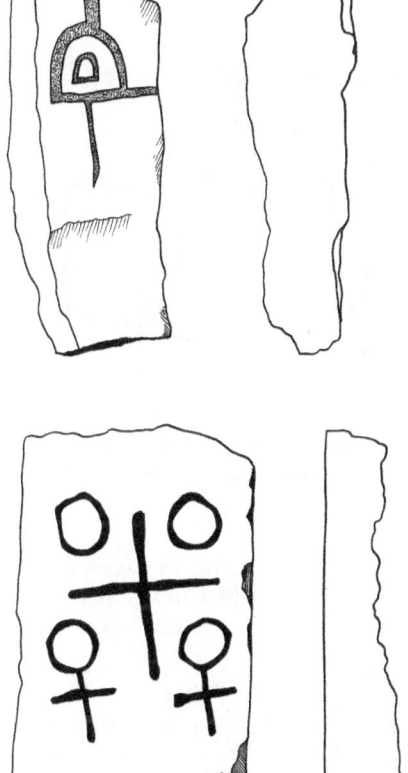

Fig. 5.13 (above left). Stele with incised object; tenth–sixth century BCE (Sader 2005, fig. 34, stele 27)

Fig. 5.14 (above right). Stele with lotus bud (?); tenth–sixth century BCE (Sader 2005, fig. 15, stele 11)

Fig. 5.15 (left). Stele with cross, discs, and ankh; tenth–sixth century BCE (Sader 2005, fig. 33, stele 26)

century through the sixth century—yielded many stelae, some plain and some with crescent/disc imagery, stelae inscribed on/within other stelae, "bottle" shaped figures, cippi, "throne-cippi" (i.e., a slightly tapered cippus object with a throne on top), and L-shaped empty thrones (Bartoloni 1976); these types of objects were not entirely absent in the later period, but they appear with greatly decreased frequency. As so much of the attention for the Carthage discoveries focused on the later periods, less detailed work has been done on the earlier examples, which are sometimes dismissed with derisive comments about the unoriginality and tedium of the motifs.

Carthage maintained an important connection with Tyre on a number of levels—indeed, the very name Carthage, for the Phoenicians qrt ḥdšt, "new city" (i.e., New Tyre), attests to the identity establishment and continued interchange

---

specific studies of Carthage by Brown 1991; Quinn 2011; Bénichou-Safar 2004; and an update on the archaeology in Pappa 2013, 149–50.

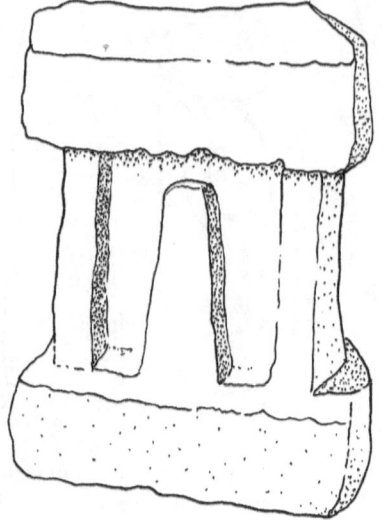
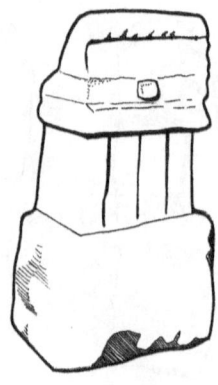

Fig. 5.16 (above left). Stele with inscribed stele in relief; Carthage; sixth century BCE (h. 50 cm) (Moscati 1988a, 614.177)

Fig. 5.17 (above right). Stele with incised "betyls"; Carthage; sixth century BCE (h. 55.5 cm) (Moscati 1988a, 614.178)

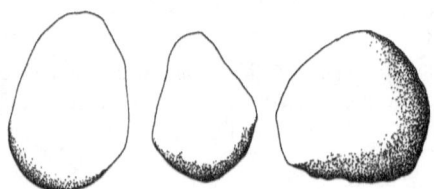

Fig. 5.18 (left). Series of ovoid stones; Carthage (Bénichou-Safar 2004, pl. XLVII, 1-3)

(Aubet 2001, 156–57; see also Günther 2000). In a recent and sophisticated analysis, Josephine Quinn argues that tophets were "collective civic spaces" where "religion, death, family, and community came together . . . in a way that gave them a peculiar power to construct and convey cultural identities for their users" (2011, 390). Thus, tophets make a most instructive site for analyzing the manner in which a colony may interact with its mother city, noting that identification *with* is to be distinguished from identification *as* in terms of ethnic belonging (2011, 390–91). Along the way, Quinn provides a helpful review of the relevant iconography associated with the various levels (2011, 391–96; following Bénichou-Safar 2004): in her analysis, the earliest period (ca. 800–650 BCE) saw very rough monuments, after which L-thrones, cippi, and small shrines make up a large portion of the material (ca. 650–525 BCE). The "stelae" then emerge in the fourth century. Quinn notes the similarity of motifs between the Phoenician mainland and Carthage in the seventh–fourth centuries generally, though we cannot dismiss the idea that motifs may have traveled west to east (instead of the assumed other way around),

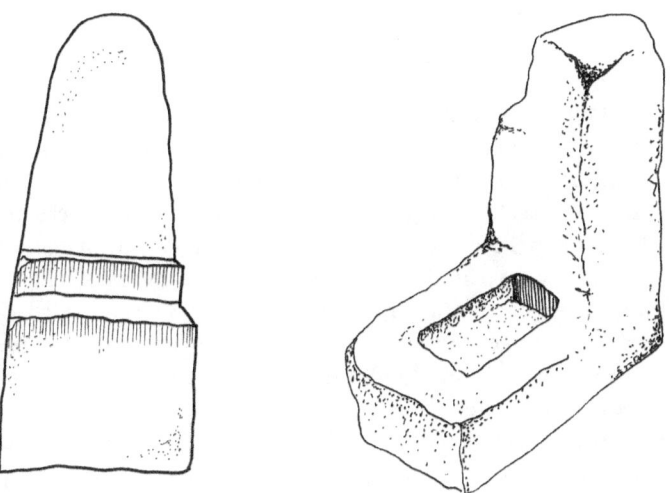

Fig. 5.19. Two L-shaped thrones; Carthage (Bénichou-Safar 2004, pl. LII, 1–2)

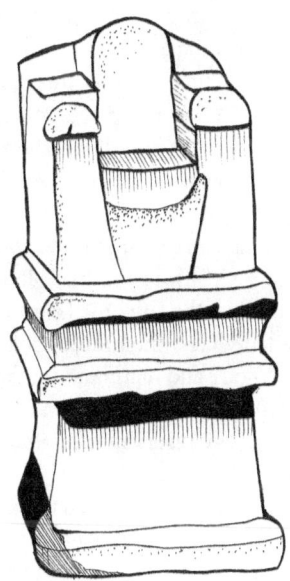

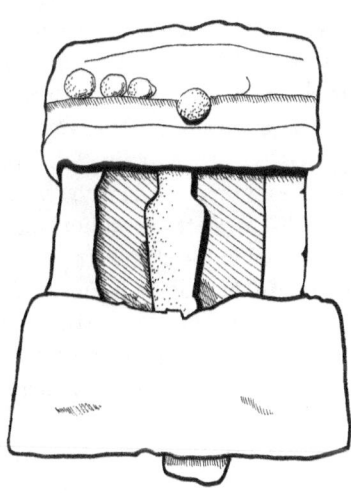

Fig. 5.20. Tiered throne; Carthage (Bénichou-Safar 2004, pl. LII, 9)

Fig. 5.21. Bottle figure in shrine; Carthage (Bénichou-Safar 2004, pl. L, 6)

and for the model shrines (*naiskoi*) in particular the closest iconographic parallels we have are from Sidon, suggesting new networks of identification in the beginning of the Persian era (2011, 396).

Most of the monuments in question here are not strictly "stelae" in the sense of tall, flat standing objects—rather, they are more like schematic shrines or houses into which miniature stelae are carved (see figs. 5.16 and 5.17). Even simpler objects, however, such as roughly worked stones and other unelaborate shapes (fig. 5.18) may have been used on their own or in tandem with cultic stands and thrones from the same period (see parallel examples from Sulcis in Bartoloni 1986, I–II); the thrones from the earlier settings, mostly empty (and treated as their own category below), range from the L-shape (fig. 5.19) to tiered examples that are hybrids of a stele in their own right with a throne or stand (fig. 5.20); other ovoid/ betyl shapes, including the bottle figure, appear as well (e.g., fig. 5.21). Devoid of figuration (with the exception of the bottle shape, discussed anon), all of these examples are truly aniconic; though some Tanit shapes do begin to appear, and although some of these aniconic forms persist long throughout the later periods (past the fourth century BCE), the archaic Carthaginian tophet stelae and stones constitute a strong repertoire of aniconographic images.

The Bar Hadad Stele, Redux

An additional stele—this one inscribed and clearly depicting a deity—must now be revisited, namely, the Bar Hadad stele featuring Melqart from the ninth century (found near Aleppo; fig. 4.7 above). I bring this piece back into the discussion at this point because, interestingly enough, Mettinger suggests that this earliest-known representation of Melqart is a false lead as an iconic piece and rather suggests the fundamentally *aniconic* nature of the Tyrian cult. How? The image here is "obviously composite," Mettinger avers; the object in Melqart's right hand, "whether a lotus or an ʿnḫ-symbol, is obviously of Egyptian origin. The style of dress has Syro-Hittite affiliations. The head-gear, hair and beard seem to indicate influences from a neo-Hittite center," and so on (1995, 94). From this, Mettinger claims that Melqart was without native images, and thus the aniconic Gadir cult—as described in the classical sources—had its roots in Tyre, the mother colony. If we can feasibly imagine such a dynamic between colony and mainland religion, as I have suggested here, this would provide (as Mettinger asserts) "just another example indicating that cultic practice is one of the most conservative of all human activities" (1995, 100; see also Mettinger 2004 on this).

On the one hand, Mettinger may have a point. Others have noticed this dearth of Melqart images in the material record, such as Sergio Ribichini, who characterizes the anthropomorphic representations of Melqart as "few and uncertain" and claims the depiction on the Bar Hadad stele "portrays him with the features of a Baal Lord of Tempest, but this is probably derived from iconographies that are not original to this deity" (1988, 110). However, the point is pushed too far. As

Fig. 5.22. Front and back of razor from Carthage with standing figure (left); Punic; scarab from Cyprus with standing figure (uncertain date and provenance; right) (both in Acquaro 1971, tav. XXVIII [photo], fig. 40 [drawing]; fig. 75.1 [scarab])

any review of Phoenician artistic trends must recognize,[20] Phoenician craftsman are famous for their blend of iconographies, and this cannot be reduced to mere bungling or heedless borrowing, even if one argues that the artisan was after the creation of a certain "look" rather than the production of subtle meanings (e.g., Brown 1992, 13–14).

Moreover, we must not be overly hasty to dismiss other early depictions of Melqart or the idea that Melqart had a cult statue in Tyre after which these images had been modeled (Culican 1960–1961, 41; Bonnet 1988, 77–90, for other possibilities for Melqart images, and 99–113, on Melqart's temples). For example, a razor from Carthage shows a figure in a pose that is extremely similar to the Melqart on the Bar Hadad stele, as does a scarab from Cyprus (fig. 5.22; Acquaro 1971, 107),[21] and even though Baal Hammon was the primary male deity at Carthage, Melqart is attested there (see also the seventh-century BCE limestone sculpture of "Herakles/Melqart" from Kazaphani [Cyprus] in Moscati 1988a, 585.10; Bonnet 2007). Obviously a figure like this could be shared through any number of channels, a "canonical" version of a cult statue from a temple being one possible avenue. At any rate, we should be open to the possibility that the depiction of Melqart on

---

20. See above at "4.1. The Phoenician Artistic Context."
21. The stance of the central figure and iconography may also be compared with a basalt stele from Qadbun (over 100 km north of Sidon, the Syrian coast), now in the Tartous Museum, depicted in Gubel 2000, 187, fig. 1.

Fig. 5.23 (above left). Single "betyl" stele; Motya; sixth–fifth century BCE; h. 47.5 cm (Moscati 1988a, 648.380)

Fig. 5.24 (above right). Twin "betyl" stele; Persian period; Burj esh-Shemali (Sader 2005, 77, fig. 67 stele 54)

Fig. 5.25 (left). Three "betyl" stele; Nora; sixth–fourth century BCE; h. 74.4 cm (Moscati 1988a, 670.509)

the Bar Hadad stele does indeed represent "native" Phoenician imagery in that the motifs have been adopted in the cosmopolitan style of the Phoenicians and thus "made Phoenician." Presumably one can show the heterogeneous nature of most "indigenous" iconographies; if we must deny the label "Phoenician" for all iconographies with mixed motifs or clear international influence, then we shall be denying the Phoenicians most of their (apparently) "native" imagery.

Ultimately, then, in summary of our discussion of the earlier stelae, we would seem to have several types of stelae that could be discussed as aniconic in the tenth–sixth-century BCE corpus: unmarked stelae, without images; stelae with nonfigural symbols that, even if related to figural ideas or models, appear without a clear anthropomorphic context; and stelae with figural/anthropomorphic images, such as the Tanit figure or other roughly depicted faces that, whether human or divine (or postmortem human spirits), gesture toward schematic as opposed to more detailed anthropomorphic representation.

Punic Stelae from the Mediterranean

From the Punic Mediterranean of the fourth century BCE and beyond we find an explosion of examples, the majority from Carthage, followed by significant data from Motya, Hadrumetum, Selinus, Constantine (Algeria), Sardinia (e.g., Nora, Sulcis, Tharros), and elsewhere. These materials push us into later periods and cannot be wantonly compared with the tenth–sixth-century BCE stelae considered above, but it is nonetheless instructive to see the persistence of aniconographic forms in many Phoenician contexts on into the Hellenistic and later eras. We find not only many stelae in these locations but also "cultic stones," betyls, and cippi of various kinds. Since our discussion of the iconography of various stele types has already given us a picture of iconic and aniconic possibilities, I will give a briefer treatment here (but see Bisi 1967; Brown 1991; Patrich 1990, 167–84; Bartoloni 1976; 1986; Falsone 1993; Berthier and Charlier 1952; Moscati 1970; 1988d and sources cited there). Significant changes can be traced in specific localities. For example, Quinn (2011, 396), building on the data analyzed by Shelby Brown (1991) as well as others, recognizes a shift in the "visual culture" of the Carthage tophet in the fourth century BCE—the earlier, rougher monuments give way to sleeker ones with gabled/pointed tops, and there is a sharp decline (though not a complete absence) in earlier forms such as pillars and the bottle shape. Greek motifs increase (e.g., the caduceus wand), and the familiar Tanit figure is ubiquitous, along with the disembodied hand of Baal Hammon.

From the Phoenician coastal mainland of the fourth–third century BCE, we have a mere three stele examples, all smoothly carved and inscribed; they are more like texts or inscriptions than "stelae" on the terms we have been discussing them here (Sader 2005, 20, 80–84). Sader identified only seven examples from the sixth–fifth centuries BCE (2005, 18–20), six of which were model shrines (*naiskoi*) and one of which was a deeply carved double-stele motif from Burg esh-Shemali, near

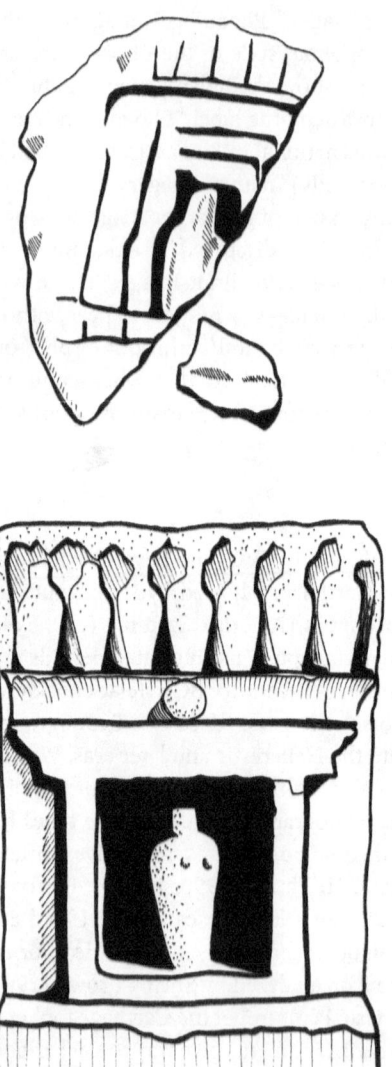

Fig. 5.26 (above left). Bottle figure stele fragment; Akhziv (Patrich 1990, 176, ill. 59a; Bisi 1967, fig. 14)

Fig. 5.27 (above right). Bottle figure stele; Nora; sixth–fourth century BCE; h. 84.3 cm (Moscati 1988d, 318)

Fig. 5.28 (left). Bottle figure stele; Nora; sixth–fourth century BCE; h. 79.7 cm (Moscati 1988a, 670.510)

Tyre (fig. 5.24; the dating of this piece is disputed, and some place it centuries later; see Quinn 2011, 410 n. 66). Wherever the twin-pillar motif appears in a Phoenician-Punic context, one may be tempted to posit an origin from a putatively early Tyrian founding myth along the lines of the Ambrosial Rocks legend or the much earlier double *stelai* described by Herodotus (see also the twin vertical objects from Motya tophet in Falsone 1993, 281, pls. 010–011), though we sometimes find many more than two stelae inscribed on such objects—often three, or groups of three (see fig. 5.25; cf. with fig. 4.17 and other triple-stelae from Nora, where they seem to have been particularly popular, in Moscati 1970, tav. VII–XIII), and often just one (fig. 5.23). The problem of "triads" of deities in the ancient Near East is notoriously difficult to pin down as a comprehensive or formal arrangement, though it is clear that triadic deity groups (e.g., a divine father, mother, and a son) were common from a very early period.

The Bottle Idol Debate

Though the "bottle idol" form fell off in popularity at Carthage, it remained a common piece of iconography in the sixth–fourth-century BCE Mediterranean, as other examples from Nora, Motya, and elsewhere demonstrate (see fig. 5.21 above). Surprisingly, only one example of this type from the mainland, at Akhziv (just south of Tyre), has been identified (fig. 5.26; see brief comments in Brown 1991, 138; Quinn 2011, 395).[22] Named for its bottle-like shape, this particular image appears predominantly within stele shrines in the same carved fashion as stelae (see examples in figs. 5.27 and 5.28; also figs. 3.2 and 5.21; see range of examples from Carthage in Bartoloni 1976, figs. 23–26).

Most relevant for our purposes here is this question: To what extent is the bottle figure strictly aniconic? On one extreme end of the spectrum is William Robertson Smith (1894, 207), who would seem to eschew attempts to see anthropomorphism in any such objects: "A cairn or rude stone pillar is not a portrait of anything, and I take it that we shall go on altogether false lines if we try to explain its selection as a divine symbol by any consideration of what it looks like." Brown reviews a battery of contradictory opinions on the matter (1991, 138–41), as interpreters have lined up to support or deny the idea that this image is aniconic (like the ovoid betyls generally) or even that it represented a mummy (Culican 1991, 498, suspects a North African Libyan origin for the shape; cf. with the comments on the African associations by Gubel 2005, 127, and another argument in Culican 1970, 39–41). Based on the presence of eyes or feet on some of the figures,[23] Brown suspects that the shapes are a baby—that is, the baby sacrificed or buried at the tophet in which the monument with the bottle shape is found (Brown 1991, 141).

---

22. On the interpretation of the shape, see Culican 1970, 34–45; Bertrandy 1992a; Mettinger 1995, 112; Brown 1991, 138–41; and earlier literature cited there.

23. See examples of the anthropomorphization of the bottle figure in Brown 1991, 264.276–77; cf. with 268.351; 272.453; and even 273.500; at points, the gabled area of the stele seems merged with the triangular body of Tanit, e.g., 264.286; 265.297–98; see other examples of the bottle figure taking on anthropomorphic form in Bisi 1967, fig. 34, d, f, g; Bartoloni 1986, tav. XXXIX, 230, among other examples like this from Sulcis; Picard 1978, pl. XVI.5; XVII.1.

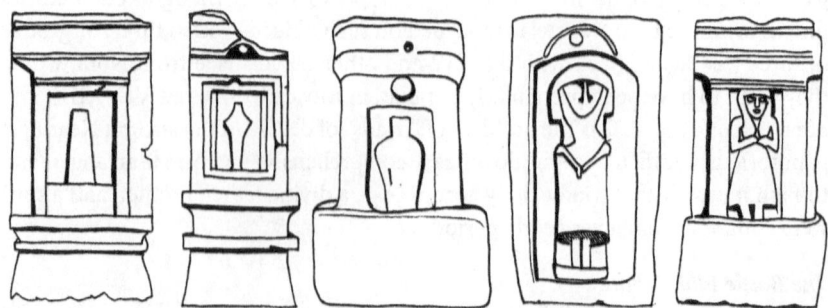

Fig. 5.29. Stelae with figures; Motya; sixth–fourth century BCE (Moscati 1988a, 648.380, 382, 381, 383, 384)

The image could have represented an offering vase or ovoid betyl without figural connotations in many of its uses and some could have found other meanings in it; a shape with this level of abstraction was obviously open to a range of uses.

But, in support of Brown's interpretation and before rushing to declare the aniconic properties of the bottle figure too quickly, we should recall David Freedberg's point about the misidentification of anthropomorphic or other representational imagery in ancient art (1989, 59)—in some cultic stones or stelae one can detect nonobvious, but still anthropomorphic, forms. A series of votive stelae with embedded figures, including the bottle figure, all from Motya and dated to roughly the same time period (the sixth–fifth centuries BCE) is instructive in this regard (fig. 5.29). Considered separately, or as pairs, each piece here is clearly distinct. However, as a group, we can better see the continuum of iconic and aniconic forms here. This is not a historical evolution of form, but rather a proclivity to depict anthropomorphically in several different ways simultaneously—the standard betyl shape on the far left is not anthropomorphic (cf. what appear to be eyes and other anthropomorphic features marked on the gabled stele itself in Brown 1991, 258.103), but the trapezoidal form next to it as well as that of the bottle figure in the center take on clearly anthropomorphic connotations when viewed side by side with similar forms crafted in greater detail. (A similar continuum could be created with the Sulcis shrine-stelae in Bartoloni 1986, tav. XXVIII–LXXVII.) We would not want to push this argument too far; clearly, there are shapes within the stele-shrine examples that simply cannot be viewed anthropomorphically so easily, such as the "lozenge" or diamond-shaped items in the earlier Carthaginian stelae (see Bartoloni 1976, tav. CIX–CXVI) or many other examples for that matter (see, from Nora, e.g., Moscati 1970, tav. XV, XVIII).

In the specific instance of the bottle figure, we cannot allow a modern arthistorical concentration on form to "compel us to draw a binary opposition between 'iconic' and 'aniconic' forms . . . and to treat them as though they were completely at odds with each other" (Gordon 1979, 11), when in fact the iconic/

Fig. 5.30. Apulian bell-krater; youth approaching Nike at altar and two youths by the stele of Nike; 380–370 BCE (Gaifman 2012, 252–53, figs. 6.7–8, faces a–b)

aniconic opposition may have been artificially drawn or misinterpreted to begin with. The addition of human features to the bottle form at Carthage does not mean that all bottle shapes are figural, nor does the coexistence of vaguely anthropoid figures along with clearly anthropomorphic images within monuments from the same location mean that all are anthropomorphic; rather, what I am suggesting here is that we may not always be able to draw thick, decisive lines around the aniconographic phenomena within these stelae. We simply do not know whether the bare stelae or the bottle shape was an avoidance of figurism—even if for economic or practical purposes—but the existence of both straightforward figurism along with nonfigurism in similar pieces tells us something about the fluidity of the iconography. (For a similar point for different materials, see Nunn 2010.)

Stelae on Stelae

One more note on the stelae: as mentioned earlier, the Phoenician fondness for stelae resulted in images of stelae being incised or drawn on/within other stelae, creating a focus on the shape and meaning of the object in a redoubled manner. On the simplest end of the spectrum, this could include the incision of a bottle shape on a stele from Carthage (Bénichou-Safar 2004, pl. XLVII.5; see fig. 3.5 above, and another example from Mozia [Sicily] in Bisi 1967, tav. XXXVIII, 1), the double stelae incised in figure 5.17, or any other number of simple betyl objects on stelae (figs. 5.10–11). More complex are examples of carefully wrought vertical stelae within a monument that itself is a type of stelae—in most cases, these monuments are more like model shrines, though it is not immediately clear what significance a stele would have within a monument like this as opposed to a craftsman simply creating a plain stele of the very monument itself (such as in figs. 5.23–25). At the very least, this phenomenon suggests the *iconization of the stele itself* as a particular kind of symbol. By using this term "iconization," I refer to the linguistic feature of iconization as an analogy; Judith Irvine and Susan Gal define iconization as a language process by which linguistic features become identified with social images, creating the appearance of an inherent linkage between the speech and the group (2000, 37–38). To what extent might the ubiquity of the Phoenician stelae have served in the Iron Age Mediterranean as a quickly identifiable "Phoenician" signal?

In her study of the Greek aniconic materials Milette Gaifman examines a parallel motif in Greek art: the representation of stelae on vases of the fifth–fourth centuries BCE to mark tombstones or for other cult purposes (Gaifman 2012, 243–69). The stelae in these instances are very recognizable, as opposed to rougher examples adopted for cultic purposes or unmarked stones in their natural settings. One purpose for this visual strategy, for Gaifman, could be a "double presentation"—both a deity and his or her stele on the same piece invites the viewer "to explore the relationship between the two." The pillar is the permanence and immovability of memorial, while the deity is (in the case of the winged Nike) mobile, a sign of dynamism (see fig. 5.30). The figures are complementary, not binaries (iconic vs. aniconic). Moreover, the very shape of the stele—as a distinct vertical marker—can play an important organizational role in a scene when juxtaposed with other figures, such as signaling transition for a character (Gaifman 2012, 261–62) or emphasizing the centrality of the stele, even if an ambiguous centrality, vis-à-vis other characters in the scene (Gaifman 2012, 264–65).

Our Phoenician stelae on stelae cannot match the narrative and mythological complexity of the Greek vases, yet the use of stelae in two respects—for visual organization and the ambiguous evocation of a deity—are certainly factors in the case of the Phoenician objects. One would not want to merely reduce the stelae in figures 5.23–25 to mere space foci, yet the shape of the larger monument may have in some cases necessitated the addition of a stele, instead of using only one, lest a single stele prove artistically unattractive in the midst of an overly large square space. Even so, the single stele focuses attention toward the center in a very simple and effective manner, whereas the stele monuments with multiple symbols encourage diffuse meditations (e.g., figs. 4.16–17, 5.15). The stelae in these cases also invoke an austere sense of mystery; they are less personalized than perhaps any other specific type of representation and allow projections of memory and divinity at multiple levels.

Summary of the Stelae

To summarize: the profusion of stelae at Phoenician sites in the Mediterranean world suggests an iconographic code of some kind, with the stele communicating across space and time. We must reckon with what could be an early and native tradition of stele use in Tyre itself, reflected not only through texts (including Ezekiel and Herodotus in the sixth and fifth centuries BCE respectively) but through newly discovered or freshly analyzed examples dating to the ninth–seventh centuries from Tyre and surrounding cites. These traditions were clearly not whole-cloth inventions for mortuary use at these sites, but rather participate in a long-standing ancient Near Eastern tradition. The question of the "aniconic" status of any particular stele must be kept open, yet even funerary use suggests a ritual context of memory and cult; there seems to be no clear preference for the nonfigural materials over the figural, but rather we find a continuum of types, ranging from the fully iconic, to isolated and schematic symbols, to the aniconic. This continuum is not evolutionary, but seems to represent simultaneous strategies, and we must take care to see the nuances of anthropomorphism where they may appear even in very simple motifs (such as the bottle idol). A potential exception to the nonevolutionary nature of the motifs appears at Carthage, where the transition from the "archaic" to the "Punic" materials from the eighth–third centuries sees a significant switch from stelae, betyls, empty thrones, and so on to the classic Tanit image and Baal Hammon hand on refined monuments. At any rate, the earlier examples from Tyre do suggest that the kind of continuity that others have suspected between mainland and colony is real and meaningful, even if in the West local traditions were an important driving force (as for the pottery and other material culture generally).

5.4. Shrines with Aniconic Objects and Empty Shrines

Another significant site for aniconic potential in the Phoenician material record comes in the form of miniature shrines—sometimes referred to as "model" shrines or by the Greek term *naiskos/naiskoi*. Many examples of this type have been published and described (see esp. Brentschneider 1991a), although relatively little analysis of the meaning and function of these objects has been carried out and far less with attention to the aniconic meaning of what is often an empty space within the shrine itself.[24] Most frequently, such shrines are of terracotta and sometimes painted. The shrine model of two flanking pillars, a roof, and perhaps sun-disc imagery on the facade could be incised as an iconographic motif on stelae, stone monuments, and various other scenes—indeed, what I had above been loosely calling "stelae" are in many instances a form of the model shrine carved into stone or coins, housing betyl-pillars, bottle figures, or fully anthropomorphic images of deities or humans (see esp. figs. 5.4; 5.16–17; 5.21; 5.23–25; 5.27–28; cf. with the

---

24. See some comments in Culican 1976; 1960–1961, 48–49; Sader 2005, 76–80; Metzger 2004; Gubel 1992; 1987, 38–39, 58–60; Stockton 1974–1975, 9–10; Dayagi-Mendels 2002, 160–62; Brentschneider 1991a, esp. 145–68; 1991b, 20; cf. with discussion focused on Israelite evidence in Zevit 2001, 328–43. Curiously, Mettinger did not make the empty or otherwise aniconic shrines a key part of his argument, but see one reference in 1995, 105.

stelae depicted and discussed from Punic Lilibeo [near Motya, Sicily] in Bisi 1967, tav. XLIV–XLV, and some updated findings at Motya in D'Andrea 2014b).

Shrines of this type may be helpfully classified as an example of what Claude Lévi-Strauss (1966, 23–25) and, more recently, Jonathan Z. Smith (2004, 224–27) identified as the tendency toward *miniaturization* in religious representation and cultic contexts (on this, see also S. Stewart 1984). Lévi-Strauss argued that miniaturized depictions of temples or even the entire cosmos are "not just projections or passive homologues of the object: they constitute a real experiment with it"; thus "the intrinsic value of a small-scale model is that it compensates for the renunciation of sensible dimensions by the acquisition of intelligible dimensions" (1966, 24). For Lévi-Strauss, the artistic enterprise itself (as product of his famous "bricoleur" type) "lies half-way between scientific knowledge and mythical or magical thought" (1966, 22). These reflections led Smith to analyze some ritual implements mentioned in Greek magical papyri for their miniaturization strategy; small-scale temples and shrines are "treated as if they were major edifices housing a divine image and a cult table" and receive sacrifice, a cultic meal, and incubation rituals (2004, 225). These rituals, before the miniaturized objects, are a *replacement* for larger temple space and thus create the immediacy of the formalized temple in an "ordinary but purified room" (2004, 225). The miniature takes on narrative identity vis-à-vis the "gigantic" or even the full size, as Susan Stewart avers (1984, 86): "The gigantic is viewed as a consuming force, the antithesis of the miniature, whose objects offer themselves to the viewer in a utopia of perfect, because individual, consumption."

The model shrine, then, functions as a portal of accessibility; commenting on plaques depicting the goddess from Tell Qasile, a Philistine coastal site, Othmar Keel and Christoph Uehlinger highlight the model-shrine motif as both an iconographic instrument of *identification*—the material goddess is to be identified with a particular divine being—and also *accessibility*, as the deity offers herself as the central motif to the worshiper (1998, 103–5, and figs. 123–26; see also discussion and examples of materials like this on 161–63, figs. 188a–b). Keel and Uehlinger see the terracotta examples of model shrines in particular as "conservative," reflecting familial religion for personal use or "house cults" (1998, 154, 162). In one of the more sustained and nuanced discussions of shrine models, in his study of Iron Age Israelite materials (although it is by no means clear all of the examples he discusses are "Israelite" per se), Ziony Zevit points to examples where the great detail of the architectural structure of the shrines suggests "real structures," that is, larger temples or shrines of which the small shrines are faithful models (2001, 326–27, 338–39, 343). Alternatively, the shrines may represent mythological or "heavenly" shrines, but nonetheless for Zevit the connection between clay realia and larger, cultic contexts is vital to understanding their function (2001, 327–28; 329–30); due to extended use in the Near East, however, these shrines could come to mark "divine presence" generally without particular reference to any one deity (Zevit 2001, 329).

This broadened symbolic function could make the shrines a vehicle for more specific use, as empty shrines could allow the epiphanic presence of a variety of deities. When the shrines are aniconic—even purely empty—they may be associated with a particular deity, a range of deities, or the empty space could accommodate a material image. In Syro-Palestinian religions, these model shrines were, according to Zevit, miniature dwelling places of the deity (betyls in that sense), representative of real shrines and wayside sites where worshipers could realize the "auspicious" presence of the deity. The models were like a "telephone," conveying a sense of "immanence" for worshipers that was different from formal, in-person temple worship (Zevit 2001, 340).

Regarding the Phoenician examples, a variety of types could have functioned as aniconic spaces—represented most conspicuously by "empty space" but also by nonfigural objects. Culican saw these shrine types as quite possibly representing larger cultic sites in the Phoenician mainland (e.g., an enthroned deity on a scarab or even the depictions on an entire seal series could be a "fuller representation of the cultic installation of Melqart as it existed in the Phoenician cities"), and the shrine models and *naiskoi* of varying kinds can even offer a "clear picture" of actual fifth-century BCE Phoenician shrines (1960–1961, 48–49). The question of whether such model shrines represent larger, "actual" shrines and even the cult images in those shrines has bedeviled interpreters; at best, one may offer guesses based on the intricacy or proportions of the architecture (as attempted for different examples by Garfinkel and Mumcuoglu 2013 discussed below; Steel 2013, 65–66). Commenting on shrine examples from Cyprus centuries before our materials in question (models from Kotsiatis and Kalopsidha) and in the process revealing something of the earlier clay model shrine traditions in Cyprus, Louise Steel notes that the shrines in question and their attendant figures may be a topos, thus not revealing the details of a local shrine but rather serving as a marker of time and space or narrating particular identities (2013, 66; on the Phoenician presence in Cyprus, see the overview in Aubet 2001, 51–54). Short of clearly excavated shrines, compared with models that bear connection to the shrine, such questions remain open to speculation.

One of the more fascinating aniconic model-shrine objects from the Phoenician mainland is the Iron Age terracotta example from Akhziv (on Akhziv as a Phoenician site, see, e.g., Dayagi-Mendels 2002; and the overview in Lipiński 2004, 302–3; see the analysis of the piece and comparative examples in Culican 1976; fig. 5.31). The object displays an odd simplicity: a clay tongue or face or strip is at center and bends sharply backward into a "head" onto which are affixed two rows of clay "buttons." Typical of the terracotta shrine models, as well as other two-dimensional shrine facades, a disc appears above the central display. Culican notes the visibility of painted red strips on the sides and top of the shrine (1976, 47). Commenting on the clay buttons, Zevit suspects that the buttons on the central figures within the shrines may have significance apart from the buttons on the temple facade/entrance (which, he thinks, may merely mark the dwelling as a

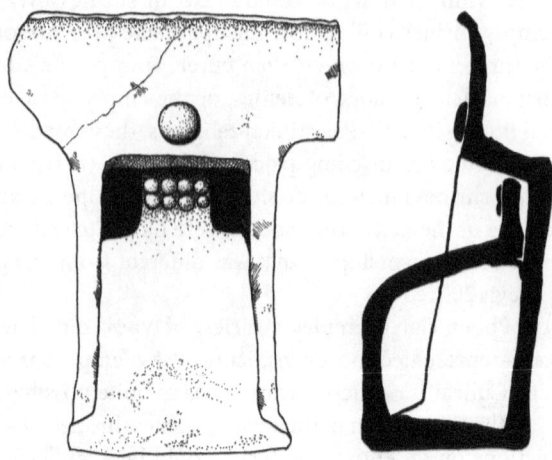

Fig. 5.31. Terracotta model shrine; Akhziv; ca. seventh century BCE (Dayagi-Mendels 2002, 161, fig. 7.25)

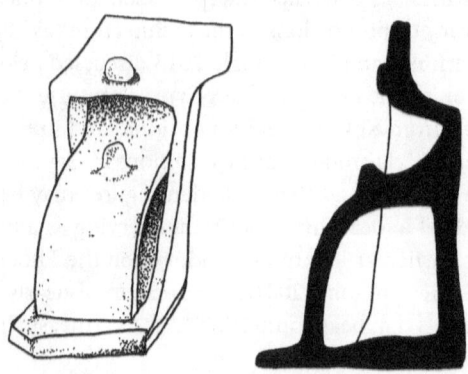

Fig. 5.32. Model shrine; Tyre al-Bass cemetery; seventh century BCE; h. 16.5 cm (Metzger 2004, 421, figs. 280–81)

shrine) and wonders whether the pattern of exactly six buttons on some objects (see examples in Culican 1976, 488–90) could represent a "divine number," along the lines of number-identification of deities in Mesopotamian traditions (Zevit 2001, 334–35; e.g., the number fifty for Marduk; see also Dayagi-Mendels 2002, 162, for a suggestion along these lines; cf. Metzger 2004, 430, who thinks these are either a crown for the deity or stars). The discs on the facade may represent astral imagery, as suggested by the prominence of the classical winged sun disc in some cases (Gubel 1992, 229; Ornan 2005a). A strikingly similar piece, proving the Akhziv shrine was not sui generis among the Phoenicians and also from the same historical context (seventh century) yet with some different elements, comes from the excavations at Tyre al-Bass (fig. 5.32). In the Tyre al-Bass shrine, the clay strip does not come to a narrow "head" at the point of contact with the back wall of the shrine and, instead of the rows of clay buttons, has only a single "lozenge" protrusion and the normal sun disc (but without crescent) on the facade top.

For Culican, the aniconic nature of the Akhziv shrine was clear (1976, 47, 49–50)—the sheer technical beauty and competence of the piece suggests aniconic intentionality, and thus the piece was a "deliberate attempt" to create an "aniconic cult object." For the Tyre al-Bass example, Martin Metzger thinks the central clay strip functioned like a *maṣṣēbâ*, representing the deity. Culican speaks of a "devolution from anthropomorphic image to an enigmatic aniconic shape" in similar examples from Amathus (Cyprus), a place with Phoenician contact in various periods (beginning in the eleventh century BCE; J. S. Smith 2008). Michal Dayagi-Mendels, the other hand, seems to leave open the possibility that the central "figure" is in fact figural, denying Culican's suggestion of aniconism in light of other, iconic depictions in similar shrines and instead suggests that the "frequent presence of a female figure [in objects like this] suggests that a female deity was also present in our shrine" (2002, 162; see also Metzger 2004, 430). It may be true that the shrine was meant to invoke a female presence, though Dayagi-Mendels seems to misunderstand the claim of aniconism here—the claim is not that the Phoenicians *never* used iconic/figural representation, but rather that this particular shrine avoids an obvious figural presentation of any deity, and this figure-avoidance is a significant Phoenician artistic-cultic trend.

To be sure, other examples from Cyprus have been brought into the discussion. Karageorghis describes several shrines from the sixth century BCE, a time during particular intense Phoenician influence (preceded by, and continuing along with, Cretan influence as early as the eleventh century; see overview in Reyes 2007). Karageorghis suspects that the aniconic phenomenon in Cyprus, but also in the Phoenician Mediterranean generally, is "of very high antiquity" (2000, 51, 54). Let us consider three examples of the type in question, all from the sixth century BCE—the first two from Amathus, discussed by Karageorghis, the third from Nicosia (see Metzger 2004, 428–29)—in light of their aniconic qualities (figs. 5.33–35). These shrines offer us not purely empty space but rather some central image, and, as with our analysis of the bottle idol figure above, one may question the figural qualities of these images. All feature central "figures" with affixed knobs/buttons below an arched facade, below a crescent/disc image marking the shrine as home to the deity (most assume a goddess, perhaps Astarte; see Karageorghis 2000, 53, on the relationship between the knobs, crown, and Astarte at Cyprus).

106 | CHAPTER FIVE

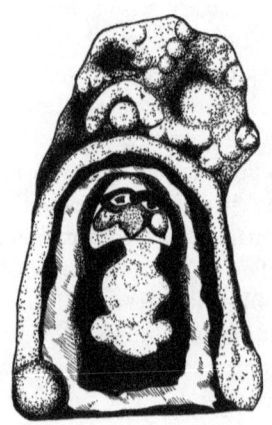
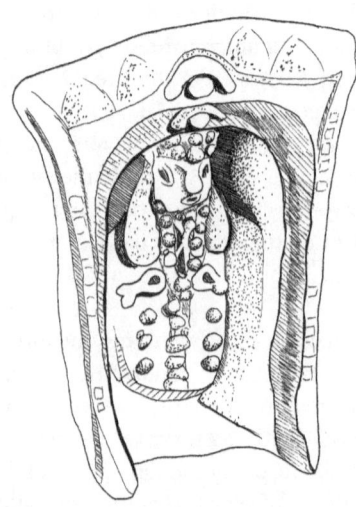

Fig. 5.33 (above left). Model shrine; Amathus (Cyprus); sixth century BCE (Karageorghis 2000, 60, fig. 5; Metzger 2004, 429, fig. 286.b)

Fig. 5.34 (above right). Model shrine; Amathus (Cyprus); sixth century BCE (Karageorghis 2000, 61–62, figs. 6–7)

Fig. 5.35 (left). Model shrine; Nicosia (Cyprus); sixth century BCE; h. 11.5 cm (photograph in Bisi 1988, 353; drawing in Metzger 2004, 429, fig. 286.c)

Of the three examples here, in the first (fig. 5.33) the shape of the central object most closely resembles the Akhziv shrine, though with six buttons on the "head" instead of eight. In the second example from Amathus (fig. 5.34), the central item is more like a pillar, even phallic, with a "body" in relief within the shrine covered in what appear to be irregular mounds or knobs similar to those at the head of other figures—in this piece, the knobs also function as an architectural detail on the top/face of the shrine. The central pillar is painted red, and at its top are what Vassos Karageorghis at least calls "two eyes." If indeed these are painted eyes—and I think they are—the craftsman has introduced anthropomorphic features that mark the image off as *iconic*, much in the way that the addition of facial

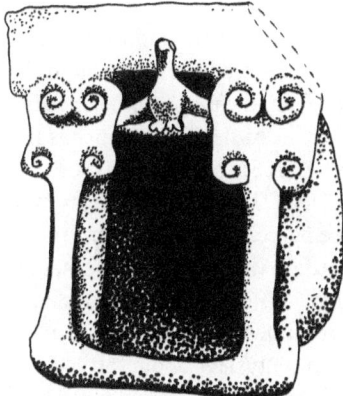

Fig. 5.36. Empty model shrine; Mount Nebo region (Jordan); ca. 900 BCE (drawing in Metzger 2004, 427, fig. 285a and Keel and Uehlinger 1998, 161, ill. 188b; photo in Brentschneider 1991a, Taf. 91, Abb. 80a–b)

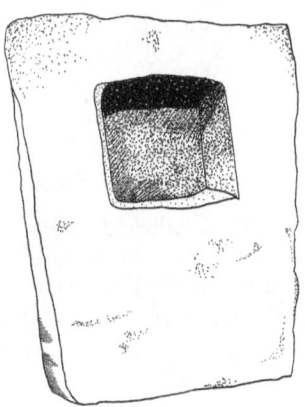 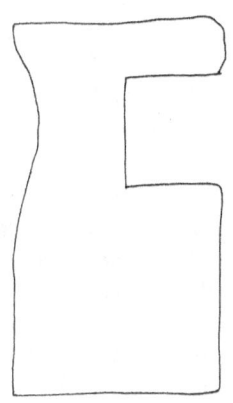

Fig. 5.37. Stele with empty niche; Tyre al-Bass cemetery; tenth–seventh century BCE; approx. h. 50 cm, w. 40 cm (Sader 2005, 64, Stele 43, fig. 50)

features on the bottle idol at Carthage transforms a potentially aniconic piece into an iconic one (Brown 1991, 141, 264.276–77). Such is the fluidity of anthropomorphic recognition.

In the final example (fig. 5.35), the figural qualities are clearest of all—divine female hair drapes down on the figure's shoulders, and the six knobs clearly form the deity's crown, which can now be clearly compared with the "head" on the "nonfigural" example in figure 5.33. The point here, as with the bottle-idol examples, is as simple as it is revealing about the aniconographic phenomenon: it is not black and white, and the reverent gaze of the viewer can pass fluidly from seeing the goddess in the more strictly aniconic setting to partly iconic and fully iconic modes. Since we have no evidence that one form was preferred over another in this historical setting in Cyprus or that pieces on different ends of this continuum were ritually differentiated, we can only assume for the moment that they represented a true continuum of acceptable options. The "aniconism" here is a function of *style*, of divine symbol, and perhaps of idiosyncratic preference in a given setting.

In addition to the stelae recovered from the tenth–seventh-century settings in and around the Tyrian mainland, we also have "shrine-stelae" and model shrine examples that now demonstrate a Phoenician mainland tradition—although all of the examples published in Sader 2005 (75–80) are from the middle or later Persian period (fifth–fourth centuries BCE; see the examples of stele-shrine niches from Sulcis in Bartoloni 1986, tav. CXXIX, 1050; CXXX, 1051; tav. CXLVIII–CLI; and also Carthage in Bénichou-Safar 2004, pl. LIV, 12). Of the several examples in this corpus, we find shrines housing betyl-pillars (see fig. 5.24 above) and presumably other objects, now lost due to the state of preservation (limited in some cases only to the upper shrine facade; see Sader 2005, 76, fig. 66, stele 53; 79, fig. 70, stele 57; 80, fig. 72, stele 59). Clearly a Late Bronze tradition of empty clay shrine objects existed, as at Tell Kamid el-Loz (thirteenth–twelfth centuries), about forty kilometers east of Sidon, but it seems that the parallel shrines that can be adduced of the empty variety to nonempty shrines (such as the Tyre al-Bass, Akhziv, and Cypriot examples above) all come from far inland, such as the parallels offered by Metzger (2004, 424–27), most of uncertain origin and dating (see fig. 5.36; also images in Culican 1976, 491, 4.A–B; 493, 6.C–D; Brentschneider 1991b, 28–31; but cf. the "empty" stelae-shrines from Punic Sulcis [Sardinia] in Bisi 1967, figs. 125–26; and Carthage in Bénichou-Safar 2004, pl. L, 8).

At any rate, of the purely empty-shrine types, the majority of interpreters agree that these shrines had but one basic purpose: to house a figure of the deity, along the lines of the Ashkelon dome-shrine with the silver calf (e.g., Stager 2006; Metzger 2004, 426; cf. with examples from Ugarit in Brentschneider 1991b, 27, abb.3a–b). A rarer group of empty functional "shrines" comes in the form of stelae with niches (Sader 2005, 19, 64–65, 76–79, 136–38, and accompanying images; see also Sader 2004, 384, fig. 253; here fig. 5.37). Again, as with empty shrines, the emptiness here could be classified as "sacred emptiness" (see Stockton 1974–1975, 9–10) to the extent that it probably served some cultic function—perhaps an imaginative projection of an invisible deity, but more likely with a votive figure or offering of some kind. Some striking stele-shrine examples from Carthage, however, clearly display multiple recessed "frames" as a method of focusing attention on the center square without any "figure" inside—the frames focus on a rectangular or square flat space, uninscribed, inviting the gaze at blank space (see examples in Bartoloni 1976, tav. LV–LXI).

In conclusion for our discussion of the shrines, the aniconic or "empty" shrines offer a distinct and indisputable nonfigural *possibility*, since the presence of the shrine itself clearly evokes at least the idea of empty cultic space where the deity resides; we simply cannot be certain about the relationship of these shrines to "official" temple or larger shrine settings or whether the shrines once housed material, figural images. In any case, the shrines suggest a "flexible material theology" that could allow worshipers to connect, as in a phone booth, to some geographically or even chronologically distant location. In the Punic western Mediterranean, the stele-shrine was much more prominent (as opposed to the clay models from Cyprus and the Levant; but note Culican 1976, 487 n. 42, who mentions a potentially empty larger shrine space at Nora; reconstructed image in Bisi 1967, tav. LVII), and these stelae-shrines could have offered variations on local cultic patterns with a perceived connection to the Phoenician mainland.

5.5. Thrones with Aniconic Objects and Empty Thrones

The use of thrones and cultic throne-stands, sometimes seemingly empty, sometimes supporting an object (and sometimes now empty but probably containing an object at some point) form yet another potential category for the investigation of Phoenician aniconographic representation. In particular, the thrones with the most obvious aniconographic possibilities are those that are empty—not just in their currently recovered state, but presumed to be empty in their original context for cultic use—as well as thrones or stands that support(ed) aniconic symbols, such as ovoid objects, pillars, and so on. Regarding the ritual use of these thrones, there seems to be little we can say with great confidence; what was suggested above about the model shrines and the miniaturization tactic applies to the thrones as well: miniature thrones suggest accessibility and communication with a larger constellation of religious ideas and cultic context, whether a formal cult site in some other location or an imaginative/ideal setting. In some cases, an enthroned aniconic object likely received veneration as a deity (e.g., fig. 5.43 below), or a now "empty" throne held such an object (figs. 5.40–41). In the case of purely empty thrones, some of these may have seated a divine image (fig. 5.39?), but for some examples this seems hardly likely—in the case of figures 5.38 and 5.42 (far left figure), the thrones appear in a funerary context, the former an L-shape object as a grave marker (and perhaps not a "throne" at all) and the latter a smaller object within a funerary urn at Carthage, perhaps as a divine symbol of Baal Hammon.

As with seemingly all other categories of evidence we have considered so far, there are parallels in earlier periods along the Levantine coast. At Ugarit, for example, we have some stelae with images that are also shaped like thrones, though it is not entirely clear they are in fact thrones. The horizontal piece on the bottom of the L-shape could allow the pieces to stand (Yon 1991, 326–27, 330, esp. 6.4 [fig. 5.5 above], 7.11, 10.a; 342, 22.a), although most stelae of this type do not have the "seat." Seated male figures of presumably El and Baal at Ugarit demonstrate the importance of the throne for these deities, and some seated figures detached from thrones were clearly meant to be paired with an otherwise "empty" throne (see Yon 1991, 337, 17.a//351, 2.a for the figures, and 350, 1.b, for a throne of this type). Of the Tyrian stelae from the ninth–seventh centuries BCE, one example could be classed under this L-shape throne category (fig. 5.38), though again, we cannot say with confidence that it is a throne, and if it were a throne, what the context would be—would a deity be expected to invisibly reside in it at the grave, or perhaps it is for the venerable deceased? In a variety of media and contexts, the enthroned

Fig. 5.38. Inscribed L-shaped stele; Tyre; eighth–seventh century BCE; inscription: *grḥmn* (Sader 2005, 37, fig. 17, stele 12)

Fig. 5.39. Astarte throne in Eshmun temple complex; Sidon; ca. fourth century BCE (Khalifeh 1997, fig. 2; Markoe 2000, 126, fig. 42)

Fig. 5.40. Stele-shrine with sphinx throne; probably from Sidon; ninth–fifth century BCE (Sader 2005, 77, fig. 68 stele 55; Gubel 1987, pl. III)

Fig. 5.41. Stele-shrine with throne; probably from Sidon; sixth–fifth century BCE (Sader 2005, 78, fig. 69a stele 56; Gubel 1987, pl. II)

figure is one of the more enduring symbols of divinity and power in the ancient Near Eastern world and could represent either king or deity (Metzger 1985); and for Phoenician examples, Eric Gubel has shown that a variety of throne/seat types were used for both male and female deities (1987, 278–79). For deities associated with major natural phenomena, such as the sun or especially the sky, a throne may serve as a symbol of the deity without an anthropomorphic image. Culican remarks on the association between a particular set of Phoenician seals representing sky deities (similar to the type described above, "4.3. Overview of Phoenician Anthropomorphic Iconography," at fig. 4.8) for which the sphinx throne is "coupled with a strong aniconographic tendency," a motif also found in other early Levantine throne scenes (1968, 82; but cf. fig. 4.13). In Culican's view, a throne can be classified as "empty" if either the structure of the throne would prevent sitting or object placement or if there are objects (e.g., stelae) inscribed on the back of the throne that would be obscured if another figure were enthroned on the seat (1968, 82 n. 138).

Some special significance seems to have been attached to the "empty throne" motif at Sidon, the earliest clear evidence for which is a fourth-century BCE throne (fig. 5.39) in the so-called Astarte chapel attached to the larger Eshmun sanctuary complex (operative from as early as the eighth century BCE and well into the Common Era; see Dunand 1967, pls. IV, VI.1).[25] The throne is not "model sized"—it sits in situ on a platform, backed into a wall niche, and could easily seat a very large human. Two stele-shrines that are probably from Sidon and date to the sixth–fifth centuries BCE (figs. 5.40–41; though some date 5.40 far earlier, to the ninth century) feature an "empty" central throne—figure 5.40 is flanked by what appear to be poorly rendered or eroded sphinx-like creatures (cf. with a similar example from the Motya tophet in Falsone 1993, 285, pl. 020), and figure 5.41 is more clearly a simple throne with straight arms (though on the side of the stele itself, an Isis-type creature stands with wings extended out and forward). In the case of figure 5.40, no clear space for an object exists (cf. Gubel 1987, 39), but in figure 5.41 there is a distinct niche in the throne that was likely meant to house a small object (but unlikely an anthropomorphic object; see images and discussion in Sader 2005, 76–78; Gubel 1987, 38–39, pls. II–III).

This tradition of the "enthroned Astarte" or enthroned objects associated with Astarte reaches far into the Hellenistic and Roman periods and features many varieties of representation in Sidon, Carthage, and elsewhere; in his argument Mettinger leaned very heavily on relatively late elements of the tradition, including items from the first several centuries CE (1995, 100–106).[26] One may hazard the assumption that even late materials preserve earlier motifs, though such assumptions must be born out in the available evidence to be valid. We are able to see a potentially empty-throne tradition at Sidon as early as the fourth century BCE (at the Eshmun temple complex, fig. 5.39) and suggestions of it in the stele-shrines (figs. 5.40–41; see Gubel et al. 2002, 82–83, and also some additional throne examples not discussed here in Nunn 2010, 167, abb. 13–14). Looking west to the Carthage tophet, the older objects there feature many varieties of empty throne (some already discussed—see figs. 5.19–20 above), ranging from purely empty thrones to enthroned pillars and betyl stones on throne-like cultic stands (fig. 5.42; cf. with similar examples in Bartoloni 1976, tav. XXII–XLVII). For Quinn (2011,

---

25. See also Stucky 1993, esp. 53–55, 107 (abb. 9 and photo 15.58–60). Culican 1968, 82, thinks the throne in question—which he erroneously associated with Eshmun (?)—is "more archaic" than the Hellenistic period, but he does not say how archaic or how this decision could be reached. On the status of Eshmun and Astarte as deities at Sidon, see discussion above at "2.2. Phoenician Religion."

26. See discussion of these materials in Stockton 1974–1975; Soyez 1972; Seyris 1959; Patrich 1990, 175–84; Falsone 1993.

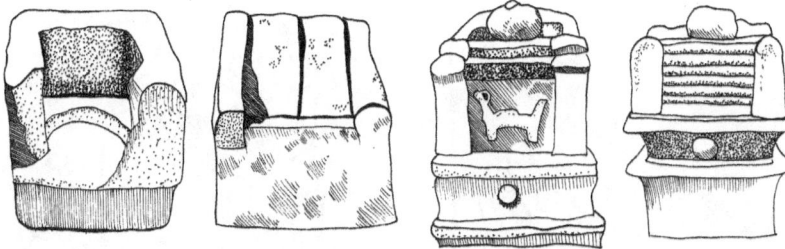

Fig. 5.42. Series of thrones from the Carthage tophet; ca. sixth century BCE (from left to right, Bisi 1967, tav. V.1, XIII.1, X.2, V.2)

392, 396), the chief status of Sidon among the mainland Phoenician sites (indeed, among all Levantine cities) beginning in the sixth century BCE coincides with parallel iconographic forms between Carthage and Sidon, and the mainland Phoenician references to Tanit, so prominent at Carthage, come predominantly from Sidon during this same period. Certainly the L-shaped thrones at Carthage, most of which can be dated to around the sixth century, can be roughly correlated to the earliest traces of the empty-throne tradition at Sidon that we have been discussing (see many examples in Bartoloni 1976, tav. XIV–XVII). All of this suggests, at least tentatively, that the later empty-throne traditions had antecedents in the earlier Iron Age and that colony and mainland city shared an iconographic register that placed emphasis on the empty thrones.

Of the later evidence that Mettinger and others have already reviewed at length, a few examples should be noted, particularly where we must circumscribe what Mettinger had considered examples of aniconism. Mettinger claims one of the Sidonian thrones (1995, 101, 103, fig. 5.10) has a "seat so steeply inclined that it must have been empty," and this is certainly possible. However, it should be noted that several of the statuary documented in Ora Negbi's (1976) study of Canaanite deities in metal, for example—some of which even come from possibly Phoenician contexts—exhibit a body shape that was made to fit on a decidedly sloped chair, perhaps even on just such an angled incline as found on the previously mentioned throne.[27] Another throne with a dedicatory inscription to Astarte from Khirbat et-Tayyiba (just south of Tyre; third–second century BCE) supports two carefully engraved stelae; in this case, especially, the iconic nature of the image is clear, since the stelae feature clearly anthropomorphic figures—possibly Astarte and a worshiper or Melqart and Eshmun (discussion in Nunn 2010, 144; 166, abb. 12;

---

27. See, e.g., Negbi 1976, 90–91, fig. 103/1648; pl. 47/1644; 49, fig. 58/1450; pl. 34/1478. It is not necessarily clear that such figures were constructed to sit on the exact type of throne cited here—or that slanted-seat figures were produced in the same time frame as the angled-seat thrones—but these examples do raise the possibility that any empty throne could certainly have been occupied by a deity cast in metal.

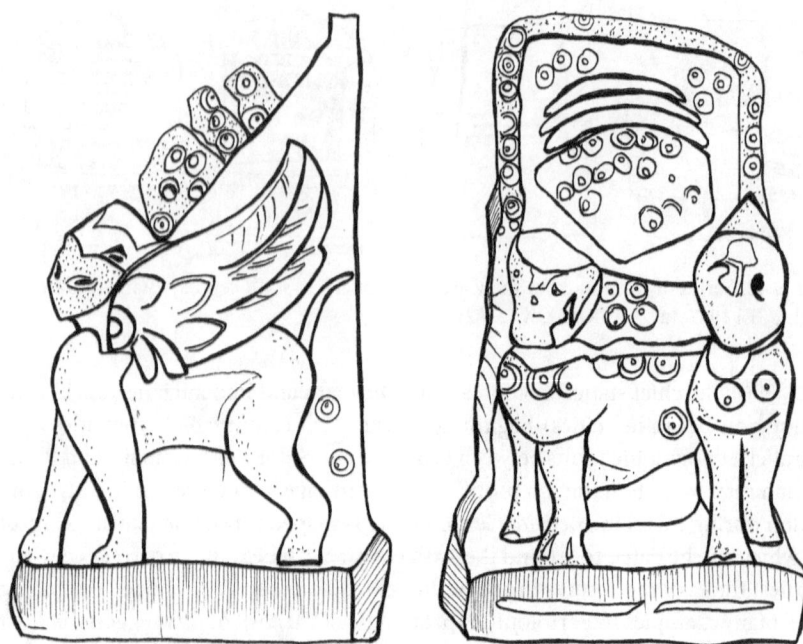

Fig. 5.43. Throne with ovoid object; Sidon; second–first century BCE (?); h. 6–7 cm (photo in Seyrig 1959, pl. X.3,5; illustration in Falsone 1993, 275, fig. 6a)

Mettinger 1995, 101; Falsone 1993, 255–56; Gubel et al. 1986, 107; 2002, 121–22). Thus Mettinger's bold proposal regarding the Punic stelae, "*stelae equal empty space!*" (1995, 106, emphasis original), that is, empty-space aniconism, obviously cannot be applied without regard to the nature of the stelae or across the board.

Mettinger does exhibit at least one clear example from Sidon where a throne holds a nonanthropomorphic egg-shaped object (fig. 5.43), which has been debated as either a token of Astarte (based a particular interpretation of anepigraphic ovoid objects in the Sidon Eshmun sanctuary that may have been associated with the goddess) or as astral imagery (Mettinger 1995, 101–2, 104–5; see also Falsone 1993, 256). The evidence does not permit a clear conclusion, though later traditions (such as Philo of Byblos) did associate Astarte with a fallen "star" (meteor?) at Tyre (discussed by Mettinger 1995, 104).[28] It is possible that the ovoid image car-

---

28. Philo of Byblos states that "Astarte placed upon her own head a bull's head as an emblem of kingship. While traveling around the world, she discovered a star which had fallen from the sky. She took it up and consecrated it in Tyre, the holy island. The Phoenicians say that Astarte is Aphrodite" (Attridge and Oden 1981, 54–55). The myth may obliquely refer to an actual meteorite; see D'Orazio 2007, 221.

ried on the "car of Astarte" on Tyrian coinage (discussed below) is a continuation of this earlier ovoid tradition connected with Astarte.

For our thrones, then, what we have found is a variety of examples—many more could be adduced—that feature a presently empty space or an enthroned object that is not clearly figural. In both of these broad cases, the objects in question are unquestionably "aniconic," though in some thrones the presence of a niche or socket for the insertion of an object means that the thrones may now only appear to us as aniconic by accident. Having said that, the aniconic, empty thrones would only become iconic if the inserted/seated piece itself was anthropomorphic—and in some cases, at least, this seems not likely (e.g., figs. 5.40–41). In other cases, we see the enshrined object, and it is certainly not iconic (e.g., figs. 5.42–43), and in the case of the empty thrones, we have some reason to doubt that the throne would be suitable for a seated figure (figs. 5.19–20, 5.38). Given the prominence of iconography for Baal Hammon in particular with that deity seated on a throne (Niehr 2008), combined with the widespread significance of Baal Hammon in various locations (but especially at Carthage) and his status as a "sky god," it may well be that this deity specifically was to be imagined on the empty thrones.

5.6. Divine Symbols and Body Parts

In this final section of potential categories of aniconism in Phoenician material culture, I want to take up the question of divine symbols or isolated anthropomorphic body parts as a type of aniconism or at least a move toward aniconic categories. We have already encountered several examples of these phenomena, so a few examples—placed within a larger ancient Near Eastern artistic framework—will suffice. Moreover, the category of the divine symbol as a potential avenue toward aniconism will give us a chance to reexamine the problem of the ovoid Astarte symbol broached above as an isolated, aniconic token of that goddess.

In summary of her rich analysis of the Mesopotamian evidence, Tallay Ornan (2005, 168–78) describes a shift in ancient Near Eastern divine imagery during the first millennium BCE—and particularly the first half of the first millennium— from anthropomorphic representation of deities toward nonanthropomorphic techniques, such as the use of symbols and emblems on seals and *kudurrus*. These divine symbols include astral imagery, mostly sun discs, stars, and crescents, as well as animals, natural elements (trees), incense altars, and other schematized shapes. One may be tempted already to locate Phoenician aniconography somewhere within this Mesopotamian movement, though we must refrain for the moment—in Ornan's analysis, at least, there were specific theological developments that prompted this shift. Rejecting the idea that divine emblems replaced figural forms so as to practically differentiate between human and divine images, Ornan rather follows Wilfred Lambert (1990) in the argument that the temple-cult image was so holy that it could not be presented casually in full anthropomorphic

Fig. 5.44. Detail of Kulamuwa inscription; king pointing to divine symbols; Zinjirli; ninth century BCE (Ornan 2005b, 275 fig. 181)

form to the masses (Ornan 2005b, 173–74; see also Ornan 2004, 103). Whatever the reason for the move to symbols, the fact is that in the Mesopotamian context it does correspond to a drastic decrease in fully anthropomorphic representation and thus suggests that the use of symbols can be directly correlated with an inclination toward aniconism.

In the ninth-century Kulamuwa inscription from Zinjirli, for example, the king gestures toward a row of divine symbols (fig. 5.42, accompanying text removed from the image here), and similar motifs from Sam'al appear in orthostats of Bar-Rakib from the eighth century. Though not clearly Phoenician, the text of the former inscription is in both Phoenician script and language (as opposed to the local Aramaic dialect), and the latter is in Phoenician script (Rollston 2010, 40; see Lipiński 2004, 109–43, on Phoenicians in Anatolia). In the case of the kings at Zinjirli, it may well be the case that emulation of other Near Eastern kings to the east provided the motivation for the depiction, and thus they tell us nothing about any distinct or early Phoenician preference for avoiding anthropomorphic divine images through symbols.

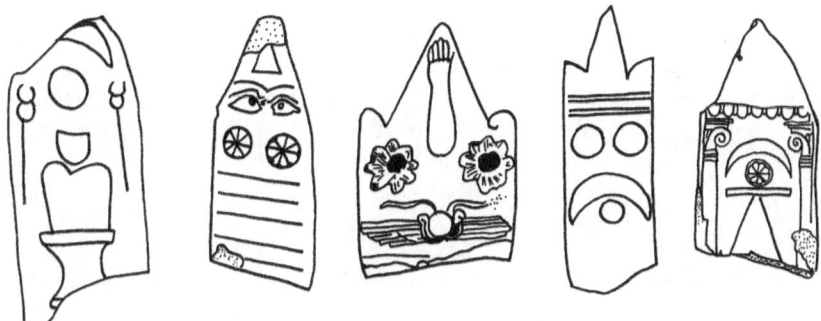

Fig. 5.45. Symbols on Carthaginian Punic tophet stelae (Brown 1991, 260, 18.229; 258, 16.103; 281, 39.568; 264, 22.289; 276, 34.521)

Perhaps it is best to identify isolated body parts that appear as divine symbols as a hybrid or partial form of aniconism—the body part becomes a shorthand identification but also conveys to the viewer the at least implicit message that the full body does not need to be viewed. For example, the footprint, which occurs on several of the Persian-period Phoenician jasper scarabs, may suggest the steps of a deity (Boardman 2003, 25, pl. 2, 1/4, 1/5, 1/6; cf. with the large footprints leading into the temple at 'Ain Dara, which Mettinger discusses in terms of aniconism [2006, 284]). Mettinger (1995, 96) singles out a particular image on a Tyrian coin of a sacrifice performed before the club of Herakles/Melqart as an example of "aniconic composition" on the basis of the use of a symbol. The later-period Carthaginian tophet stelae frequently utilize body parts and symbols (Picard 1975; 1978), most pervasively the raised hand (see fig. 4.16 above), the disc and crescent, and the caduceus (fig. 5.45). The ubiquitous Tanit image itself trends toward a divine symbol, even as it is clearly anthropomorphic, to the point that it could be nearly merged with the gabled triangle stele top in some cases (Brown 1991, 264, 22.286) or the solar imagery completely merged and identified as Tanit's head (1991, 276, 34.521, example at far right in fig. 5.45 here). Creativity abounds in such moves, and we witness the fluid ease with which the anthropomorphic and nonanthropomorphic merge together and pull apart. We certainly cannot locate the Mesopotamian evolution Ornan describes toward the symbol on the Carthage stelae, however, and we cannot even definitively pronounce the symbols in these stelae as *divine* symbols, except perhaps for Tanit herself and possibly the hand (if it is Baal Hammon). To the extent that the caduceus represents passage through the underworld on a Greek model, then it could be drawn into the orbit of divine aniconism, as could (mutatis mutandis) the solar disc, crescent, and even floral imagery.

Finally, one additional word on the ovoid betyl of Astarte. Henri Seyrig (1959, 48–51) easily conflates the Sidonian sphinx thrones and many ovoid objects within the general orbit of Astarte and cites Philo of Byblos's falling-star myth to describe the origin of the ovoid symbol (see also the review in Soyez 1972, 153–60). The

Fig. 5.46. Reverse of two Sidonian coins with "car of Astarte" (Hill 1910, pl. 25 no. 4; pl. 24, no. 8)

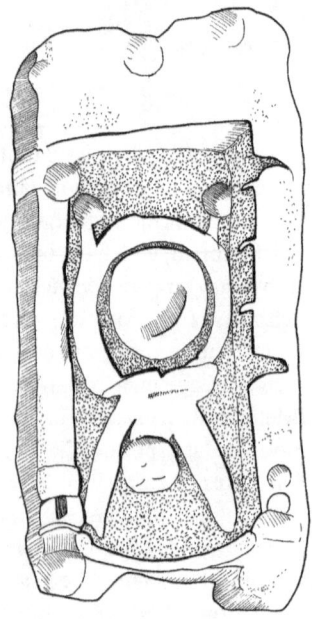

Fig. 5.47. Clay shrine plaque with figure; Sidon (Soyez 1972, pl. II.7; Sader 2005, 125 fig. 108)

basic question revolves around the confidence with which we can see the object on the Sidonian coins—riding on the so-called car of Astarte—as reflective of a much earlier tradition involving enthroned cultic stones related to Astarte or other deities; in his initial publication, Maurice Dunand saw a connection between the iconography of certain ovoid objects in the Sidonian Astarte chapel and the later images on Sidonian currency (1967, 43). The coins themselves are not as clear as one would wish them to be (see images in Hill cxiii, pl. XXIII.9, 10, 17; pl. XXIV.5–9; pl. XXV.4; Soyez 1972, pl. I), but in some of the examples the central image appears to be an ovoid object on a stand, flanked by two more small objects of the same kind on smaller stands (e.g., at left in fig. 5.46). In other cases, there is a chance that object is supported by a sphinx-type creature on either side (at right in fig. 5.46). The major interpreters of the ovoid object have all adduced a clay shrine object from Sidon with a potentially anthropomorphic figure at center (fig. 5.47) as if it somehow explains the object on the coins (often without saying exactly what that relationship might be); along with Sader (2005, 125), I find the image on the clay plaque to be remarkably similar to the Tanit sign, and, as the body of the goddess, the disc that forms the head and the disc at the womb (?) could become pars pro toto symbols of the deity and thus preserve a signal of anthropomorphic form in a manner that the original meaning is quickly lost. Even if this development has merit, we cannot rule out the conflation of the astral imagery from Philo with local understandings that change through time (or even divergent interpretations in the same time/place).

5.7. Comparanda: Aniconism in Mesopotamia, Egypt, Israel, and Greece

Much detailed and original work has already been done on the aniconisms of some other ancient Near Eastern and Mediterranean groups—particularly ancient Israel—and my goal here is not to repeat the contours of this research in detail. Rather, for each broad category, I give an overview of what aniconic material we may have by following what recent and relatively programmatic work has been done up to this point and then focus the discussion on potential avenues of connection with the Phoenicians (whether by historical/genealogical influence between groups or simply at the level of shared visual tactics). Of particular interest is the question of *why* any particular group engaged with aniconographic forms. Are the reasons practical, economic, or due to material constraints in a given medium? Political? Religious? And how would we know?

To be sure, there are data from the Roman Empire in the West and the Nabateans in the East—falling too far outside of the chronological range of my focus here—that provide fascinating typological parallels to Phoenician and other aniconisms. For example, the Nabateans, a southern Levantine and Arabian desert group receiving literary attestation as early as the late fourth century BCE but whose aniconic material culture is more prominent in the second or first century BCE, were famous for their abstention from anthropomorphic images (see Patrich 1990, 21–49; Mettinger 1995, 57–68; Healey 2001, 181–210). While past work at a major Nabatean temple site like Khirbet et-Tannur had focused on figural images, Joseph Patrich declares these images "not a true reflection of the Arabian-Nabatean tradition"—rather, stelae (*mṣb/nṣb*) took pride of place in representing the deities, often in striking square or rectangular geometrical shapes but also in the form of empty niches and ovoid betyl shapes of the type examined above (Patrich 1990, 50, and images at 54, ill. 6; 57, ill. 7; 77, ill. 19; 78–79, ills. 21–23; on the Tannur temple, see now McKenzie 2013). The aniconography of the Nabateans even reached iconoclasm under the reign of Obodas III (30–9 BCE), though Patrich argues against a long, evolutionary process of development for the non-figuration: along with its distinct language and script, Nabatean art "emerged in an act of innovation" and expressed "natural uniqueness, self-consciousness, and pride" (1990, 166). The aniconic trend in the southern desert regions continued on into pre-Islamic Arabia (review in Mettinger 1995, 69–76; and also Shenkar 2008) and, more famously and programmatically, Islam (see Grabar 2003; Pregill 2009; Natif 2011), where the intent on breaking with the "idolatrous" past drove aniconographic and iconoclastic programs.[29]

Mesopotamia

Outside of Israel (discussed below), the long history of Mesopotamian art offers a fascinating and complicated picture of iconic depiction and aniconic possibility that does not easily admit to summary. Though he found some empty thrones, betyl objects, symbol worship, and the like in both Mesopotamia and Egypt, Mettinger did not find much by way of truly aniconic practice or theology (1995, 39–56), though more nuanced and recent studies (especially Ornan 2005b) have highlighted the significant use of nonanthropomorphic symbols, emblems, and other representational techniques to the point that we must take the evidence from Assyria and Babylonia, especially in the middle of the first millennium BCE, as a potential avenue of contact for the Phoenicians—though few would be willing to claim artistic influence from east to west. (Usually the Phoenicians are viewed as the innovators, themselves influenced by Egypt.)

Politically, at least, the relationship between the Phoenicians and ancient Near Eastern empires—particularly Assyria in the eighth century and Persia in the sixth century—has been characterized and debated as a push and pull between the needs of empire for tribute and the Phoenician expansion westward. Beginning most prominently with Susan Frankenstein's famous thesis (1979), namely, that the Phoenicians colonized the Mediterranean in order to pay metal tribute to the Assyrians, various suggestions for the expansion ensued that involved overpopulation at Tyre (Aubet 2001, 76–79) and other political factors of trade (see the helpful overview in Demand 2011, 221–55; and Fletcher 2012; as well as Pappa 2013, 177–88, who cites many factors for the expansion). It seems only reasonable to leave open the possibility that iconographic influence specifically penetrated from Mesopotamia to the Phoenicians, but perhaps a better view would be to see whatever Phoenician aniconic tendencies we can find as part of a larger, more general trend toward nonfigural forms for deities in the first millennium generally.

In particular, Ornan offers the most comprehensive and compelling analysis of the Mesopotamian evidence to date (2005b; see also, e.g., Ornan 1995, 2004, 2014). Even though anthropomorphism dominated and figural forms were "probably . . . the prevailing focus of the cult in Mesopotamian shrines," Ornan argues that "in certain periods divine non-anthropomorphic representations became

---

29. The Qur'an prohibits idolatry at many points, but it is the later hadiths that specify prohibitions on the making of iconic images.

the norm" (2005b, 13). In summary of her conclusions, Ornan finds that Middle Babylonian and Middle Assyrian seals (in roughly the second half of the second millennium) offer the greatest variety among all media types for divine images, while *kuddurus* from the same period feature divine emblems. During this period, Ornan sees Babylonian influence on the Assyrians (2005b, 58–59). In the first millennium, especially the ninth–sixth centuries, the Babylonians depicted deities anthropomorphically only inside of their proper temples as a cult statue—otherwise, the form is the symbol, that is, various conventional emblems (see Black and Green 1992 for a catalogue of symbols and Collon 1987 for a collection of seal images). The neo-Assyrians of the first millennium, on the other hand, seem to have severely downplayed anthropomorphic images of their deities—indeed, we currently have no extant "free-standing" images of specifically Assyrian deities (Ornan 2005b, 73), and only Ninurta appears as a monumental-sized wall relief in human form (87), even as many deities appear in smaller glyptic media (a more "conservative" medium, Ornan argues, which preserved older anthropomorphic ideals as opposed to the "innovative" monumental form; 98–108). Ornan argues that the Assyrian need to exalt the king, who visually becomes "the only protagonist" (2005b, 15; see also Ornan 2014; 1993), prompted this Assyrian figural deity abstention (on the analysis of the king in this role, see Machinist 2006, 186–88). Overall, for both the first millennium Babylonians and Assyrians, symbols and emblems predominate (Ornan 2005b, 109).

Even accepting these broad trends as Ornan delineates them, among which the aniconic innovations are most central for our purposes, it is still the case, as Ornan herself readily acknowledges, that the iconic-aniconic continuum in the Mesopotamian evidence admits to fluidity, change, and context-specific variety. The cases of the *kuddurus* and the Sippar tablet stand as cases in point. For the Sippar tablet, the interplay between the anthropomorphic deity and the solar-disc narrates the politics of the image, absence, and reimaging of the deity (fig. 5.48; Woods 2004; Ornan 2005b, 63–66). As the inscription beneath the scene tells us (see translation in Woods 2004, 83–89), Shamash voluntarily (?) vacated his Ebabbar temple in Sippar during a time of turmoil, creating a two hundred year anthropomorphic cult statue absence. During this interim, the sun-disc symbol served in its place, but the tablet celebrates the creation of a new cult statue under Nabu-apla-iddina II (ninth century BCE), based on an allegedly archaic model found by a priest.

Woods and Ornan agree that the tablet features genuinely archaic motifs, but interpret the visual scene with differing emphases. For Ornan (2005, 65–66), the large sun disc is "the most telling visual feature," and indeed the central sun disc is the largest discrete object and the focal point of the attention, thus marking the rise of the symbol here already at the dawn of the first millennium. For Woods (2004, 76–77), although both disc and Shamash are overwhelming, the anthropomorphic deity is ranked above the disk (evidenced by the more elaborate throne for the anthropomorphic figure), and the scene highlights the

Fig. 5.48. Detail of stone tablet of Nabu-apla-iddina (text removed); ninth century BCE (Woods 2004, 26, fig. 1)

anthropomorphic deity at right through a tripartite movement from left to right, signaling the cult hierarchy from human, to symbol, to anthropomorphic deity. In favor of Woods's argument, we may simply notice that the tablet itself is a celebration of the installation of the new anthropomorphic form (with the symbol relegated to a time of divine absence), while Ornan is correct to place the centrality of the sun disc in the first millennium iconographic context of emblems. The basic point here is that we need not conceive of the iconic and aniconic as an either-or scenario (on this point for related materials, see also Nunn 2010, 136–41)—both appear prominently here on the Sippar tablet—but clearly this scene and its accompanying narrative invites us to read the interplay between emblem and deity as a point of cultic deliberation.

In the case of the *kudurrus*—Kassite boundary stones from the second half of the second millennium BCE—symbols for deities abound, though here again we would be incorrect to posit a sweeping aniconographic trend (Seidl 1989; Slanski 2003). In one of the more famous and visually stimulating examples, the twelfth-century *kudurru* of Meli-shipak (fig. 5.49), some two dozen symbols, emblems, and signs refer to various deities (e.g., horned crowns in the top tier for Anu and Enlil, the vertical pointed spade in the middle tier for Marduk; see Mettinger 1995, 45, with more elaborate discussion in Seidl 1989, 80–81, and the chart of symbols

Fig. 5.49. Kudurru of Meli-shipak; recovered at Susa; twelfth century BCE (photo in Seidl 1989, Taf. 15.a; illustration in Ornan 1995, 49, fig. 25)

in the back matter). Though such a scene may provide, as Ornan argues (1995, 48–49), a "precedent" for later symbol use, anthropomorphic forms still appear regularly enough on other *kudurrus* (see Cornelius 1997, 34, on this point), and Mesopotamian divine iconography underwent alternating trends—from nonanthropomorphic forms in early periods (third millennium), to bold anthropomorphism in the second millennium, and then over to a preference for nonanthropomorphic symbols again in the first millennium, thus complicating any analysis of a specific object in isolation (Ornan 1995, 49; 2005b, 45–48).

Egypt

Although Egyptian religion would seem to be the anthropomorphic example par excellence in the ancient world and its influence on the Phoenicians in this respect as with iconography generally is beyond dispute from the second millennium on through the Iron Age (e.g., Frankfort 1970, 310; Markoe 1990, 16–23; 2000, 15–17, 145–46; Winter 2010c), one particular ruler and era, Akhenaten in the Amarna era (mid-fourteenth century BCE), introduced an arguably monotheistic religion with a sun disc as the only "image" of the deity and even attempted to obliterate all of the older elements of Egyptian religion and iconography (Redford 1984; 2013, esp. 26–29; Assmann 2001, esp. 198–220, and Assmann's older work cited there; Assmann 2011; and now Hoffmeier 2015; overview in Cornelius 1997, 23–30). Akhenaten's iconoclasm was not unprecedented in the ancient Near Eastern world (see May 2012, secs. 1–2), but seemed to have been more coherent and sweeping than other comparable examples. Significantly, the sun god Aten's primary association was the sun, or even light itself; the coidentity of the deity and the natural phenomenon of the sun certainly lends itself to the aniconism Akhenaten sought to impose on Egypt, and Jan Assmann argues that the quasi-philosophical complexity with which light and sun are discussed is "an item of explicit theology," "congealed into an orthodoxy" that "is attempting a precise definition of the essence of god." The "immanence" of Aten required "a fresh definition" and a repudiation of other expressions (Assmann 2001, 210). The iconography of this movement was a simple disc, out of which rays of light like outstretched hands emanate (e.g., Redford 2013, 24, fig. 11).

For Akhenaten all of this was a deeply personal theology, whatever the precedence for solar veneration in the prior era or continuation of Aten's characteristics in Egyptian religion, as his solar worship was increasingly fused with "divine filiation," centering on his relationship with his father in the form of the sun disc, approached only by Akhenaten himself, who also merged his own identity with the disc (Redford 2013, 28–29). The idiosyncrasy of these views as they relate to aniconic worship prevents us from comparing it to the Phoenicians in any specific way, although we should notice the association here between aniconism and the visibility of the sun, recalling the distinct possibility that solar worship was a primary feature of Phoenician religion from an early period (Azize 2005)—to paraphrase Lucian, what need is there to create images of that which everyone can see?

Outside of the Akhenaten sun-disc issue, Mettinger points to several other avenues for Egyptian aniconism (1995, 49–56; see Roth 2006 on divine emblems in Egypt). Not only Aten but also Amun experienced a "spiritualization" that led to descriptors such as "the One who made himself into millions," an active wind and air deity who was both omnipresent and invisible in this respect, a god "whose being nobody knows, and of whom there do not exist sculptures by artists" (Mettinger 1995, 49–50). Amun's iconography apparently included enthroned objects, at least some of which are nonfigural and appear rather like the betyl-stones of the

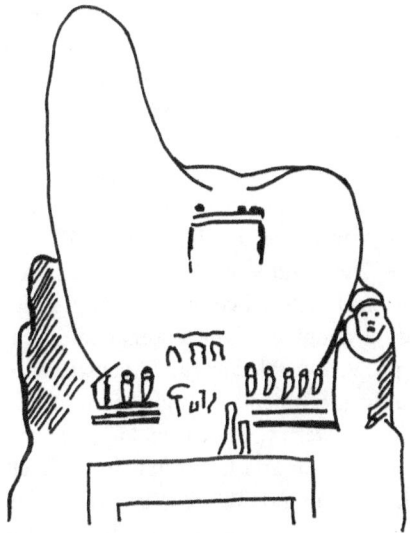

Fig. 5.50. Object from Karnak (left) and "omphalos" figure from Napata (Nubia) (right); Egypt; Persian or Ptolemaic period (?) (Mettinger 1995, 53, figs. 2.12–13)

later Punic examples reviewed above (fig. 5.50; Mettinger 1995, 52–53, figs. 2.9–13, and literature cited there). As with the Mesopotamian examples and essentially all "aniconic" phenomena in the ancient world, lest we imagine that the Amun cult at Thebes was entirely aniconic and focused on objects like this, we must recognize the "ample attestations" of anthropomorphic imagery for this deity that coexisted with the allegedly nonfigural forms (Mettinger 1995, 53).

Israel

As Iron Age Phoenicia's closest mainland neighbor in the Levant for which we have evidence of aniconism—most prominently in the texts of the Hebrew Bible—ancient Israel makes for a culturally and historically natural comparative avenue. The Bible's position even in the modern period has led to immense scrutiny of its proscription of the divine image, and the understanding of Israel's religion in this respect has explicitly or implicitly motivated nearly every one of the many scholarly investigations of the iconography of ancient Israel.[30] There are many dif-

---

30. The amount of secondary literature on Israelite iconism/aniconism is expansive; the following relatively recent sources (representing only the last two decades) have been helpful for me and represent a variety of perspectives: Mettinger 2006; 2004; 2001; 1997; 1995; Keel and Uehlinger 1998, esp. 354–91; Uehlinger 2006; 1996; 1993; Lewis 2013; 2005; 1998; Schmidt 1995; 2002; Sass 1993; Hendel 1988; 1997; B. Sommer 2009, esp. 150–59; Becking 2006; Zevit 2001, 332–43; Evans 1995.

ferent kinds of evidence and avenues that could be pursued here, but I will focus on three things in particular: the evidence for cultic influence between Israel and Phoenicia; two types of aniconographic evidence that Israel shares with Phoenicia, namely, stelae and shrine models; and the explanation others have given for why Israel pursued an aniconographic religious agenda.

On a strictly archaeological analysis, Israel clearly engaged with Phoenician material culture on the level of pottery, precious goods, and architecture (see, e.g., reviews in Crouch 2014, 28–29; Geva 1982; examples in Mazar 1992, 376–79, 464–75, 502–7). The Hebrew Bible imagines Israel and Judah in close connection with the Phoenicians in matters of religion and material culture in two primary instances: the marriage between Ahab and the daughter of the Sidonian king Ethbaal (= Ittobaal), Jezebel and the building projects enabled by the Phoenicians for both David and Solomon—most significantly, the Israelite temple in Jerusalem.[31] The biblical narrators present the interaction between the northern kingdom and Phoenicia in entirely negative terms, as Jezebel imports her prophets of "Baal" (a biblical cipher for any number of deities that are not Yahweh) into the North and persecutes Yahwistic prophets so that Elijah must defeat them and cleanse Israel of their influence (1 Kgs 18–19; a later northern king, Jehu, massacres the Baal prophets who have apparently risen up again in 2 Kgs 10). The reference to a "house of ivory" for Ahab (1 Kgs 22:39) may indicate a luxury good trade to Israel, and the excavations at Samaria that produced many ivory pieces from this period confirm the existence of these goods (cf. with Amos 3:15; 6:4; Ps 45:8 [Heb. 45:9]; Mazar 2007, 163; cf. Suter 2010, who argues that the ivory production was local, not imported from Phoenicia). The cedar and cypress wood Hiram delivers to Solomon reflects the well-known Phoenician timber trade (see Treumann 2009; Markoe 2000, 93–95; Nam 2012, 81–83), although such trade was not restricted to the tenth century BCE. The prominent role given to cherubim in the temple decoration would certainly reflect the Phoenician specialization in sphinx motifs (see 1 Kgs 6:23–36; Gubel 1987). Drawing on Josephus's famous passage in *Against Apion* (1.16–20; text and commentary in Barclay 2007, 72–74) recounting Hiram's temple building and reforms and Tyre, Culican argued that Hiram and Solomon

---

31. The so-called primeval history in Genesis only seems to know of Sidon, not Tyre (see Gen 10:15; 10:19; cf. with Gen 49:13, part of an allegedly archaic poem), and Sidon is the primary Phoenician city mentioned in the narratives of the premonarchic period; see Josh 11:8; 19:28 (Tyre appears incidentally in Josh 19:29, whereas Sidon is called "Mighty Sidon" or "Sidon the Great" [ṣîdôn rabbâ] in Josh 19:28); Judg 1:31; 10:6; 18:28 (Peckham 1976). See 2 Sam 5 // 1 Chr 14 for the account of David's interaction with Hiram; 1 Kgs 5, 7, and 9 // 2 Chr 2 for Solomon's interactions with Hiram; 1 Kgs 16:31–34 on Ahab's marriage to Jezebel; and then the drama involving Elijah and Jezebel's Baal prophets in 1 Kgs 17–19. Jezebel makes further appearances in 1 Kgs 21 (encouraging Ahab to take Naboth's vineyard) and then in 2 Kgs 9, where she dies. Prophets rant against Tyre and Sidon—predominantly Tyre—in Isa 23; Jer 47:4; 27:13; Ezek 26–28; Amos 1:9–10; and Zech 9, among other places.

alike utilized a central empty-throne tradition to enshrine their respective "sky gods" (1968, 82).

Ultimately, it is difficult to know how we are supposed to assess these references; despite marshaling small pieces of evidence for this or that, historians have not been able to offer specific or compelling arguments for how we might definitively judge the nature of the encounter. On the one hand, there are narrative incongruences and problems that raise immediate suspicion—the presence of Hiram as a building comrade during the reigns of both David and Solomon, spanning at least four decades, is possible (see A. R. Green 1983, 391) but comes off, prima facie, as a way of linking the major kings of the unified monarchy with a prestigious and nearby regional power esteemed for their precious building materials (e.g., Liverani 2005, 308–29). The Elijah stories have not typically impressed scholars for their historical merit—J. Maxwell Miller and John Hayes (2006, 314) discount Elijah's interaction with the Jezebel's Baal priests on the assumption that Yahweh monotheism did not exist during this period—although more incidental notices regarding Hiram and disputes over cities (2 Sam 5:11–12; 1 Kgs 5:1–12; 9:10–14) are antiquarian notices with little propagandizing purpose and would not be particularly helpful to invent out of whole cloth, especially in light of the negative image of the Phoenicians as a religiously corrupting group in the northern kingdom (see Brettler 2007, 322; for a maximal historical view in this respect, see, e.g., Peckham 1976; Provan, Long, and Longman 2003, 251–56; even Liverani 2005, 111–12, and Miller and Hayes 2006, 311–16, seem to accept the general nature of the Israel-Phoenicia connection in early periods, as does A. R. Green 1983). Then again, perhaps all along the narrator intended to paint Solomon in a negative light through his association with the Phoenicians (Hays 2003, 166–67, 171). The Hebrew Bible presents us with a very complex mixture of legend, history, and ideological storytelling, although in the case of the Phoenician connection to Solomon and the temple, we must admit that some of the material and iconographic details of the alleged exchange are tantalizing and may represent accurate memories of the tenth century BCE (Briquel-Chatonnet 1992).

Aside from the textual description of the temple in the Bible, what types of material evidence from Israel would be instructive for understanding Phoenician aniconography (or vice versa)? The dearth of male anthropomorphic images from the Iron Age within the boundaries of ancient Israel is striking. Although making an exact count of "goddesses" recovered from the Iron Age context of Israel and Judah is complicated by the problems involved with identifying the meaning and purpose of the Judean pillar figurines (see now Darby 2014; and the earlier study of Kletter 1996), it is safe to say that there are many more female anthropomorphic images than male images. True, several contenders for this elusive male divine figure have surfaced, but none of them uncontested or unambiguous (e.g., Gilmour 2009; de Hulster 2009a; 2009b, 203–5; Dever 1974, 74, 41.2; Keel and Uehlinger 1998, 346, ill. 337a–b; Schmidt 2002; and a list of other examples in Hendel 1997, 212–19 and Lewis 1998, 42–43). Perhaps due to the lack of material evidence, scholars of ancient Israel have turned to exploring aniconism as a literary phenomenon—that is, studying nonanthropomorphic descriptions of the deity (e.g., as fire, darkness, or isolated body parts, visualizations of certain kinds of space, or the words in a book itself as aniconism; see Lewis 2005, 106–8; 2013; Middlemas 2013; George 2012; van der Toorn 1997b).

Two types of evidence are instructive for our purposes. First, given the Phoenician predilection for using stelae, the Israelite *maṣṣēbôt* phenomenon is significant (see, e.g., Bloch-Smith 2006; LaRocca-Pitts 2001, 205–28; Zevit 2001, 142–47, 217–18, 256–66; B. Sommer 2009, 49–57; Keel and Uehlinger 1998, 33–35, 50–53). These biblically proscribed objects (e.g., Exod 23:24; 34:13; Lev 26:1; Deut 7:5; 12:3; 16:22) formed the central place in Mettinger's case for Israelite aniconism. Following Uzi Avner (1984), Mettinger tended to see all stone-pillar traditions as explicitly cultic (1995, 32–34), considering the Phoenician stele tradition as the functional equivalent of "empty space" aniconism (1995, 106) and then analyzing at great length examples of Israelite *maṣṣēbôt* at locations such as Arad, Lachish, Beth-Shemesh, Tirzah, Megiddo, the "Bull Site" near Dothan, Taanach, and Tel Dan (1995, 140–91) to conclude that Israel's cult shared features with other West Semitic cults in their use of open-air shrines featuring blood sacrifice and centered on the use of aniconic objects (primarily stelae) (1995, 191–94). Mettinger was justifiably criticized for an over-reliance on the *maṣṣēbôt* (e.g., Lewis 1998, 40–42), though in her cautious review of potential sites for legitimate *maṣṣēbâ* use in public and sacred spaces Elizabeth Bloch-Smith affirms the cultic character of *maṣṣēbôt* at Tell el-Farʿah (N), Lachish, Tel Dan, Shechem, the Bull Site, Hazor, and Arad (2006, 72–77). The largely uninscribed nature of these Israelite *maṣṣēbôt* stands in contrast to many of the Phoenician examples discussed above (inscribed with text and/or images).

The model shrines constitute a second area for comparison.[32] A recent discovery (2011) of a tenth-century BCE limestone model at Khirbet Qeiyafa (thirty kilometers southwest of Jerusalem) revived interest in the Israelite empty-shrine phenomenon (Garfinkel and Mumcuoglu 2013; 2015; fig. 5.51). Situated among other cultic paraphernalia, Yosef Garfinkel and Madeleine Mumcuoglu compare the piece to regional palace and temple architecture, specifically to the biblical Solomon, and suggest (with some caution), based on features such as the recessed door frames, roof, and proportions of the doorway (10 × 20 cm, the same as the Mishnah's description of the Second Temple at 10 × 20 cubits), that the shrine may be a model of existing Solomonic architecture in contemporary tenth-century Jerusalem. The shrine's status as "empty," however, is questionable. The photos indicate what appears to be a small but distinct irregular square recess in the back floor of the "empty" space, which, if intentional and not caused by the break and

---

32. See discussion of shrine model examples and function above at "5.4. Shrines with Aniconic Objects and Empty Shrines."

reconstruction of the piece—the excavators think it is indeed intentional—would be a support niche for an object (see photos in Garfinkel and Mumcuoglu 2013, 140-41, figs. 4-6; and now Garfinkel and Mumcuoglu 2015, fig. 36, for a close-up of the floor).[33] The smooth space inside the shrine, in any case, would easily support a small object.

Here, as with our Phoenician examples reviewed above, the case for the empty-space aniconism is ambiguous and, more specifically in the present case, seems quite an unlikely confirmation of the completely aniconic character of the Solomonic temple cult. The focus I have given to the fluidity and interplay between iconic and aniconic techniques among the Phoenicians could help us analyze one of Israel's most famous shrine-model examples, the so-called Taanach cult stand (fig. 5.52; here I draw on my own earlier work presented in Doak 2007; for full analyses of this object, see Hestrin 1987; Beck 1994; Keel and Uehlinger 1998, 154-60; Taylor 1993, 24-37; Hadley 2000, 169-80; Oggiano 2005, 70-75, among many others). As others have rightly pointed out, this "cult stand" is better analyzed as a shrine model, albeit of a peculiar type that is potentially unique to the Levant (Frick 2000, 115; but not without iconographic precedence in Anatolia; see Beck 1994, 356-57). On the stand itself, the evidence for this involves the use of stylized architectural columns (top tier), the function of the second tier as an entrance to the shrine, and the sun disc at the very top, so common to shrine models (i.e., the sun is not "striding on" the back of the top animal as in the style of an Anatolian or Levantine war god; on this point, see Beck 1994, 372).

The intense debate over this shrine has focused on the meaning of each individual tier, the identity of the animal at the top tier, the nature of the empty space in the second tier, and the identity of the deity or deities for whom the shrine was made or whom it directly or indirectly represents (essentially, every aspect of the piece). Rather than review and critique each aspect of the problem in detail at the moment, I would like to suggest a strong possibility that has not yet been adequately considered: the Taanach shrine is dedicated to a female deity, probably Astarte (or less likely, Anat), and simultaneously presents this deity iconically and aniconically, both with nonanthropomorphic symbols and anthropomorphically. Alhough they think the shrine could possibly be related to Baal, Keel and Uehlinger (1998, 160) instructively point to the horse as the primary "attribute animal" of Anat and Astarte in the early Iron Age, a fact that could push us to see the top-tiered animal as indeed a horse (and not a bull-calf; note that Darby 2014, 333, points out the fact that "almost every cult stand [from the Levant, of the broad type discussed here] combines female figurine with zoomorphic images"). Moreover, some have asserted a strong link between Late Bronze and early Iron Age terra-

---

33. I thank Professor Garfinkel for sending me a detailed photo of the floor of the shrine from Garfinkel and Mumcuoglu 2015 (fig. 36) and confirming the nature of the recess (personal communication; March 26, 2015).

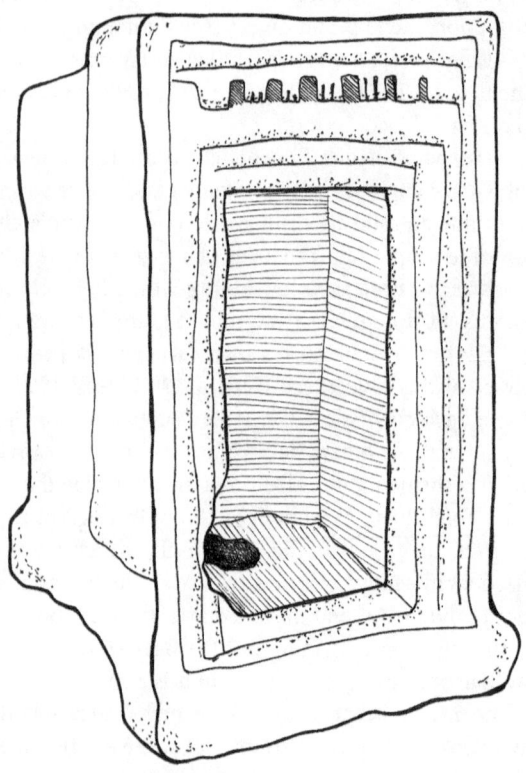

Fig. 5.51. Model shrine from Kh. Qeiyafa; tenth century BCE; h. 35 cm (Garfinkel and Mumcuoglu 2013, 140–41, figs. 4–6)

cotta figural images and the worship of female deities (Keel and Uehlinger 1998, 160), though the issue has not reached a consensus. No single feature of the stand requires a male deity, yet we do have several features—the horse, the sphinx figures (if they can be compared to the Phoenician sphinxes related to Astarte worship), the standing caprids, and of course the blatantly anthropomorphic female figure in the bottom tier—that suggest a goddess.

The figural female deity at the bottom of the stand is but one way to invoke the goddess here, and the empty space (very likely the entrance to the shrine), the lion- and horse-attribute animals, and even the sun disc all nonanthropomorphically gesture toward the focus of worship at the shrine. If this analysis is accurate—it is admittedly speculative but not more so than other interpretations of the shrine—then the Taanach shrine serves as one more striking example of the simultaneous use of iconic and aniconic representations in discreet settings or culturally in a given place/period in the first millennium at Phoenician sites as well as the ancient Near East broadly.

Of all the complex examples of aniconism from the ancient world we have been considering thus far, ancient Israel is apparently the only group that offered a

Fig. 5.52. Taanach shrine; tenth century BCE; h. 21.2 cm (illustration in Keel and Uehlinger 1998, 159, ill. 184; photo in Hestrin 1987, 62–63, figs. 1–2 and Taylor 1993, pl. 1a–d)

textual explanation for an image prohibition (but compare with the Egyptian text in Mettinger 1995, 49–50):

> I am YHWH your God, who brought you out from the land of Egypt, from the house of slavery. There shall not be any other gods before me, nor shall you make for yourself an idol [*pesel*], or any image [*tĕmûnâ*] which is in the heavens above or the earth below or in the waters under the earth. You shall not bow down to them or worship them. (Exod 20:2–5; see also Deut 5:6–9, and various statements in Deut 4)

Not content to leave the issue at the Lord's inscrutability, interpreters have offered myriad explanations for the command, most often focusing on Israel's struggle to become unique in its religio-historical environment through a decisive break with the past and with their contemporary neighbors in cultic matters (Hendel 1988, 368–72, helpfully summarizes some prominent earlier views in this regard, as does Evans 1995, 196–97). Assmann (2011, 20) speaks of Israel's "radical disenchantment with the world" through its divine-image prohibition, and Feder (2013) cites multiple motivations against the "other," whether perceived within the community or outside of it in ancient Israel.[34]

Ronald Hendel (1988; 1997, 225–28) offers a different argument that relies heavily on Israel's supposedly early and persistent bias against kingship. He claims that "once the image of the king was rejected, the image of the god, which was essentially a mirror image of the king, was also rejected" (1988, 378). Since the image of El on the sphinx throne was stock imagery for deity and king in the ancient Near East, Israel rejected the entire iconographic package of anthropomorphic divine icon and royal legitimacy. (Gottwald [1979, 687–88] pursues a somewhat similar line of reasoning, not mentioned in Hendel's article.) This view is attractive in that it takes into consideration some aspects of the Israelite rejection of the past and makes it politically relevant for the nation from an early stage. Mettinger offers a different theory, but one that likewise takes account of Israel's iconographic inheritance (as opposed to Hendel's disinheritance) from pre-Iron Age Canaan and beyond (1995, 195): as a result of his important study, he declares that Israelite aniconism was not an "innovation" and not the result of "theological reflection" at all—rather, it was an "inherited convention of religious expression which only later formed the basis for theological reflection" (1995, 195). In other words, Israel inherited its aniconic forms, most prominently the stele but also empty spaces, symbols, and other objects, and simply accepted them as such; only later did the justifications arise, post facto. A theory like this may be easily overlooked because of its banality, but historical development is sometimes banal: aniconism may be an accident, although not one that must remain meaningless forever.

Greece

Finally, we must look not only to the east but also west to the Aegean world in order to see comparisons for Phoenician aniconism in the Iron Age. Gaifman's recent study of Greek aniconism serves as both a helpful introduction to the topic as well as a penetrating analysis of several categories of evidence (2012; see also Gaifman 2010a; 2010b). The Aegean and Phoenician presence in the broader Mediterranean world throughout the Iron Age ensured contact on a number of levels (see,

---

34. Evans 1995, 200, similarly speaks of "differentiation," and see also Lewis 1998, 52–53; in fact, as Assmann points out (2011, 20), Deut 4:15–20 itself basically gives a version of this same explanation. If Ben-Tor's suggestion about statue mutilation at Hazor has merit (2006, 8–9, fig. 5), then this would be very visceral evidence of Israel's violent reaction to the past in the form of iconoclasm. (Note that Ben-Tor does not rule out the decapitation of this particular figure as the result of "its very long period of use.")

e.g., various essays in Dietler and López-Ruiz 2009)—most famously, the Greeks had borrowed the Canaanite alphabet from the Phoenicians (e.g., McCarter 1975; Woodward 1997), but influence flowed between the Near Eastern world and the West as mediated by the Phoenicians in areas of religion, myth (see López-Ruiz 2010), literature, and material culture (see review of the issue and sources listed in Doak 2012, 25–31).

On parallel with the classical authors who commented on Phoenician imageless worship, Greek authors such as Pausanias did the same for Greek religion, documenting what he called *argoi lithoi* ("unwrought stones"), sacred natural features, and other aniconic objects of particular interest (Gaifman 2012, 47–63). For Pausanias, as Gaifman puts it, "there is no fundamental contradiction between the aniconic and the fully figural; the two are part and parcel of the same landscape," but this is not to say that aniconic representations were not noticed for what they were and recognized as anonymous, mythical symbols of local traditions (2012, 74–75). For the classical Greek world, the Platonic notion of the invisible deity would come to suggest both that humans needed images for worship and yet that some gods were, by their very nature, completely unseen (Gaifman 2012, 103–8; see 47–130 for Greek textual descriptions of aniconic worship).

For the material evidence Gaifman traces, Greek aniconism falls into two broad categories: "rough rocks" and pillar-type objects such as stelae or columns. Some inscribed rocks may have marked sacred precincts (Gaifman 2012, 136–57) or even suggested some sense of the numinous on their own, as Gaifman demonstrates for the category of explicitly enshrined stones (2012, 157–80). For example, and with obvious functional connection to the potentially empty thrones discussed above,[35] at the island of Chalke (near Rhodes) a "double rock-cut throne" was discovered, dating as early as the fourth century BCE, carved in stone and inscribed with the words *DIOS* and *EKAT* (i.e., Zeus and Hekate; fig. 5.53). As a carefully sculpted piece the double throne is hardly a "rough stone," yet it represents the kind of spontaneous "theophany" that may accompany the recognition of a deity—especially those associated with natural phenomena (like Zeus)—and manifest itself in aniconographic form. Gaifman suggests that these life-sized thrones were not meant to hold objects or serve as real seats; rather, the hollowness could be "anticipatory, suggesting a possible manifestation of the two gods and their powers at the site" (2012, 163–65). This situation of worship is reminiscent of the comments cited above ("3.2. Defining the Aniconic") by Fritz Blakolmer, who focused on the element of ritual in terms of "epiphany"—in the Bronze Age materials he discussed, Blakolmer suggests that the cultic image was not the center of attention, but rather "the deity itself" (2010, 49). Aniconic worship could certainly have functioned this way, drawing anticipatory attention for a climactic moment.

---

35. See "5.5. Thrones with Aniconic Objects and Empty Thrones."

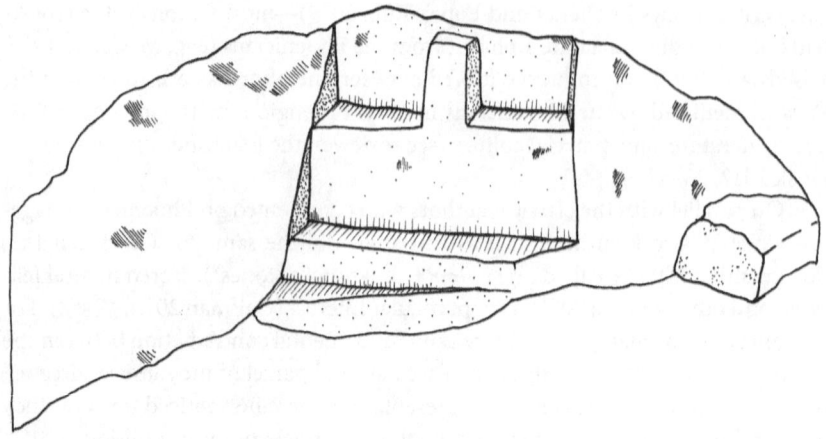

Fig. 5.53. Double rock-cut thrones of Zeus and Hekate; Chalke (near Rhodes); fourth–first century BCE (Gaifman 2012, 164, fig. 4.17)

The Greek stelae create problems of interpretation that we had encountered for the Phoenician examples. Does the location of or incision on the stele relate to cultic function and thus justify the use of a term like *aniconism*? No single picture of the use of the stelae emerges for the Greek world, though again Gaifman is careful to highlight the "liminal" nature of the evidence: as spatial markers and funerary monuments, stelae are sometimes "semi-figural" (see examples in 2012, 235–39), not merely flat and strictly "aniconic," thus rendering "the figural and non-figural into one homogenous entity in a visual assertion of their place betwixt and between" (2012, 241). On the whole Gaifman's study helpfully insists on the ambiguity and liminality of the aniconic phenomena in Greece, just as we have we have observed it for the Phoenicians and other groups. Aniconism preserves or creates a moment when things are possible—and for the Greeks but perhaps even more for their interpreters, aniconism eventually became the iconic movement placed at the center and foundation of Greek art.

5.8. Phoenician Aniconism—Why?

Having now considered the evidence to this extent, I am prepared to offer a series of explanations for why and under what circumstances the Phoenicians may have employed aniconic representations. Such explanations are, to my knowledge, almost completely lacking in the secondary literature up to this point and perhaps with good reason: the data we have are ambiguous in so many cases, and we can probably automatically rule out a single explanation for all "Phoenician" materials that could fall under into aniconism category. Nevertheless, if the study of aniconism in the ancient world as an aspect of the history of religion is to move forward at all, we must at least attempt to go beyond mere cataloging and into more speculative areas of interpretation. The following suggestions are presented in roughly descending order of confidence in the plausibility of the explanation, although I think all of these ideas deserve consideration as tentative analyses of Phoenician nonanthropomorphic religious representations.

The Inevitable, the Mixed, the Practical, and the Economic?

Broadly defined as the abstention from anthropomorphic depiction in specific circumstances, aniconism is a natural and inevitable part of all religious systems, both ancient and modern—even for those systems that heavily employ anthropomorphic images. Conversely, at least insofar as human bodies cannot be removed from any religious activity involving humans, anthropomorphism is a natural and inevitable part of all religious systems. The question, then, is always about *how* nonfigural space is used and the *extent* to which anthropomorphism is seen as central and significant within a system (Freedberg 1989). Stepping back to this very broad vantage point, then, we are justified in treating all iconographic systems as "mixed" to some degree, ranging from strictly aniconic groups (e.g., Islam) where the living human figure is the only permitted visible image of its type all the way to strikingly polytheistic and anthropomorphic religious (e.g., ancient Near Eastern religions generally or some forms of Hinduism) where nonfigural symbols, body parts, or suggestively noniconic space will be used to at least invoke or frame iconic forms.

As we have seen repeatedly—not only for the Phoenicians but for ancient Mesopotamian, Egyptian, and Greek religions as well—aniconic forms functioned alongside iconic forms. It seems clear enough that the Phoenicians had no objection to the human form, and yet, looking backward through the eyes of Greek and Roman authors into the still-cloudy early history of key sites like Sidon and Tyre, we have been able to discern a specific preference for stelae and other nonanthropomorphic objects. Even in these instances, however, aniconism can appear not from an acute theological or ideological motivation but rather as the result of "practical" concerns, such as the need for visual space, uniformity, or decoration on a particular medium. Economic factors may also play a role—certainly the production of thousands of stelae for mortuary purposes (at Carthage, Hadrumetum, Motya, Sulcis), for example, in a short period of time could itself drive artistic innovation toward aniconism, and in a variety of imaginable circumstances those who via their status could afford to commission more elaborate scenes for stelae, model shrines, and so on may have done so, while others simply could not. In still other cases, crude-looking objects or schematized pieces could feasibly be in-process sculptures destined for more elaborate form (Moscati 1969).

Within the Context of Broader Iconographic Trends in the Ancient Near Eastern and Mediterranean Worlds?

Notwithstanding the complex debate concerning the amount of direct religious influence exerted by the Mesopotamian powers over the Levant during periods of conquest (see, e.g., Machinist 2003), we can reasonably infer some cross-pollination of iconographic trends that may have resulted in a broad, Syro-Mesopotamian trend toward avoiding certain kinds of representation. Given the Assyrian and Babylonian involvement in major Phoenician cities during the eighth–sixth centuries BCE, Ornan's thesis (2005b) about the trend toward symbols and away from iconism could be considered for our materials, though we should be duly suspicious about whether the *motivation* behind the trend even within a context of artistic influence can be correlated. Not every instance of iconographic influence would need to carry with it identical understandings of the iconography or reasons for the iconographic choices, however. On analogy with Mettinger's culminating suggestion about Israelite aniconism (1995), that is, that it was at first a tradition that grew out of the borrowing of forms (such as stelae) from earlier aniconic cults and only later acquired sophisticated theological rationale, the fact that Mesopotamians exhibited a broad and well-documented trend away from anthropomorphism suggests that Phoenician religious iconography concurrently exhibited this same trend. In the main medium in which the Mesopotamian non-anthropomorphic trend is most obvious, glyptic art, Keel and Uehlinger notice a proliferation of divine symbols/emblems among ancient Israelites at the same time that Phoenician motifs also become more widespread in the same medium (1998, 141–47; on this, see also Sass 1993, 244), a correlation that does not imply causation but which is nonetheless suggestive. Again, this would not be to say that the Phoenicians adopted an ideological motivation along the lines of Israel's textual image prohibitions as represented in the Hebrew Bible—as far as we know, they clearly did not (e.g., Bonnet 1988, 100)—nor would it be to suggest that the prohibitions in the Hebrew Bible were in effect during the early Iron Age at all.

Rather, the suggestion is that the broader first-millennium ancient Near Eastern trend had concomitant expression in the smaller kingdoms in the Levant. Thus we need not assume that either the Phoenicians or the Israelites provided a "context" for the other's aniconism, insofar as a context is typically understood (among scholars of ancient Israelite religion, at least) to imply direct influence. Even so, a more thorough familiarity with materials such as the Phoenician items that I have examined in this study could help scholars of the Hebrew Bible and the iconography of ancient Israel see the range of what one prolific image-producing group was doing in the West Semitic world of the Iron Age. As evidence continually mounts to show the intense interconnectedness of the Mediterranean during the Phoenician period, students of the iconography must look more deeply into the Aegean world as well for analogies and comparison, not only Egypt and Mesopotamia. The eclectic nature of Phoenician art should continue to make us aware of all of these connections—to the north, the south, the east, and the west of the northern Levantine coast—and prevent us from making unwarranted assumptions about any supposed lack of an iconic core to Phoenician material culture.

The Relationship between Aniconism and Natural Phenomena?

I remain intrigued by Lucian's comment in *De Dea Syria* regarding the imageless "throne of Helios," for which there is no reason to craft an image since "what reason is there to make statues of those gods who appear in the open air?" They are visible to everyone in the natural state, and thus tokens of the deity—vacant thrones, empty shrines, or other simple markers—are not only "enough" to suggest divine presence but may also be the appropriate and maximal visual expressions in a given setting. The Phoenician veneration of the sun or other natural phenomena as primary deities may have been a distinct (but not unparalleled) emphasis among West Semitic groups (Azize 2005, esp. 127–94, for hints of the earlier tradition; compare with Taylor 1993). Philo of Byblos averred that the Phoenicians acknowledged "among things of nature . . . as gods only the sun, the moon, and other planets," which perhaps does not isolate only these entities as deities but does recognize their centrality at least for Philo (see text in Attridge and Oden 1981, 32–33).

Also, with profound connections to seafaring, water could function in this role as well. The earliest Tyrian and Sidonian coins from the fourth century BCE, for example, prominently bear seafaring motifs (e.g., the plates in Elayi and Elayi 2004; 2009), and in the Sidonian Eshmunazar's fifth-century inscription, the king turns in lines 16–18 particularly toward calling Sidon "Sidon-Land-by-the-Sea" (*ṣdn 'rṣ ym*) in concert with his description of a shrine ("house," *bt*) for Astarte and a mountain shrine from Eshmun, who is called "the prince of the sanctuary of the Ydll-Spring" (*'n ydll*) (text from Gibson 1982; *KAI* 14). The fact that nearly all deities in the ancient world were connected with some natural feature(s) mitigates the value of this connection, but it remains intriguing, especially for deities like Baal Hammon, who functioned as a "sky deity" and was likely associated with the empty-throne tradition reviewed above.

A Political and Colonial Explanation?

The Phoenicians did not rule over an "empire" in any typical sense of the word, at least as we would understand it on the Mesopotamian model; their colonial network was city-based, not pan-"Phoenician," and the economic motivations seem to have played a primary role far and above any strict religious fidelity among linked sites. Having admitted that, to maintain control over any complex economic process the participants must remain symbolically, politically, ideologically, and materially linked in conversation, a process that involved shared language, myth, and other cultic factors (Álvarez Martí-Aguilar forthcoming; Dietler 2009; Sanmartí 2009; cf. with Quinn 2012–2013, 29–33, who speaks of the establishments of Punic tophets as a key part of colonial symbol establishment). The question of how cities like Tyre and Sidon could stay in the appropriate level of engagement with or control over this conversation with their colonies remains elusive, but would have required no small amount of effort, especially given the great distance between the mainland and the far western Mediterranean (a distance that was more looming, to be sure, in the earliest centuries of exploration and colonization).

What does this mean for aniconism? Perhaps in a geographical situation where contact between parties was relatively rare, the visual flexibility of aniconic motifs served as a distinct, simple, and open touchpoint between mainland city and Mediterranean colony (and/or among disparate colonies). Such a geo-visio-religio-political strategy would certainly be very different from, say, the Roman pantheonic approach, through which images of conquered regions could be taken into symbolic and literal captivity under the aegis of Roman control, displaying the political dominance of the center over the periphery. The proliferation of aniconic images could represent a different, more flexible way for a colonial network to deal with images and connect with hybridized contexts involving indigenous groups. The ritual logic of aniconic images, which relies on apophatic projection to suggest meaning, presents a more fluid, dynamic, and discrete visual model and could have communicated an ideology of flexibility that more particularistic figural models could not as ably convey. One might think that multiple, obvious divine images of a certain kind would accomplish colonial control effectively, but perhaps the truth is simply that the Phoenicians did not exert this rigorous kind of ideological control. The evidence we have does suggests cultic continuity between, say, Tyre and Gadir, and thus an explanation that links mainland with western Mediterranean on the level of visual meaning has potential to illuminate the emerging sense of shared aniconographic visual culture among diverse groups.

Aniconism and the Image of the King?

What little we know about the early Phoenician city-states tells us that they fostered a robust view of kingship; the Phoenician economic model required strong and relatively centralized power structures in the mainland cities, and the epigraphic evidence from Byblos, Sidon, and Tyre attests to monarchies in traditional acts of memory preservation, building projects, and cultic establishment (see above at "2.1. Who Were the Phoenicians?"). We do not have specific details on royal involvement in local cults beyond these types of inscriptions, although at Late Bronze Age Ugarit we do know that the king played a central role in almost all of the extant rituals (see Pardee 2002 and Niehr 2014) and the Israelite prophet Ezekiel's sixth-century BCE pillories against the king of Tyre in Ezek 26–28 evoke the image of a ritually obsessed king, perhaps even claiming divinity for himself (Ezek 28:2). Along these lines, one may wonder whether Ornan's explanation for the Assyrian abstention from portraying the deity—namely, to draw focus on the royal figure of the king as the sole power (Ornan 2014; 2005b, 15; 2004, 113; cf.

with Winter 2010a)—could have functioned for the Phoenician reticence in some cases for male anthropomorphic imagery (as already suggested briefly by Lipiński 1970, 51).[36]

This explanation stands in clear contrast from Hendel's account of Israelite aniconism (1988), which involves a putative bias against kingship in ancient Israel; because deity and king could become so easily conflated and were, in Hendel's view, in the perception of early Israel, the image of the enthroned god (= king) could not be tolerated. These two explanations—Ornan's for the Assyrians and Hendel's for the Israelites—are clearly two ends of the same spectrum, and if the Phoenicians were to fit in here anywhere, it would be on the Assyrian side. As "king of the city," the Tyrian Melqart (*mlk-qrt*) may have been viewed as an ancestral-deity figure for the Tyrian kings, a fact that would reinforce the high view of kingship for at least Tyre. One may compare this notion with Philo's opinion that the earliest Phoenicians began by worshiping humans, who were only later considered gods and then honored with "temples and also consecrated steles and staves in their name [*stēlas te kai rabdous aphieroun ex onomatos*]" (Attridge and Oden 1981, 32–33). Admittedly, if this aniconographic explanation were true of the Phoenicians, we would expect to see prominent images of the king even vaguely along the lines of what we find for the Neo-Assyrians, and we do not (the exception perhaps being the "royal" figures on Persian-period seals in fig. 4.8).

---

36. In Lipiński's view (1970, 51) it was specifically the status of Melqart as the eponymous deified ancestor of the Tyrian monarchy and visible/earthly husband to Astarte that meant no male image was needed at the temple: "Melqart nous apparaît ainsi comme l'éponyme deifié des rois de Tyr. Ceux-ci sont en quelque sorte ses manifestations visibles et les epoux terrestres de sa parèdre Astarte. C'est vraisemblablement pour cette raison, et non en vertu d'une aversion sémitique pour les représentations anthropomorphiques de la divinité, que les temples de melqart, 'roi de la cité,' ne contenaient pas de statue de culte."

6

Conclusions

What is at stake for the various interpreters of Phoenician aniconism, outside of the sheer joy of historical discovery? Indeed, "the sheer joy of historical discovery" is never enough, since it does not answer the question of the choice of this group, in this time period, for these materials. Why did anyone care about aniconism at all, and why would anyone care today? We may posit a threefold framework of reception, beginning with the Hellenistic and Roman authors, the earlier modern interpreters of aniconism such as J. J. I. Döllinger, William Robertson Smith, and others in the nineteenth century, and then our own contemporary world. What was at stake given each of these interpretive horizons? For much of the interpretive history, it seems, evolutionary ideas toward some religious goal—the perceived religious superiority of one's own period on the scale, perhaps—played a large role, certainly for the Greek and Roman authors who were proud of their intellectual and philosophical achievements but also for those in the modern period, for which aniconism would become a flexible category that could either prove the primitive minds of the early aniconic worshipers or serve as a way of vaunting the religious sublimity of those who had the foresight to see the divine at such an elevated, abstract level. Even for interpreters today in the *Religionsgeschichte* trajectory, not to mention those with theological interests in Judeo-Christian history, the comparative task has often meant a focus on aniconism on the strict and polarized terms of the biblical image prohibition and all that it came to entail (e.g., monotheism). Though we can disavow the biblical influence here, we must wonder whether the use of the very term *aniconism* and the history of scholarship devoted to it has charted an overly rigid path for the analysis of material culture for too many disparate groups.

What of the Phoenicians themselves? Aside from tracing something of this history of research into broader questions of aniconism as a religious practice, in this study I have sought to reach back to the Iron Age Mediterranean and Near Eastern contexts of Phoenician identity and material culture to see what we can say about Phoenician divine representation in this respect. A vaguely pessimistic sense of the extent to which all of the items, as a group or individually, belong under the rubric "Phoenician" lingers among the pages of this study; this is not cynicism or a kind of historical minimalism, but rather a recognition that identities in this Iron Age Mediterranean context were not always as obvious or stable as we would want them to be for purposes of tidy scholarly categorization. Moreover, a synthetic study of this type introduces a certain "flatness" into the images, as the collection of iconography puts the images into a two-dimensional comparative context for a specific purpose—decidedly not the purpose for which the images were created and not the situation in which they were used. Consider the size of some of the objects we have examined—for example, "Seyrig's throne," the sphinx-throne object supporting the ovoid betyl (fig. 5.43), is a mere six centimeters in height, hardly larger than a board-game piece. On the printed page, placed alongside other objects, one gets a distorted sense of scale, which could prevent us from even wondering how an object this small could clearly encode notions of ritual, of divine representation, and of cultic space.

Thus a synthesis of this type, conducted in search of such an elusive concept as aniconism among a group as elusive as the Phoenicians, is bound to encounter many uncertainties, and there are many questions a study like this could only begin to address. Indeed, the study of Phoenicians is getting increasingly complicated, and a plethora of both primary data and secondary literature spanning the Mediterranean world calls for new syntheses and attempts at addressing some issues, and what I hope to have accomplished here is to create one such synthesis around one particular question. Further study of Phoenician temples and open-air spaces may reveal nuances of aniconic ritual that I was not able to explore here, and my most basic hope is that I have provided a helpful configuration of materials and sources to serve as a new clearinghouse for future and better efforts to understand particular aniconic contexts with a deeper understanding of very particular historical and archaeological environments.

Even so, this project has found positive results. Though some previous studies had used the terminology of aniconism to describe Phoenician religious representation for isolated objects, regions, or historical periods, this study is the first to attempt to collect and describe a much wider range of data—coroplastic art, sculpture in metal, scarabs and seals, coinage, temple architecture, and more—representative of what we now possess from mainland cities and colonies that come under the umbrella of Phoenician identity and influence. A coherent pattern of Phoenician engagement in nonfigural divine representation emerges, and the Phoenicians played a role in the dissemination and popularization of this type of representation. The case for Phoenician aniconism is, I believe, more robust than others had been able to say (e.g., Tryggve Mettinger), but it is also much more complicated than previous interpreters such as Mettinger have allowed or could allow within the natural limits of their studies. Wherever possible, I have skewed my focus toward examples from the coastal Phoenician mainland and toward earlier examples than Mettinger did, as my sense was that he downplayed the earlier material, especially if it was anthropomorphic (even though some significant materials had not been excavated let alone published during the early–mid 1990s).

On the level of the iconography itself, I have argued that Phoenician aniconism had multiple contexts and influences: connections exist with Egypt (which was the main artistic influence generally) as well as Mesopotamia and the Levant, but the Greek world must also be included in the conversation as an important environment for studying aniconism. It is no longer permissible to dismiss Phoenician art as a careless mélange of motifs, and the diversity of Phoenician divine representation suggests that we must acknowledge the existence of a continuum of, and interplay between, anthropomorphic figurism and aniconism. Some objects that had been previously categorized as "aniconic" must be reevaluated in light of their figural possibilities, while other forms, such as unadorned stelae, could by their association with a mortuary cult be drawn back into the conversation of aniconism.

As for an explanation of Phoenician aniconism, no single factor can be expected to sweep over every example. I have suggested that, in some cases, practical issues such as artistic concerns, economics, and availability of materials can "invent" aniconism, though this does not rule out the possibility that the Phoenicians participated in a larger first-millennium trend toward nonanthropomorphic depictions or even that factors of colonial cohesion and identity with the mainland could have prompted the use of open, flexible images that remain usable for the widest variety of people. Simple forms like stelae could serve as simple yet distinct points of visual contact between a Mediterranean colony and the memory (or imaginative projection) of a temple in Tyre with prominent stelae. It is even possible that the prominence of the king in the Phoenician mainland obviated the need for anthropomorphic images in some circumstances.

In the end, the study of Phoenician aniconism—and Phoenician iconography and art generally—forces us to face the very difficult question of Phoenician identity in the Iron Age Mediterranean, a question that does not admit to simple answers. Rather than abandoning the quest to understand Phoenician iconography in lieu of this problem, or, on the other hand, insisting on an overly rigid sine qua non for Phoenician identity, we must remain content to observe identifiable trends and incorporate new material into a broad framework as it becomes available.

Bibliography

Abdy, Richard. 2012. "The Severans." Pages 499–513 in *The Oxford Handbook of Greek and Roman Coinage*. Edited by William E. Metcalf. Oxford: Oxford University Press.

Acquaro, Enrico. 1971. *I Raisoi Punici*. SS 41. Rome: Consiglio Nazionale Delle Ricerche.

———. 1988. "Bronzes." Pages 422–35 in *The Phoenicians: Under the Scientific Direction of Sabatino Moscati*. New York: Abbeville.

Albright, William F. 1942. "A Votive Stele Erected by Ben-Hadad I of Damascus to the God Melcarth." *BASOR* 87:23–29.

Alexandropoulos, Jacques. 1992. "Numismatique." *DCPP* 319–27.

Almagro Gorbea, María José. 1980. *Corpus de las terracotas de Ibiza*. Madrid: Consejo Superior de Investigaciones Científicas.

Álvarez Martí-Aguilar, Manuel. forthcoming. "The Network of Melqart: Tyre, Gadir, Carthage and the Founding God." In *Warlords, War and Interstate Relations in the Ancient Mediterranean 404 BC–AD 14*. Edited by Toni Ñaco del Hoyo and Fernando López-Sanchez. Leiden: Brill.

Amadasi Guzzo, Maria Giulia. 2005. "Melqart nelle iscrizioni fenicie d'Occidente." Pages 45–52 in *Il Mediterraneo di Herakles. Studi e ricerche*. Edited by Paolo Bernardini and Raimondo Zucca. Rome: Carocci.

Amadasi Guzzo, Maria Giulia, and José Ángel Zamora López. 2012–2013. "The Epigraphy of the Tophet." *SEL* 29–30:159–92.

Anderson, William P. 1990. "The Beginnings of Phoenician Pottery: Vessel Shape, Style, and Ceramic Technology in the Early Phases of the Phoenician Iron Age." *BASOR* 279:35–54.

Aruz, Joan, Sarah B. Graff, and Yelena Rakic, eds. 2014. *Assyria to Iberia at the Dawn of the Classical Age*. New York: Metropolitan Museum of Art, distributed by Yale University Press.

Astour, Michael C. 1965. "Origin of the Terms 'Canaan,' 'Phoenician' and 'Purple.'" *JNES* 36:346–50.

Assmann, Jan. 2001. *The Search for God in Ancient Egypt*. Translated by D. Lorton. Ithaca, NY: Cornell University Press. First published as *Ägypten: Theologie und Frömmigkeit einer frühen Hochkultur*. Stuttgart: Kohlhammer, 1984.

———. 2011. "What's Wrong with Images?" Pages 19–31 in *Idol Anxiety*. Edited by Josh Ellenbogen and Aaron Tugendhaft. Stanford: Stanford University Press.

Attridge, Harold W., and Robert A. Oden., eds. and trans. 1976. *Lucian of Samosata: The Syrian Goddess (De Dea Syria)*. GRRS 1. TT 9. Missoula, MT: Scholars Press.

———. 1981. *Philo of Byblos: The Phoenician History. Introduction, Critical Text, Translation, Notes*. CBQMS 9. Washington, DC: Catholic Biblical Association of America.

Aubet, María Eugenia. 1982. *El santuario púnico de Es Cuieram*. TMAI 8. Ibiza: Museo Arqueológico de Ibiza.

———. 2001. *The Phoenicians and the West: Politics, Colonies, and Trade*. Translated by Mary Turton. 2nd ed. Cambridge: Cambridge University Press.

———, ed. 2004. *The Phoenician Cemetery of Tyre-Al Bass: Excavations, 1997–1999*. BAALHS 1. Beirut: Ministère de la Culture, Direction générale des antiquités.

———. 2006. "Burial, Symbols and Mortuary Practices in a Phoenician Tomb." Pages 37–47 in *Across Frontiers: Etruscans, Greeks, Phoenicians and Cypriots: Studies in Honour of David Ridgway and Francesca Romana Serra Ridway*. Edited by E. Herring, I. Lemos, F. Lo Schiavo, L. Vagnetti, R. Whitehouse, and J. Wilkins. ASSM 6. London: Acccordia Research Institute, University of London.

———. 2008. "Political and Economic Implications of the New Phoenician Chronologies." Pages 179–91 in *Beyond the Homeland: Markers in Phoenician Chronology*. Edited by Claudia Sagona. ANESS 28. Leuven: Peeters.

———. 2010. "The Phoenician Cemetery of Tyre." *NEA* 73:144–55.

———. 2013. "Phoenicia during the Iron Age II Period." Pages 706–16 in *The Oxford Handbook of the Archaeology of the Levant: c. 8000–332 BCE*. Edited by Margaret L. Steiner and Ann E. Killebrew. Oxford: Oxford University Press.

Aune, David E. 1995. "Herakles." *DDD* 765–71.

Avishur, Yitzhak. 2000. *Phoenician Inscriptions and the Bible: Select Inscriptions and Studies in Stylistic and Literary Devices Common to the Phoenician Inscriptions and the Bible*. Tel Aviv: Archaeological Center.

Avner, Uzi. 1984. "Ancient Cult Sites in the Negev and Sinai Deserts." *TA* 11:115–31.

Azize, Joseph. 2005. *The Phoenician Solar Theology: An Investigation into the Phoenician Opinion of the Sun found in Julian's Hymn to King Helios*. GNES 15. Piscataway, NJ: Gorgias.

Bahrani, Zainab. 2003. *The Graven Image: Representation in Babylonia and Assyria*. Philadelphia: University of Pennsylvania Press.

Barclay, John M. G., trans. 2007. *Against Apion*. Vol. 10 of *Flavius Josephus: Translation and Commentary*. Edited by S. Mason. Leiden: Brill.

Bardill, Jonathan. 2012. *Constantine, Divine Emperor of the Christian Golden Age*. Cambridge: Cambridge University Press.
Barnett, Richard David. 1957. *Catalogue of the Nimrud Ivories in the British Museum*. London: Trustees of the British Museum.
Bartoloni, Piero. 1976. *Le Stele Arcaiche del Tofet di Cartagine*. CSF 8. Rome: Consiglio Nazionale Delle Richerche.
———. 1986. *Le Stele di Sulcis: Catalogo*. CSF 24. Rome: Consiglio Nazionale Delle Richerche.
Baumgarten, Albert I. 1981. *The Phoenician History of Philo of Byblos: A Commentary*. Leiden: Brill.
Beck, Pirhiya. 1994. "The Cult-Stands from Taanach: Aspects of the Iconographic Tradition of Early Iron Age Cult Objects in Palestine." Pages 352–81 in *From Nomadism to Monarchy: Archaeological and Historical Aspects of Early Israel*. Edited by Israel Finkelstein and Nadav Na'aman. Jerusalem: Israel Exploration Society.
Becking, Bob. 2006. "The Return of the Deity: Iconic or Aniconic?" Pages 53–62 in *Essays on Ancient Israel in Its Ancient Near Eastern Context: A Tribute to Nadav Na'aman*. Edited by Yairah Amit, Ehud Ben Zvi, Israel Finkelstein, and Oded Lipschits. Winona Lake, IN: Eisenbrauns.
Bénichou-Safar, Hélène. 2004. *Le tophet de Salammbô à Carthage: Essai de reconstitution*. CEFR 342. Rome: Ecole française de Rome.
Ben-Tor, Amnon. 2006. "The Sad Fate of Statues and the Mutilated Statues of Hazor." Pages 3–16 in *Confronting the Past: Archaeological and Historical Essays on Ancient Israel in Honor of William G. Dever*. Edited by Seymour Gitin, J. Edward Wright, and J. P. Dessel. Winona Lake, IN: Eisenbrauns.
Berlejung, Angelika. 1997. "Washing the Mouth: The Consecration of Divine Images in Mesopotamia." Pages 45–72 in *The Image and the Book: Iconic Cults, Aniconism, and the Rise of Book Religion in Israel and the Ancient Near East*. Edited by Karel van der Toorn. Leuven: Peters.
———. 2009. "Aniconism; I. Hebrew Bible/Old Testament." *EBR* 1:1210–15.
Berthier, André, and L'Abbé René Charlier. 1952. *Le Sanctuaire Punique d'El-Hofra a Constantine*. Planches. Paris: Arts et Métiers Graphiques.
Bertrandy, François. 1992a. "Idole-bouteille." *DCPP* 227–28.
———. 1992b. "Signe de Tanit." *DCPP* 416–18.
Besançon, Alain. 2000. *The Forbidden Image: An Intellectual History of Iconoclasm*. Chicago: University of Chicago Press.
Betlyon, John Wilson. 1982. *The Coinage and Mints of Phoenicia: The Pre-Alexandrine Period*. HSM 26. Chico, CA: Scholars Press.
Bierling, Marilyn R., ed. and trans. 2002. *The Phoenicians in Spain: An Archaeological Review of the Eighth–Sixth Centuries B.C.E.* Winona Lake, IN: Eisenbrauns.
Bijovsky, Gabriela. 2005. "The Ambrosial Rocks and the Sacred Precinct of Melqart in Tyre." Pages 829–34 in *XIII Congreso Internacional de Numismatica*,

Madrid—2003. Actas-Proceedings-Actes I. Edited by Carmen Alfaro, Carmen Marcos Alonso, and Paloma Otero Morán. Madrid: Ministerio de Cultura.

Bikai, Patricia Maynor. 1978. *The Pottery of Tyre*. Warminster: Aris and Phillips.

———. 1987. "The Phoenician Pottery." Pages 1–19 in *La nécropole d'Amathonte, Tombes 113-367. Vol. 2, Céramiques non chypriotes*. Edited by Vassos Karageorghis, Olivier Picard, and Christiane Tytgat. EC 8. Nicosia: Leventis.

———. 1992. "The Phoenicians." Pages 131–41 in *The Crisis Years: The Twelfth Century B.C.* Edited by W. A. Ward and M. S. Joukowsky. Dubuque: Kendall Hunt.

Birney, Kathleen, and Brian R. Doak. 2011. "Funerary Iconography on an Infant Burial Jar from Ashkelon." *IEJ* 61:32–53.

Bisi, Anna Maria. 1967. *Le Stele Puniche*. SS 27. Rome: Università di Roma.

———. 1986. "Le 'Smiting God' dans les Milieux Phéniciens d'Occident: Un Réexamen de la Question." *SP IV* 169–87.

———. 1988. "Terracotta Figures." Pages 328–53 in *The Phoenicians: Under the Scientific Direction of Sabatino Moscati*. Edited by Sabatino Moscati. New York: Abbeville.

Bittel, Kurt. 1976. *Die Hethiter: Die Kunst Anatoliens vom Ende des 3. Bis zum Anfang des 1. Jahrtausends vor Christus*. Munich: Beck.

Black, Jeremy, and Anthony Green. 1992. *Gods, Demons and Symbols of Ancient Mesopotamia: An Illustrated Dictionary*. Illustrated by Tessa Rickards. Austin: University of Texas Press.

Blakolmer, Fritz. 2010. "A Pantheon without Attributes? Goddesses and Gods in Minoan and Mycenean Iconography." Pages 21–61 in *Divine Images and Human Imaginations in Ancient Greece and Rome*. Edited by Joannis Mylonopoulos. Leiden: Brill.

Bloch-Smith, Elizabeth. 2005. "*Maṣṣēbôt* in the Israelite Cult: An Argument for Rendering Implicit Cultic Criteria Explicit." Pages 28–39 in *Temple and Worship in Biblical Israel*. Edited by John Day. LHBOTS 422. London: T&T Clark.

———. 2006. "Will the Real *Massebot* Please Stand Up: Cases of Real and Mistakenly Identified Standing Stones in Ancient Israel." Pages 64–79 in *Text, Artifact, and Image: Revealing Ancient Israelite Religion*. Edited by Gary M. Beckman and Theodore J. Lewis. BJS 346. Providence: Brown Judaic Studies.

———. 2014. "Archaeological and Inscriptional Evidence for Phoenician Astarte." Pages 167–94 in *Transformation of a Goddess: Ishtar-Astarte-Aphrodite*. Edited by D. T. Sugimoto. OBO 263. Fribourg: Academic Press; Göttingen: Vandenhoeck & Ruprecht.

Boardman, John. 2000. "Iconography and Archaeology: Some Problems East and West." Pages 393–96 in *Images as Media: Sources for the Cultural History* of the Near East and the Eastern Mediterranean (1st Millennium BCE). Edited by Christoph Uehlinger. OBO 175. Fribourg: Academic Press; Göttingen: Vandenhoeck & Ruprecht.

———. 2003. *Classical Phoenician Scarabs: A Catalogue and Study*. Studies in Gems and Jewlery 2. BARIS 1190. Oxford: Archaeopress.

Bonatz, Dominik. 2007. "The Iconography of Religion in the Hittite, Luwian, and Aramaean Kingdoms." *IDD* 1–29.

Bonnet, Corinne. 1988. *Melqart: Cultes et Mythes de l'Héraclès Tyrien en Méditerranée*. SP 8. Leuven: Peeters.

———. 1996. *Astarté: Dossier documentaire et perspectives historiques*. CSF 37. Rome: Consiglio nazionale delle ricerche.

———. 2007. "Melqart." *IDD* 1–4.

———. 2015. *Les enfants de Cadmos: Le paysage religieux de la Phénicie hellénistique*. AH 63. Paris: de Boccard.

Bóttero, Jean. 1992. *Mesopotamia: Writing, Reasoning, and the Gods*. Translated by Zainab Bahrani and Marc Van De Mieroop. Chicago: University of Chicago Press. First published 1987.

Boyle, Alan. 2014. "Ancient Phoenician Relics Unearthed in Lebanon." *NBC News Online*, May 21, 2014. http://www.nbcnews.com/science/science-news/ancient-phoenician-relics-unearthed-lebanon-n110361.

Brentschneider, Joachim. 1991a. *Architekturmodelle in Vorderasien und der östlichen Ägäis vom Neolithikum bis in das 1. Jahrtausend: Phänomene in der Kleinkunst an Beispielen aus Mesopotamien, dem Iran, Anatolien, Syrien, der Levante und dem ägäischen Raum unter besonderer Berückichtigung der bau- und der religionsgeschichtlichen Aspekte*. AOAT 229. Kevelaer: Butzon & Berker; Neukirchen-Vluyn: Neukirchener Verlag.

———. 1991b. "Götter in Schreinen." *UF* 23:13–32.

Brettler, Marc Zvi. 2007. "Method in the Application of Biblical Source Material to Historical Writing (with Particular Reference to the Ninth Century BCE)." Pages 305–36 in *Understanding the History of Ancient Israel*. Edited by H. G. M. Williamson. Oxford: Oxford University Press.

Briquel-Chatonnet, Françoise. 1992. *Les relations entre les cites de la côte phénicienne et les royaumes d'Israël et e Juda*. OLA 46. SP 12. Leuven: Peeters.

Brown, Brian Arthur, and Marian H. Feldman, eds. 2014. *Critical Approaches to Ancient Near Eastern Art*. Berlin: de Gruyter.

Brown, Shelby. 1991. *Late Carthaginian Child Sacrifice and Sacrificial Monuments in Their Mediterranean Context*. JSOT/ASOR Monograph Series 3. Sheffield: Sheffield Academic.

———. 1992. "Perspectives on Phoenician Art." *BA* 55:6–24.

Bunnens, Guy. 1979. *L'expansion phénicienne en méditerranée: Essai d'interprétation fondé sur une analyse des traditions littéraires*. EPAHA 17. Brussels: Institut historique belge de Rome.

Burkert, Walter. 1979. *Structure and History in Greek Mythology and Ritual.* SCL 47. Berkeley: University of California Press.

Cagni, Luigi. 1977. *The Poem of Erra.* Malibu: Udena.

Camille, Michael. 2003. "Simulacrum." Pages 35–48 in *Critical Terms for Art History.* Edited by Robert S. Nelson and Richard Shiff. 2nd ed. Chicago: University of Chicago Press.

Cancik, Hubert. 1988. "Ikonoklasmus." Pages 217–21 in *Handbuch religionswissenschaftlicher Grundbegriffe.* Edited by Hubert Cancik, Burkhard Gladigow, and Matthias Laubscher. Stuttgart: Kohlhammer.

Cecchini, Serena Maria. 1997. "La stele di Amrit. Aspetti e problem iconografici e iconologici." *CMAO* 7:83–100.

Celestino, S., and Carolina López-Ruiz. Forthcoming. *Tartessos and the Phoenicians in Iberia.* Oxford: Oxford University Press.

Chiarenza, Nicola. 2013. "On Oriental Persistence in the Hellenistic Town of Soluntum: A New Hypothesis about the Statue of an Enthroned Goddess." Pages 945–54 in *Identity and Connectivity: Proceedings of the 16th Symposium on Mediterranean Archaeology, Florence, Italy, 1–3 March 2012.* Edited by Luca Bombardieri Anacleto D'Agostino, Guido Guarducci, Valentina Orsi, and Stefano Valentini. Vol. 2. BARIS 2581. Oxford: Archaeopress.

Ciafaloni, D. 1995. "Iconographie et iconologie." Pages 535–49 in *La civilisation phénicienne et punique: Manuel de recherche.* Edited by Véronique Krings. HO 1/20. Leiden: Brill.

Ciasca, Antonia. 1988. "Masks and Protomes." Pages 354–69 in *The Phoenicians: Under the Scientific Direction of Sabatino Moscati.* Edited by Sabatino Moscati. New York: Abbeville.

Clifford, Richard J. 1990. "Phoenician Religion." *BASOR* 279:55–64.

Collins, Billie Jean. 2005. "A Statue for the Deity: Cult Images in Hittite Anatolia." *CIDRANE* 13–42.

Collon, Dominique. 1987. *First Impressions: Cylinder Seals in the Ancient Near East.* Chicago: University of Chicago Press; London: British Museum Press.

Colvin, Stephen. 2014. *A Brief History of Ancient Greek.* Chichester: Wiley-Blackwell.

Cornelius, Izak. 1997. "The Many Faces of God: Divine Images and Symbols in Ancient Near Eastern Religions." Pages 21–43 in *The Image and the Book: Iconic Cults, Aniconism, and the Rise of Book Religion in Israel and the Ancient Near East.* Edited by Karel van der Toorn. Leuven: Peters.

———. 2004. *The Many Faces of the Goddess: The Iconography of the Syro-Palestinian Goddesses Anat, Astarte, Qedeshet, and Asherah c. 1500–1000 BCE.* OBO 204. Fribourg: Academic Press; Göttingen: Vandenhoeck & Ruprecht.

Crawford, Cory D. 2014. "Relating Image and Word in Ancient Mesopotamia."

Pages 241–64 in *Critical Approaches to Ancient Near Eastern Art*. Edited by Brian A. Brown and Marian H. Feldman. Berlin: de Gruyter.
Cross, Frank Moore. 2002. "Appendix 1: Phoenician Tomb Stelae from Akhziv." Pages 169–73 in Michal Dayagi-Mendels, *The Akhziv Cemeteries: The Ben-Dor Excavations, 1941–1944*. IAAR 15. Jerusalem: Israel Antiquities Authority.
Crouch, C. L. 2014. *The Making of Israel: Cultural Diversity in the Southern Levant and the Formation of Ethnic Identity in Deuteronomy*. VTSup 162. Leiden: Brill.
Culican, William. 1960–1961. "Melqart Representations on Phoenician Seals." *AN* 2:41–54.
———. 1968. "The Iconography of Some Phoenician Seals and Seal Impressions." *AJBA* 1.1:35–50.
———. 1970. "Problems of Phoenicio-Punic Iconography—A Contribution." *AJBA* 1.3:28–57.
———. 1976. "A Terracotta Shrine from Achzib." *ZDPV* 92:47–53.
———. 1980. "Phoenician Incense Stands." Pages 85–101 in *Oriental Studies: Essays Presented to B. S. J. Isserlin*. Edited by Rifaat Y. Ebied and M. J. L. Young. Leiden: Brill.
———. 1982. "The Repetoire of Phoenician Pottery." Pages 45–78 in *Phönizier im Westen: Die Beiträge des Internationalen Symposiums über "Die phönizische Expansion im Westlichen Mittelmeerraum" in Köln vom 24. bis 27. April 1979*. Edited by Hans Georg Niemeyer. MB 6. Mainz: von Zabern.
———. 1991. "Phoenicia and Phoenician Colonization." Pages 461–546 in *The Assyrian and Babylonia Empires and Other States of the Near East, from the Eighth to the Sixth Centuries B.C.* Vol 3.2 of *The Cambridge Ancient History*. Edited by John Boardman and I. E. S. Edwards. Cambridge: Cambridge University Press.
D'Andrea, Bruno. 2014a. *I tofet del Nord Africa dall'età arcaica all'età romana (VIII sec. a.C.–II sec. d.C.)*. CSF 45. Rome: Fabrizio Serra editore.
———. 2014b. "Nuove stele dal Tofet di Mozia." *VO* 18:123–44.
Darby, Erin. 2014. *Interpreting Judean Pillar Figurines: Gender and Empire in Judean Apotropaic Ritual*. FAT 2/69. Tübingen. Mohr Siebeck.
Dayagi-Mendels, Michal. 2002. *The Akhziv Cemeteries. The Ben-Dor Excavations, 1941–1944*. IAAR 15. Jerusalem: Israel Antiquities Authority.
Dearman, J. Andrew, and J. Maxwell Miller. 1983. "The Melqart Stele and the Ben-Hadads of Damascus: Two Studies." *PEQ* 115:95–101.
de Hulster, Izaak J. 2009a. "A Yehud Coin with a Representation of a Sun Deity and Iconic Practice in Persian Period Palestine: An Elaboration on TC 242.5/BMC XIX 29." Early Jewish Monotheisms website. September. http://www.monotheism.uni-goettingen.de/resources/dehulster_tc242.pdf.

———. 2009b. *Iconographic Exegesis in Third Isaiah*. FAT 2/36. Tübingen: Mohr Siebeck.
Deleuze, Gilles. 1990. *The Logic of Sense*. Translated by M. Lester and C. Stivale. Edited by C. V. Boundas. New York: Columbia University Press.
Demand, Nancy H. 2011. *The Mediterranean Context of Early Greek History*. New York: Wiley & Sons.
Delz, Josef, ed. 1987. *Silius Italicus: Punica*. Stuttgart: Teubner.
Dever, William G. 1974. *Gezer II: Report of the 1967–70 Seasons in Fields I and II*. Jerusalem: Hebrew Union College.
Dirven, Lucinda. 1997. "The Author of 'De Dea Syria' and His Cultural Heritage." Numen 44:153–79.
Dick, Michael Brennan. 1999. "Prophetic Parodies of Making the Cult Image." Pages 1–53 in *Born in Heaven, Made on Earth: The Making of the Cult Image in the Ancient Near East*. Edited by Michael Brennan Dick. Winona Lake, IN: Eisenbrauns.
———. 2005. "The Mesopotamian Cult Statute: A Sacramental Encounter with Divinity." *CIDRANE* 43–67.
Dietler, Michael. 2009. "Colonial Encounters in Iberia and the Western Mediterranean: An Exploratory Framework." Pages 3–48 in *Colonial Encounters in Ancient Iberia: Phoenician, Greek, and Indigenous Relations*. Edited by Michael Dietler and Carolina López-Ruiz. Chicago: University of Chicago Press.
Dietler, Michael, and Carolina López-Ruiz, eds. 2009. *Colonial Encounters in Ancient Iberia: Phoenician, Greek, and Indigenous Relations*. Chicago: University of Chicago Press.
Doak, Brian R. 2007. "A Re-evaluation of the Iconographic Motifs of the Taʿanach Cult Stand." Paper presented at the SBL Annual Meeting, San Diego, CA, November 18.
———. 2012. *The Last of the Rephaim: Conquest and Cataclysm in the Heroic Ages of Ancient Israel*. IS 7. Boston: Ilex Foundation; Washington D.C.: Center for Hellenic Studies, via Harvard University Press.
Docter, Roald F., et al. 2008. "New Radiocarbon Dates from Carthage: Bridging the Gap between History and Archaeology?" Pages 379–422 in *Beyond the Homeland: Markers in Phoenician Chronology*. Edited by Claudia Sagona. ANESS 28. Leuven: Peeters.
Döllinger, Johann Joseph Ignaz von. 1862. *The Gentile and the Jew in the Courts of the Temple of Christ: An Introduction to the History of Christianity*. Translated by N. Darnell. London: Longman, Green, Longman, Roberts, and Green.
Dommelen, Peter van. 2014. "Punic Identities and Modern Perceptions in the Western Mediterranean." Pages 42–57 in *The Punic Mediterranean: Identities and Identification from Phoenician Settlement to Roman Rule*.

Edited by Josephine Crawley Quinn and Nicholas C. Vella. BSRS. Cambridge: Cambridge University Press.

Dommelen, Peter van, and Mireia López-Bertran. 2013. "Hellenism as Subaltern Practice: Rural Cults in the Punic World." Pages 273–99 in *The Hellenistic West: Rethinking the Ancient Mediterranean*. Edited by Jonathan R. W. Prag and Josephine Crawley Quinn. Cambridge: Cambridge University Press.

D'Orazio, Massimo. 2007. "Meteorite Records in the Ancient Greek and Latin Literature: Between History and Myth." Pages 215–26 in *Myth and Geology*. Edited by Luigi Piccardi and W. Bruce Masse. GSSP 273. London: Geological Society of London.

Doumet-Serhal, Claude, ed. 2011–2012. *And Canaan Begat Sidon His Firstborn: A Tribute to Dr. John Curtis on his 65th Birthday*. In collaboration with Anne Rebate and Andrea Resek. AHL 34–35. Winona Lake, IN: Eisenbrauns.

———. 2013. *Sidon: Fifteen Years of Excavations; On the Occasion of the Exhibition Sidon "The Best of Fifteen Years."* 3 September–3 November 2013, Sidon. Beirut: The Lebanese British Friends of the National Museum.

Dunand, Maurice. 1939. "Stèle araméenne dediée à Melqart." *BMB* 3:65–76.

———. 1966. "Rapport préliminaire sur les fouiles de Sidon." *BMB* 19:103–5.

———. 1967. "Rapport préliminaire sur les fouiles de Sidon." *BMB* 20:27–44.

———. 1969. "Rapport préliminaire sur les fouiles de Sidon." *BMB* 20:101–7.

Eissfeldt, Otto. 1935. *Molk als Opferbegriff im Punischen und Hebräischen und das Ende des Gottes Moloch*. BRA 3. Halle: Niemeyer.

Elayi, Josette. 1982. "Studies in Phoenician Geography During the Persian Period." *JNES* 41:83–110.

Elayi, Josette, and Alain Gérard Elayi. 2004. *Le Monnayage de la Cité Phénicienne de Sidon à l'Époque Perse (Ve–IVe s. av. J.-C.)*. 2 vols. SuppTrans 11. Paris: Gabalda.

———. 2009. *The Coinage of the Phoenician City of Tyre in the Persian Period (5th–4th cent. BCE)*. OLA 188. SP 20. Leuven: Peeters.

———. 2014. *A Monetary and Political History of the Phoenician City of Byblos in the Fifth and Fourth Centuries B.C.E.* HACL 6. Winona Lake, IN: Eisenbrauns.

Elkins, James. 2011. "Introduction." Pages 1–12 in *What Is an Image?* Edited by James Elkins and M. Naef. SATI 2. University Park: Pennsylvania State University Press.

Elkins, J., and Maja Naef, eds. 2011. *What is an Image?* SATI 2. University Park: Pennsylvania State University Press.

Ellenbogen, Josh, and Aaron Tugendhaft, eds. 2011. *Idol Anxiety*. Stanford: Stanford University Press.

Evans, Carl D. 1995. "Cult Images, Royal Policies and the Origins of Aniconism."

Pages 192–212 in *The Pitcher Is Broken: Memorial Essays for G. W. Ahlström*. Edited by Steven W. Holloway and Lowell K. Handy. JSOTSup 190. Sheffield: Sheffield Academic.

Falsone, Gioacchino. 1986. "Anath or Astarte? A Phoenician Bronze Statuette of the Smiting Goddess." *SP IV* 53–76.

———. 1993. "An Ovoid Betyl from the Tophet at Motya and the Phoenician Tradition of Round Cultic Stones." *JMS* 3:245–85.

Feder, Yitzhaq. 2013. "The Aniconic Tradition, Deuteronomy 4, and the Politics of Israelite Identity." *JBL* 132:251–74.

Feldman, Marian H. 2014. *Communities of Style: Portable Luxury Arts, Identity, and Collective Memory in the Iron Age Levant*. Chicago: University of Chicago Press.

Fine, Steven. 2005. *Art and Judaism in the Greco-Roman World: Toward a New Jewish Archaeology*. Cambridge: Cambridge University Press.

Fitzmyer, Joseph A. 1966. "The Phoenician Inscription from Pyrgi." *JAOS* 86:285–97.

Fletcher, Richard Nathan. 2012. "Opening the Mediterranean: Assyria, the Levant and the Transformation of Early Iron Age Trade." *Antiquity* 86.331:211–20.

Frankenstein, Susan. 1979. "The Phoenicians in the Far West: A Function of Neo-Assyrian Imperialism." Pages 263–94 in *Power and Propaganda: A Symposium on Ancient Empires*. Edited by Mogens Trolle Larsen. Copenhagen: Akademisk.

Frankfort, Henri. 1970. *The Art and Architecture of the Ancient Orient*. Pelican History of Art. 4th ed. New York: Penguin.

Frazer, James G. 1890. *The Golden Bough: A Study in Comparative Religion*. Vol. 1. Reprint, Cambridge Library Collection. Cambridge: Cambridge University Press, 2012.

Freedberg, David. 1989. *The Power of Images: Studies in the History and Theory of Response*. Chicago: University of Chicago Press.

Frick, Frank S. 2000. *Tell Taannek 1963–1968 IV/2: The Iron Age Cultic Structure*. Birzeit: Palestine Institute of Archaeology.

Gaifman, Milette. 2008. "The Aniconic Image of the Roman Near East." Pages 37–72 in *The Variety of Local Religious Life in the Near East in the Hellenistic and Roman Periods*. Edited by T. Kaizer. Leiden: Brill.

———. 2010a. "Aniconism and the Notion of 'Primitive' in Greek Antiquity." Pages 63–86 in *Divine Images and Human Imaginations in Ancient Greece and Rome*. Edited by Joannis Mylonopoulos. Leiden: Brill.

———. 2010b. "Pausanias and Modern Perceptions of Primordial Greeks." *CRJ* 2:254–86.

———. 2012. *Aniconism in Greek Antiquity*. Oxford: Oxford University Press.

———. 2012–2013. "Baal Hammon and Tinnit in Carthage: The Tophet Between the Origin and the Expansion of the Colonial World." *SEL* 29–30:49–64.

Garbati, Giuseppe. 2012. "Fingere l'identità fenicia. Melqart 'di/sopra ṣr.'" *RSF* 40:159–74.

Garfinkel, Yosef, and Madeleine Mumcuoglu. 2013. "Triglyphs and Recessed Doorframes on a Building Model from Khirbet Qeiyafa: New Light on Two Technical Terms in the Biblical Descriptions of Solomon's Palace and Temple." *IEJ* 63:135–63.

———. 2015. *Solomon's Temple and Palace in Light of New Archeological Discoveries*. Jerusalem: Koren (Hebrew).

Garr, W. Randall. 2003. *In His Own Image and Likeness: Humanity, Divinity, and Monotheism*. CHANE 15. Leiden: Brill.

Geer, Russel M., trans. 1954. *Diodorus Siculus: Library of History; Volume X, Books 19.66–20*. LCL 390. Cambridge: Harvard University Press.

George, Mark K. 2012. "Israelite Aniconism and the Visualization of the Tabernacle." *JRS* 8:40–54.

Geva, Shulamit. 1982. "Archaeological Evidence for the Trade between Israel and Tyre?" *BASOR* 248:69–72.

Gibson, John C. L. 1982. *Textbook of Syrian Semitic Inscriptions*. Vol. 3. Phoenician Inscriptions. Oxford: Clarendon.

Gilmour, Garth. 2009. "An Iron Age II Pictorial Inscription from Jerusalem Illustrating Yahweh and Asherah." *PEQ* 141.2:87–103.

Gitin, Seymour, J. Edward Wright, and J. P. Dessel, eds. 2006. *Confronting the Past: Archaeological and Historical Essays on Ancient Israel in Honor of William G. Dever*. Winona Lake, IN: Eisenbrauns.

Gladigow, Burkhard. 1988. "Anikonische Kulte." Pages 472–73 in *Handbuch religionswissenschaftlicher Grundbegriffe*. Vol. 1. Edited by Hubert Cancik, Burkhard Gladigow, and M. Laubscher. Stuttgart: Kohlhammer.

González Blanco, Antonino, Gonzalo Matilla Séiquer, and Alejandro Egea Vivancos, eds. 2004. *El mundo púnico: religion, antropología y cultura material. Actas II Congreso Internacional del Mundo Púnico, Cartagena, 6–9 de abril de 2000*. Cartagena, Spain: Universidad de Murcia.

Goodman, Nelson. 1974. *Languages of Art*. Indianapolis: Hackett.

Goodrich, Peter. 1999. "The Iconography of Nothing: Blank Spaces and the Representation of Law in Edward VI and the Pope." Pages 89–114 in *Law and the Image: The Authority of Art and the Aesthetics of Law*. Edited by C. Douzinas and L. Nead. Chicago: University of Chicago Press.

Gordon, Richard L. 1979. "The Real and the Imaginary: Production and Religion in the Graeco-Roman World." *Art History* 2:5–34. Reprinted in R. L. Gordon, *Image and Value in the Graeco-Roman World: Studies in Mithraism and Religious Art*. Aldershot, UK: Variorum, 1996.

Gottwald, Norman K. 1979. *The Tribes of Yahweh: A Sociology of the Religion of a Liberated Israel, 1250–1050 B.C.E.* Maryknoll, NY: Orbis.

Grabar, Oleg. 2003. "From the Icon to Aniconism: Islam and the Image." *Museum International* 55:46–53.
Green, Alberto Ravinell Whitney. 1983. "David's Relations with Hiram: Biblical and Josephan Evidence for Tyrian Chronology." Pages 373–97 in *The Word of the Lord Shall Go Forth: Essays in Honor of David Noel Freedman in Celebration of His Sixtieth Birthday*. Edited by Carol L. Meyers and Michael Patrick O'Connor. Winona Lake, IN: Eisenbrauns; Philadelphia: ASOR.
———. 1995. "Ancient Mesopotamian Religious Iconography." *CANE* 3:1837–55.
Gubel, Éric. 1983. "Art in Tyre in the First and Second Iron Age." Pages 23–52 in *Redt Tyrus/Sauvons Tyr: Histoire phénicienne/Fenicische Geschiedenis*. Edited by Éric Gubel, Edward Lipiński, and Brigitte Servais-Soyez. SP 1. OLA 25. Leuven: Peeters.
———. 1987. *Phoenician Furniture: A Typology Based on Iron Age Representations with Reference to the Iconographical Context*. SP 7. Leuven: Peeters.
———. 1992. "Naos, Naiskos." *DCPP* 308–9.
———. 1993. "The Iconography of Inscribed Phoenician Glyptic." Pages 101–29 in *Studies in the Iconography of Northwest Semitic Inscribed Seals; Proceedings of a Symposium Held in Fribourg on April 17–20, 1991*. Edited by Benjamin Sass and Christoph Uehlinger. OBO 125. Fribourg: Academic Press; Göttingen: Vandenhoeck & Ruprecht.
———. 2000. "Multicultural and Multimedia Aspects of Early Phoenician Art, c. 1200–675 BCE." Pages 185–213 in *Images as Media: Sources for the Cultural History of the Near East and the Eastern Mediterranean (First Millennium BCE)*. Edited by Christoph Uehlinger. OBO 175. Fribourg: Academic Press; Göttingen: Vandenhoeck & Ruprecht.
———. 2005. "Phoenician and Aramean Bridle-Harness Decoration: Examples of Cultural Contact and Innovation in the Eastern Mediterranean." Pages 111–48 in *Crafts and Images in Conflict: Studies on Eastern Mediterranean Art of the First Millennium BC*. Edited by Claudia E. Suter and Christoph Uehlinger. Fribourg: Academic Press; Göttingen: Vandenhoeck & Ruprecht, 2005.
Gubel, Éric, et al. 1986. *Les Pheniciens et le Monde Méditerraneen*. Brussels: Général de Banque.
———. 2002. *Art phénicien: La sculpture de tradition phénicienne*. Paris: Musée de Louvre, Départment des Antiquités Orientales.
Gubel, Éric, Edward Lipiński, and Brigitte Servais-Soyez, eds. 1983. *Redt Tyrus/Sauvons Tyr: Histoire phénicienne/Fenicische Geschiedenis*. SP 1. OLA 25. Leuven: Peeters.
Gunter, Ann C. 2009. *Greek Art and the Orient*. Cambridge: Cambridge University Press.
Günther, Linda Marie. 2000. "Legende und Identität: Die 'Verwandtschaft' zwischen Karthago und Tyros." Pages 161–65 in *Actas del IV congreso interna-*

cional de estudios fenicios y púnicos 1. Edited by Manuela Barthélemy and María Eugenia Aubet Semmler. Cádiz: Universidad de Cádiz.

Hackett, Jo Ann. 2004. "Phoenician and Punic." Pages 365–85 in *The Cambridge Encyclopedia of the World's Ancient Languages*. Edited by Roger D. Woodard. Cambridge: Cambridge University Press.

Hadley, Judith M. 2000. *The Cult of Asherah in Ancient Israel and Judah: Evidence for a Hebrew Goddess*. UCOP 57. Cambridge: Cambridge University Press.

Halliwell, Stephen. 2002. *The Aesthetics of Mimesis: Ancient Texts and Modern Problems*. Princeton: Princeton University Press.

Hallo, William W. 1983. "Cult Statue and Divine Image: A Preliminary Study." Pages 1–17 in *More Essays on the Comparative Method*. Vol. 2 of *Scripture in Context*. Edited by William W. Hallo, James C. Moyer, and Leo G. Purdue. Winona Lake, IN: Eisenbrauns.

Hallo, William W., et al., eds. 1997–2000. *The Context of Scripture*. 3 vols. Leiden: Brill.

Harden, Donald B. 1963. *The Phoenicians*. London: Thames & Hudson.

Hays, J. Daniel. 2003. "Has the Narrator Come to Praise Solomon or to Bury Him? Narrative Subtlety in 1 Kings 1–11." *JSOT* 28:149–74.

Healey, John F. 2001. *The Religion of the Nabateans: A Conspectus*. RGRW 136. Leiden: Brill.

Hendel, Ronald S. 1988. "The Social Origins of the Aniconic Tradition in Early Israel." *CBQ* 50:365–82.

———. 1997. "Aniconism and Anthropomorphism in Ancient Israel." Pages 205–28 in *The Image and the Book: Iconic Cults, Aniconism, and the Rise of Book Religion in Israel and the Ancient Near East*. Edited by Karel van der Toorn. Leuven: Peters.

Herring, Stephen L. 2013. *Divine Substitution: Humanity as the Manifestation of Deity in the Hebrew Bible and the Ancient Near East*. FRLANT 247. Göttingen: Vandenhoeck & Ruprecht.

Hestrin, Ruth. 1987. "The Cult Stand from Ta'anach and Its Religious Background." Pages 61–77 in *Phoenicia and the East Mediterranean in the First Millennium B.C.* Edited by Edward Lipiński. SP 5. Leuven: Peeters.

Hill, George Francis. 1910. *Catalogue of the Greek Coins of Phoenicia*. Bologna: Forni.

Hirt, Alfred. 2015. "Beyond Greece and Rome: Foundation Myths on Tyrian Coinage in the Third Century AD." Pages 190–226 in *Foundation Myths in Ancient Societies: Dialogues and Discourses*. Edited by Naoíse Mac Sweeney. Philadelphia: University of Pennsylvania Press.

Hoffmeier, James K. 2015. *Akhenaten and the Origins of Monotheism*. Oxford: Oxford University Press.

Hoftijzer, Jacob, and Karel Jongeling. 1995. *Dictionary of the North-West Semitic*

Inscriptions. Parts 1 and 2. With Appendixes by Richard C. Steiner, Adina Mosak Moshavi, and Bezalel Porten. Leiden: Brill.

Holter, Knut. 1995. *Second Isaiah's Idol-Fabrication Passages*. BBET 28. Bern: Peter Lang.

Hundley, Michael B. 2013. *Gods in Dwellings: Temples and Divine Presence in the Ancient Near East*. WAWSup 3. Atlanta: SBL Press.

Huntington, Susan L. 1990. "Early Buddhist Art and the Theory of Aniconism." *AJ* 49:401–8.

Hurowitz, Victor Avigdor. 2006. "What Goes in Is What Comes Out: Materials for Creating Cult Statues." Pages 3–23 in *Text, Artifact, and Image: Revealing Ancient Israelite Religion*. Edited by Gary M. Beckman and Theodore J. Lewis. BJS 346. Providence: Brown Judaic Studies.

Hvidberg-Hansen, F. O. 1979. *La déessee TNT: Une etude sur la religion canaanéo-punique*. 2 vols. Copenhagen: Gad.

Irvine, Judith T., and Susan Gal. 2000. "Language Ideology and Linguistic Differentiation." Pages 35–84 in *Regimes of Language: Ideologies, Polities, and Identities*. Edited by Paul V. Kroskrity. Santa Fe: School of American Research Press.

Jacobsen, Thorkild. 1987. "The Graven Image." Pages 15–32 in *Ancient Israelite Religion: Essays in Honor of Frank Moore Cross*. Edited by Patrick D. Miller Jr., Paul D. Hanson, and S. Dean McBride. Philadelphia: Fortress.

Jones, Christopher P., ed. and trans. 2005. *Philostratus: The Life of Apollonius of Tyana; Books V–VIII*. LCL. Cambridge: Harvard University Press.

Joukowsky, Martha Sharp, ed. 1992. *The Heritage of Tyre: Essays on the History, Archaeology, and Preservation of Tyre*. Dubuque: Kendall Hunt.

———. 1997. "Byblos." *OEANE*.

Kaldellis, Anthony, and Carolina López-Ruiz. 2009. "BNJ 790: Philon of Byblos." In *Brill's New Jacoby (Fragments of Ancient Historians)*. Edited by Ian Worthington. Leiden: Brill Online. http://www.brill.nl/brillsnewjacoby.

Katzenstein, H. Jacob. 1997. *The History of Tyre from the Beginning of the Second Millennium B.C.E. until the Fall of the Neo-Babylonian Empire in 538 B.C.E.* 2nd rev. ed. Jerusalem: Ben Gurion University of the Negev Press.

Karageorghis, Vassos. 1993. *Late Cypriote II–Cypro-Geometric III*. Vol. 2 of *The Coroplastic Art of Ancient Cyprus*. Nicosia: Leventis Foundation.

———. 2000. "Aniconic representations of divinities in Cypriote 'Naïskoi.'" Pages 51–62 in *Actas del IV congreso internacional de estudios fenicios y púnicos. Cádiz, 2 al 6 de Octubre de 1995*. Vol. 1. Edited by María Eugenia Aubet and Manuela Barthélemy. Cádiz: Servicio de Publicaciones, Universidad de Cádiz.

Katz, Maya Balakirsky. 2009. "Aniconism; II. Judaism; A. Second Temple and Hellenistic Judaism." *EBR* 1:1215–17.

Keel, Othmar, and Christoph Uehlinger. 1998. *Gods, Goddesses, and Images of God*

in Ancient Israel. Translated by Thomas H. Trapp. Minneapolis: Fortress.
Khalifeh, Issam Ali. 1997. "Sidon." *OEANE.*
King, Philip J., and Lawrence E. Stager. 2001. *Life in Biblical Israel.* Library of Ancient Israel. Louisville: Westminster John Knox.
Kletter, Raz. 1996. *The Judean Pillar-Figurines and the Archaeology of Asherah.* BARIS 636. Oxford: Tempus Reparatum.
Knapp, A. Bernard. 2014. "Mediterranean Archaeology and Ethnicity." Pages 34–49 in *A Companion to Ethnicity in the Ancient Mediterranean.* Edited by Jeremy McInerney. Chichester: Wiley-Blackwell.
Krahmalkov, Charles R. 2001. *A Phoenician-Punic Grammar.* HO 54. Leiden: Brill.
Krings, Véronique, ed. 1995a. *La civilisation phénicienne et punique. Manuel de recherche.* HO 1/20. Leiden: Brill.
———. 1995b. "La Literature Phénicienne et Punique." Pages 31–38 in *La civilisation phénicienne et punique: Manuel de recherche.* Edited by Véronique Krings. HO 1/20. Leiden: Brill.
Kristensen, Troels Myrup. 2013. *Making and Breaking the Gods: Christian Responses to Pagan Sculpture in Late Antiquity.* ASMA 12. Aarhus: Aarhus University Press.
Lambert, Wilfred G. 1990. "Ancient Mesopotamian Gods: Superstition, Philosophy, Theology." *RHR* 207: 115–30.
LaRocca-Pitts, Elizabeth C. 2001. *"Of Wood and Stone": The Significance of Israelite Cultic Items in the Bible and its Early Interpreters.* HSM 61. Winona Lake, IN: Eisenbrauns.
Lemche, Niels Peter. 1991. *The Canaanites and Their Land: The Tradition of the Canaanites.* JSOTSup 110. Sheffield: JSOT Press.
Levene, David S., ed. 1997. *Tacitus: The Histories.* First translated by W. H. Fyfe. Oxford: Oxford University Press.
Lévi-Strauss, Claude. 1966. *The Savage Mind.* Chicago: University of Chicago Press.
Lewis, Theodore J. 1989. *Cults of the Dead in Ancient Israel and Ugarit.* HSM 39. Atlanta: Scholars Press.
———. 1998. "Review: Divine Images and Aniconism in Ancient Israel." *JAOS* 118:36–53.
———. 2005. "Syro-Palestinian Iconography and Divine Images." *CIDRANE* 69–107.
———. 2013. "Divine Fire in Deuteronomy 33:2." *JBL* 132:791–803.
Linder, Elisha. 1973. "A Cargo of Phoenician-Punic Figurines." *Archaeology* 26:182–87.
Lipiński, Edward. 1970. "La fête de l'ensevelissement et de la résurrection de Melqart." Pages 30–58 in *Actes de la XVIIe Recontre Assyriologique Internationale.* Edited by André Finet. Ham-sur-Heure: Comité belge de recherches en Mésopotamie.

———. 1975. *Studies in Aramaic Inscriptions and Onomastics.* Vol. 1. OLA 1. Leuven: Peeters.
———. 1995. *Dieux et déesses de l'univers phénicien et punique.* OLA 64. SP 14. Leuven: Peeters.
———. 2004. *Itineraria Phoenicia.* OLA 127. SP 18. Leuven: Peeters.
Liverani, Mario. 2003. *Israel's History and the History of Israel.* Translated by Chiara Peri and Philip R. Davies. London: Equinox.
Llewellyn-Jones, Lloyd. 2013. *King and Court in Ancient Persia: 559–331 BCE.* Edinburg: Edinburg University Press.
López-Ruiz, Carolina. 2010. *When the Gods Were Born: Greek Cosmogonies and the Near East.* Cambridge: Harvard University Press.
———. 2011. "Phoenicians." Pages 659–61 in *The Homer Encyclopedia.* Edited by Margalit Finkelberg. Malden, MA: Wiley-Blackwell.
———. 2015. Philo of Byblos's *Phoenician History* and Cultural Identity in the Roman East. Paper presented at the 13th Annual Meeting of the Midwestern Consortium for the Study of Ancient Religions. University of Chicago, March 7, 2015.
Machinist, Peter. 1984. "Rest and Violence in the Poem of Errsa." Pages 222–26 in *Studies in Literature from the Ancient Near East by Members of the American Oriental Society, Dedicated to Samuel Noah Kramer.* Edited by Jack M. Sasson. New Haven: American Oriental Society.
———. 2003. "Mesopotamian Imperialism and Israelite Religion: A Case Study from the Second Isaiah." Pages 237–64 in *Symbiosis, Symbolism and the Power of the Past: Canaan, Ancient Israel and Their Neighbors; Centennial Symposium of the W. F. Albright Institute of Archaeological Research and the American Schools of Oriental Research.* Edited by William G. Dever and Seymour Gitin. Winona Lake, IN: Eisenbrauns.
———. 2006. "Kingship and Divinity in Imperial Assyria." Pages 152–88 in *Text, Artifact, and Image: Revealing Ancient Israelite Religion.* Edited by Gary M. Beckman and Theodore J. Lewis. BJS 346. Providence: Brown Judaic Studies.
———. 2014. "Anthropomorphism in Mesopotamian Religion." Pages 67–100 in *Göttliche Körper—Göttliche Gefühle: Was leisten anthropomorphe und anthropopathische Götterkonzepte im Alten Orient und im Alten Testament?* Edited by Andreas Wagner. OBO 270. Fribourg: Academic Press; Göttingen: Vandenhoeck & Ruprecht.
Marín Ceballos, María Cruz Marin. 2004. "Observaciones en torno a los pebeteros en forma de cabeza femenina." Pages 319–35 in *El mundo púnico: Religión, antropología y cultura material; Estudios Orientales 5–6, 2001–2002.* Edited by Antonino González Blanco, Gonzalo Matilla Séiquer, and Alejandro Egea Vivancos. Murcia: Universidad de Murcia.
———, ed. 2011a. *Cultos y ritos de la Gadir fenicia.* Cádiz: Servicio de publicaciones de la Universidad de Cádiz.

———. 2011b. "La singularidad religiosa de Gadir en el mundo fenicio-púnico." Pages 213–22 in *Fenicios en Tartesos: Nuevas Perspectivas*. Edited by Manuel Álvarez Martí-Aguilar. BARIS 2245. Oxford: Archaeopress.
Marín Ceballos, María Cruz Marin, and Fréderique Horn, eds. 2007. *Imagen y culto en la Iberia prerromana: los pebeteros en forma de cabeza femenina*. SM 9. Sevilla: Servicio de Publicaciones de la Universidad de Sevilla.
Marín Ceballos, María Cruz Marin, and Ana Ma Jiménez Flores. 2005. "Los sacerdotes del temple de Melqart en Gadir según el testimonio de Silio Itálico." Pages 1195–1202 in *Atti del V Congresso internazionale di studi fenici e punici. Marsala-Palermo, 2–8 ottobre 2000*. Vol. 3. Edited by Manuel Álvarez Martí-Aguilar. Palermo: Università degli Studi di Palermo, Facoltà di Lettere e Filosofia.
Marion, Jean-Luc. 1991. *God without Being: Hors-Texte*. Translated by Thomas A. Carlson. Chicago: University of Chicago Press. First published 1982.
———. 2011. "What We See and What Appears." Pages 152–68 in *Idol Anxiety*. Edited by Josh Ellenbogen and Aaron Tugendhaft. Stanford: Stanford University Press.
Markoe, Glenn E. 1985. *Phoenician Bronze and Silver Bowls from Cyprus and the Mediterranean*. CS 26. Berkeley: California University Press.
———. 1990. "The Emergence of Phoenician Art." *BASOR* 279:13–26.
———. 1997. "Phoenicians." *OEANE*.
———. 2000. *Phoenicians*. London: British Museum Press.
Massa, Aldo. 1977. *The Phoenicians*. Translated by David Macrae. Geneva: Minerva.
May, Natalie Naomi, ed. 2012. *Iconoclasm and Text Destruction in the Ancient Near East and Beyond*. COIS 8. Chicago: University of Chicago Press.
Mazar, Amihai. 1992. *Archaeology of the Land of the Bible, 10,000–586 B.C.E.* Anchor Bible Reference Library. New York: Doubleday.
———. 2007. "The Divided Monarchy: Comments on Some Archaeological Issues." Pages 159–79 in *The Quest for the Historical Israel: Debating Archaeology and the History of Early Israel*, by Israel Finkelstein and Amihai Mazar. SBLABS 17. Atlanta: Society of Biblical Literature.
McCarter, P. Kyle. 1975. *The Antiquity of the Greek Alphabet and the Early Phoenician Scripts*. HSM 9. Missoula, MT: Scholars Press.
Merker, Gloria S. 2000. *The Sanctuary of Demeter and Kore: Terracotta Figurines of the Classical, Hellenistic, and Roman Periods*. Vol. 18.4 of *Corinth: Results of Excavations Conducted by the American School of Classical Studies at Athens*. Princeton: American School of Classical Studies at Athens.
Mettinger, Tryggve N. D. 1995. *No Graven Image? Israelite Aniconism in Its Ancient Near Eastern Context*. CBOTS 42. Stockholm: Almqvist & Wiksell.
———. 1997. "Israelite Aniconism: Developments and Origins." Pages 173–204 in *The Image and the Book: Iconic Cults, Aniconism, and the Rise of Book Re-*

ligion in Israel and the Ancient Near East. Edited by Karel van der Toorn. Leuven: Peters.

———. 2001. *The Riddle of Resurrection: "Dying and Rising Gods" in the Ancient Near East*. Stockholm: Almqvist & Wiksell.

———. 2004. "The Absence of Images: The Problem of the Aniconic Cult at Gades and Its Religio-Historical Background." *SEL* 21:89–100.

———. 2006. "A Conversation with My Critics: Cultic Image or Aniconism in the First Temple?" Pages 273–96 in *Essays on Ancient Israel in Its Near Eastern Context: A Tribute to Nadav Na'aman*. Edited by Yairah Amit, Ehud Ben Zvi, Israel Finkelstein, and Oded Lipschits. Winona Lake, IN: Eisenbrauns.

Metzger, Martin. 1985. "Der Thron als Manifestation der Herrschermacht in der Ikonographie des vorderen Orients und im Alten Testament." Pages 250–96 in *Charisma und Institution*. Edited by Trutz Rendtorff. Gütersloh: Gütersloher Verlagshaus.

———. 2004. "Two Architectural Models in Terracotta." Pages 420–36 in *The Phoenician Cemetery of Tyre-Al Bass: Excavations, 1997–1999*. Edited by María Eugenia Aubet. BAALHS 1. Beirut: Ministère de la Culture, Direction générale des antiquités.

Metzler, Dieter. 1985–1986. "Anikonische Darstellungen." Pages 96–113 in *Approaches to Iconology*. Vols. 4–5 of *Visible Religion: Annual for Religious Iconography*. Leiden: Brill.

Michel, Patrick. 2014. *Le Culte des Pierres à Emar à l'époque Hittite*. OBO 266. Fribourg: Academic Press; Göttingen: Vandenhoeck & Ruprecht.

———. 2015. "Worshipping Gods and Stones in Late Bronze Age Syria and Anatolia." Pages 53–66 in *Mesopotamia in the Ancient World: Impact, Communities, Parallels; Proceedings of the Seventh Symposium of the Melammu Project Held in Obergurgl, Austria, November 4–8, 2013*. Edited by Robert Rollinger and Erik van Dongen. MS 7. Münster: Ugarit-Verlag.

Middlemas, Jill. 2013. "Divine Presence in Absence: Multiple Imaging as Literary Aniconism in the Prophets." Pages 183–211 in *Divine Presence and Absence in Exilic and Post-Exilic Judaism: Studies of the Sofja Kovalevskaja Research Group on Early Jewish Monotheism*. Vol. 2. Edited by Nathan MacDonald and Izaak J. de Hulster. Tübingen: Mohr Siebeck.

Miller, J. Maxwell, and John H. Hayes. 2006. *A History of Ancient Israel and Judah*. 2nd ed. Louisville: Westminster John Knox.

Miller, Patrick D., Jr., Paul D. Hanson, and S. Dean McBride, eds. 1987. *Ancient Israelite Religion: Essays in Honor of Frank Moore Cross*. Philadelphia: Fortress.

Mitchell, W. J. T. 1986. *Iconology: Image, Text, Ideology*. Chicago: University of Chicago Press.

McKenzie, Judith S., et al. 2013. *Architecture and Religion*. Vol. 1 of *The Nabataean Temple at Khirbet et-Tannur, Jordan; Final Report on Nelson Glueck's 1937 Excavation*. AASOR 67. Boston: ASOR.

Moscati, Sabatino. 1968. *The World of the Phoenicians*. Translated by Alastair Hamilton. London: Weidenfeld & Nicolson.

———. 1969. "Iconismo e aniconismo nelle più antiche stele puniche." *OA* 8:59–67.

———. 1970. *Le Stele Puniche di Nora: Nel Museo Nazionale di Cagliari; With a catalogue by M. L. Uberti*. SS 35. Rome: Consiglio Nazionale delle Ricerche.

———, ed. 1988a. *The Phoenicians: Under the Scientific Direction of Sabatino Moscati*. New York: Abbeville.

———. 1988b. "Arts and Crafts." Pages 244–47 in *The Phoenicians: Under the Scientific Direction of Sabatino Moscati*. Edited by Sabatino Moscati. New York: Abbeville.

———. 1988c. "Statuary." Pages 284–91 in *The Phoenicians: Under the Scientific Direction of Sabatino Moscati*. Edited by Sabatino Moscati. New York: Abbeville.

———. 1988d. "Stelae." Pages 304–27 in *The Phoenicians: Under the Scientific Direction of Sabatino Moscati*. Edited by Sabatino Moscati. New York: Abbeville.

———. 1988e. "Stone Reliefs." Pages 300–303 in *The Phoenicians: Under the Scientific Direction of Sabatino Moscati*. Edited by Sabatino Moscati. New York: Abbeville.

Mylonopoulos, Joannis, ed. 2010. *Divine Images and Human Imaginations in Ancient Greece and Rome*. Leiden: Brill.

Na'aman, Nadav. 1994. "The Canaanites: A Rejoinder." *UF* 26:397–418.

———. 1999. "Four Notes on the Size of Late Bronze Age Canaan." *BASOR* 313:31–37.

Nam, Roger. 2012. *Portrayals of Economic Exchange in the Book of Kings*. BIS 112. Leiden: Brill.

Naster, Paul. 1986. "AMBROSIAI PETRAI: Dans les textes et sur les Monnaies de Tyr." *SP IV* 361–71.

Natif, M. 2011. "The Painter's Breath and Concepts of Idol Anxiety in Islamic Art." Pages 41–55 in *Idol Anxiety*. Edited by Josh Ellenbogen and Aaron Tugendhaft. Stanford: Stanford University Press.

Negbi, Ora. 1976. *Canaanite Gods in Metal: An Archaeological Study of Ancient Syro-Palestinian Figurines*. Tel Aviv: Tel Aviv University Institute of Archaeology.

Niehr, Herbert. 2008. "Baal Hammon." *IDD* 1–3.

———. 2014. "Körper des Königs und Körper der Götter in Ugarit." Pages 141–70 in *Göttliche Körper—Göttliche Gefühle: Was leisten anthropomorphe und anthropopathische Götterkonzepte im Alten Orient und im Alten Testament?* Edited by Andreas Wagner. OBO 270. Fribourg: Academic Press; Göttingen: Vandenhoeck & Ruprecht.

Novak, Barbara, and Brian O'Doherty. 1998. "Rothko's Dark Paintings: Tragedy and Void." Pages 264–81 in *Mark Rothko*. Edited by Jeffrey Weiss. New Haven: Yale University Press.

Núñez Calvo, Francisco Jesús. 2008. "Phoenicia." Pages 19–95 in *Beyond the Homeland: Markers in Phoenician Chronology*. Edited by Claudia Sagona. ANESS 28. Leuven: Peeters.

Nunn, Astrid. 2008. "Die Phönizier und ihre südlichen Nachbarn in der achämenidischen und frühhellenistischen Zeit: Ein Bildervergleich." Pages 95–123 in *Israeliten und Phönizier: ihre Beziehungen im Spiegel der Archäologie und der Literatur des Alten Testaments und seiner Umwelt*. Edited by Markus Witte and Johannes Friedrich Diehl. OBO 235. Fribourg: Academic Press; Göttingen: Vandenhoeck & Ruprecht.

———. 2010. "Bildhaftigkeit und Bildlosigkeit im Alten Orient: Ein Widerspruch?" Pages 131–68 in *Von Göttern und Menschen: Beiträge zu Literatur und Geschichte des Alten Orients. Festschrift für Brigitte Groneberg*. Edited by Dahlia Shehata, Frauke Weiershäuser, and Kamran Vincent Zand. Leiden: Brill.

———. 2014. "Mesopotamische Götter und ihr Körper in den Bildern." Pages 51–66 in *Göttliche Körper—Göttliche Gefühle: Was leisten anthropomorphe und anthropopathische Götterkonzepte im Alten Orient und im Alten Testament?* Edited by Andreas Wagner. OBO 270. Fribourg: Academic Press; Göttingen: Vandenhoeck & Ruprecht.

Oden, Robert A. 1977. *Studies in Lucian's De Syria Dea*. HSM 15. Missoula, MT: Scholars Press.

Oggiano, Ida. 2005. *Dal terreno al divino: Archeologia del culto nella Palestina del primo millennio*. Rome: Carroci.

Onnis, Francesca. 2014. "The Influence of the Physical Medium on the Decoration of a Work of Art: A Case Study of the 'Phoenician' Bowls." Pages 159–84 in *Critical Approaches to Ancient Near Eastern Art*. Edited by Brian A. Brown and Marian H. Feldman. Berlin: de Gruyter.

Oppenheim, A. Leo. 1977. *Ancient Mesopotamia: Portrait of a Dead Civilization*. Rev. ed. Chicago: University of Chicago Press.

Ornan, Tallay. 1993. "The Mesopotamian Influence on West Semitic Inscribed Seals: A Preference for the Depiction of Mortals." Pages 52–73 in *Studies in the Iconography of Northwest Semitic Inscribed Seals: Proceedings of a Symposium Held in Fribourg on April 17–20, 1991*. Edited by Benjamin Sass and Christoph Uehlinger. OBO 125. Fribourg: Academic Press; Göttingen: Vandenhoeck & Ruprecht.

———. 2004. "Idols and Symbols: Divine Representation in First Millennium Mesopotamian Art and its Bearing on the Second Commandment." *TA* 31:90–121.

———. 2005a. "A Complex System of Religious Symbols: The Case of the Winged Disc in Near Eastern Imagery of the First Millennium BCE." Pages 207–41 in *Crafts and Images in Conflict: Studies on Eastern Mediterranean Art of the First Millennium BC*. Edited by Claudia E. Suter and Christoph

Uehlinger. Fribourg: Academic Press; Göttingen: Vandenhoeck & Ruprecht.

———. 2005b. *The Triumph of the Symbol: Pictorial Representation of Deities in Mesopotamia and the Biblical Image Ban*. OBO 213. Fribourg: Academic Press; Göttingen: Vandenhoeck & Ruprecht.

———. 2014. "A Silent Message: Godlike Kings in Mesopotamian Art." Pages 569–95 in *Critical Approaches to Ancient Near Eastern Art*. Edited by Brian A. Brown and Marian H. Feldman. Berlin: de Gruyter.

Pappa, Eleftheria. 2013. *Early Iron Age Exchange in the West: Phoenicians in the Mediterranean and the Atlantic*. ANESS 43. Leuven: Peeters.

Pardee, Dennis. 2002. *Ritual and Cult at Ugarit*. WAW 10. Atlanta: Society of Biblical Literature.

———. 2009. "A New Aramaic Inscription from Zincirli." *BASOR* 356:51–71.

Patrich, Joseph. 1990. *The Formation of Nabataean Art: Prohibition of a Graven Image among the Nabateans*. Jerusalem: Magnes.

Peckham, Brian. 1987. "Phoenicia and the Religion of Israel: The Epigraphic Evidence." Pages 79–99 in *Ancient Israelite Religion: Essays in Honor of Frank Moore Cross*. Edited by Patrick D. Miller Jr., Paul D. Hanson, and S. Dean McBride. Philadelphia: Fortress.

———. 2014. *Phoenicia: Episodes and Anecdotes from the Ancient Mediterranean*. Winona Lake, IN: Eisenbrauns.

Perrot, Georges, and Charles Chipiez. 1885. *History of Art in Phoenicia and its Dependencies*. 2 vols. Translated by Walter Armstrong. London: Chapman & Hall.

Picard, Colette. 1975. "Les Représentations de Sacrifice Molk sur les ex-Voto de Carthage." *Karth* 17:67–138.

———. 1978. "Les Représentations de Sacrifice Molk sur les Stèles de Carthage." *Karth* 17:5–116.

Pitard, Wayne. 1988. "The Identity of the Bir Hadad of the Melqart Stela." *BASOR* 272:3–21.

Popko, Maciej. 1993. "Anikonische Götterdarstellungen in der Altanatolischen Religion." Pages 319–27 in *Ritual and Sacrifice in the Ancient Near East: Proceedings of the International Conference Organized by the Katholieke Universiteit Leuven from the 17th to the 20th of April 1991*. Edited by Jan Quaegebeur. OLA 55. Leuven: Peeters.

Porter, Anne. 2014. "When the Subject *Is* the Object: Relational Ontologies, the Partible Person and Images of Naram-Sin." Pages 597–617 in *Critical Approaches to Ancient Near Eastern Art*. Edited by Brian A. Brown and Marian H. Feldman. Berlin: de Gruyter.

Prag, Jonathan R. W. 2014. "*Phoinix* and *Poenus*: Usage in Antiquity." Pages 11–23 in *The Punic Mediterranean: Identities and Identification from Phoenician Settlement to Roman Rule*. Edited by Josephine Crawley Quinn and Nicholas C. Vella. BSRS. Cambridge: Cambridge University Press.

Pregill, Michael. 2009. "Aniconism; III. Islam." *EBR* 1:1219–24.
Pritchard, James B. 1978. *Recovering Sarepta, A Phoenician City: Excavations at Sarafand, Lebanon, 1969–1974, by the University Museum of the University of Pennsylvania.* Princeton: Princeton University Press.
———. 1988. *The Objects from Area II, X. The University Museum of the University of Pennsylvania Excavations at Sarafand, Lebanon.* Vol. 4 of *Sarepta.* PULSEA 2. Beirut: L'Université Libanaise.
Provan, Iain, V. Philips Long, and Tremper Longman III. 2003. *A Biblical History of Israel.* Louisville: Westminster John Knox.
Quinn, Josephine Crawley. 2011. "The Cultures of the Tophet: Identification and Identity in the Phoenician Diaspora." Pages 388–413 in *Cultural Identity in the Ancient Mediterranean.* Edited by Erich Gruen. Los Angeles: Getty Research Institute.
———. 2013. "Tophets in the 'Punic World.'" *SEL* 29–30:23–48.
Quinn, Josephine Crawley, and Nicholas C. Vella, eds. 2014. *The Punic Mediterranean: Identities and Identification from Phoenician Settlement to Roman Rule.* BSRS. Cambridge: Cambridge University Press.
Rawlinson, George. 1889. *The Story of the Nations.* Vol. 18 of *Phœnicia.* 2nd ed. London: Fischer Unwin; New York: Putnam's Sons.
Redford, Donald B. 1984. *Akhenaten, the Heretic King.* Princeton: Princeton University Press.
———. 2013. "Akhenaten: New Theories and Old Facts." *BASOR* 369:9–34.
Reinhold, Gotthard G. G. 1986. "The Bir-Hadad Stele and the Biblical Kings of Aram." *AUSS* 24:115–26.
Reyes, A. T. 1994. *Archaic Cyprus: A Study of the Textual and Archaeological Evidence.* Oxford: Oxford University Press.
———. 2007. "The Iconography of Deities and Demons in Cyprus." *IDD* 1–19.
Ribichini, Sergio. 1988. "Beliefs and Religious Life." Pages 104–25 in *The Phoenicians: Under the Scientific Direction of Sabatino Moscati.* Edited by Sabatino Moscati. New York: Abbeville.
———. 1990. "Qualche osservazione sull'antropomorfismo delle divinità fenicie e puniche." *Semitica* 39:127–33.
———. 1995. "Melqart." *DDD* 1053–58.
Rich, Sara A. 2012. "'She Who Treads on Water': Religious Metaphor in Seafaring Phoenicia." *AWE* 11:19–34.
Robins, Gay. 2005. "Cult Statues in Ancient Egypt." *CIDRANE* 1–12.
Röllig, Wolfgang. 1995a. "L'Alphabet." Pages 193–214 in *La civilisation phénicienne et punique: Manuel de recherche.* Edited by Véronique Krings. HO 1/20. Leiden: Brill.
———. 1995b. "Phoenician and the Phoenicians in the Context of the Ancient Near East." Pages 203–14 in *I Fenici: Ieri Oggi Domani: Ricerche, scoperte, progetti (Roma 3–5 marzo 1994).* Rome: Gruppo editoriale internazionale.

Rollston, Christopher A. 2008. "The Dating of the Early Royal Byblian Inscriptions: A Response to Benjamin Sass." *Maarav* 15:57-93.
———. 2010. *Writing and Literacy in the World of Ancient Israel: Epigraphic Evidence from the Iron Age*. SBLABS 11. Atlanta: Society of Biblical Literature.
———. 2014. "The Iron Age Phoenician Script." Pages 74-108 in *"An Eye for Form": Epigraphic Essays in Honor of Frank Moore Cross*. Edited by Jo Ann Hackett and Walter E. Aufrecht. Winona Lake, IN: Eisenbrauns.
Roth, Ann Macy. 2006. "The Representation of the Divine in Ancient Egypt." Pages 24-37 in *Text, Artifact, and Image: Revealing Ancient Israelite Religion*. Edited by Gary M. Beckman and Theodore J. Lewis. BJS 346. Providence: Brown Judaic Studies.
Sader, Hélène. 1991. "Phoenician Stelae from Tyre." *Berytus* 39:101-26.
———. 1992. "Phoenician Stelae from Tyre." *SEL* 9:53-79.
———. 2004. "VIII. The Stelae." Pages 383-94 in *The Phoenician Cemetery of Tyre-Al Bass: Excavations, 1997-1999*. Edited by María Eugenia Aubet. BAAL-HS 1. Beirut: Ministère de la Culture, Direction générale des antiquités.
———. 2005. *Iron Age Funerary Stelae from Lebanon*. CAM 11. Barcelona: Laboratorio de Arquelogia, Universidad Pompeu Fabra de Barcelona.
———. 2013. "The Northern Levant during the Iron Age I Period." Pages 607-23 in *The Oxford Handbook of the Archaeology of the Levant: C. 8000-332 BCE*. Edited by Margaret L. Steiner and Ann E. Killebrew. Oxford: Oxford University Press.
Sagona, Claudia., ed. 2008. *Beyond the Homeland: Markers in Phoenician Chronology*. ANESS 28. Leuven: Peeters.
Saidah, Roger. 1969. "Archaeology in the Lebanon, 1968-1969." *Berytus* 18:119-42.
San Nicolas, María Pilar. 2000. "Interpretación de los santuarios fenicios y púnicos de Ibiza." Pages 675-90 in *Actas del IV Congreso Internacional de Estudios Fenicios y Púnicos, Cádiz, 2-6 Octubre 1995, 675-90*. Edited by María Eeugenia Aubet and Manuela Barthélemy. Cádiz: Servicio de publicaciones de la Universidad de Cádiz.
Sanders, Seth L. 2013. "The Appetites of the Dead: West Semitic Linguistic and Ritual Aspects of the Katumuwa Stele." *BASOR* 369:85-105.
Sanmartí, Joan. 2009. "Colonial Relations and Social Change in Iberia (Seventh to Third Centuries BC)." Pages 49-88 in *Colonial Encounters in Ancient Iberia: Phoenician, Greek, and Indigenous Relations*. Edited by Michael Dietler and Carolina López-Ruiz. Chicago: University of Chicago Press.
Sass, Benjamin. 1993. "The Pre-Exilic Hebrew Seals: Iconism vs. Aniconism." Pages 194-256 in *Studies in the Iconography of Northwest Semitic Inscribed Seals: Proceedings of a Symposium Held in Fribourg on April 17-20, 1991*. Edited by Benjamin Sass and Christoph Uehlinger. OBO 125. Fribourg: Academic Press; Göttingen: Vandenhoeck & Ruprecht.

Sass, Benjamin, and Christoph Uehlinger, eds. 1993. *Studies in the Iconography of Northwest Semitic Inscribed Seals: Proceedings of a Symposium Held in Fribourg on April 17–20, 1991*. OBO 125. Fribourg: Academic Press; Göttingen: Vandenhoeck & Ruprecht.
Saur, Markus. 2010. "Ezekiel 26–28 and the History of Tyre." *SJOT* 24:208–21.
Schmidt, Brian B. 1995. "The Aniconic Tradition: On Reading Images and Viewing Texts." Pages 75–106 in *The Triumph of Elohim: From Yahwisms to Judaisms*. Edited by Diana V. Edelman. Leuven: Peeters.
———. 1996. *Israel's Beneficent Dead: Ancestor Cult and Necromancy in Ancient Israelite Religion and Tradition*. Winona Lake, IN: Eisenbrauns.
———. 2002. "The Iron Age Pithoi Drawings from Horvat Temon or Kuntillet 'Ajrud: Some New Proposals." *JNES* 2:91–125.
Schniedewind, William M. 2013. *A Social History of Hebrew: Its Origins through the Rabbinic Period*. Oxford: Oxford University Press.
Schreiber, Nicola. 2003. *The Cypro-Phoenician Pottery of the Iron Age*. CHANE 13. Leiden: Brill.
Schwartz, J. H., F. D. Houghton, L. Bondioli, and R. Macchiarelli. 2012. "Bones, Teeth, and Estimating Age of Perinates: Carthaginian Infant Sacrifice Revisited." *Antiquity* 86:738–45.
Segert, Stanislav. 1976. *A Grammar of Phoenician and Punic*. Munich: Beck.
Seidl, Ursula. 1989. *Die Babylonischen Kudurru-Reliefs: Symbole Mesopotamischer Gottheiten*. OBO 87. Fribourg: Academic Press; Göttingen: Vandenhoeck & Ruprecht.
Seyrig, Henri. 1959. "Antiquités syriennes." *Syria* 36:38–89.
Shea, William H. 1979. "The Kings of the Melqart Stele." *Maarav* 1:159–76.
Shenkar, Michael. 2008. "Aniconism in the Religious Art of Pre-Islamic Iran and Central Asia." *BAI* 22:239–56.
Sheriff, John K. 1989. *The Fate of Meaning: Charles Peirce, Structuralism, and Literature*. Princeton: Princeton University Press.
Skinner, Joseph E. 2012. *The Invention of Greek Ethnography: From Homer to Herodotus*. Oxford: Oxford University Press.
Slanski, Kathryn E. 2003. *The Babylonian Entitlement narûs (kudurrus): A Study in Form and Function*. Boston: ASOR.
Smith, Joanna S. 2008. "Cyprus, the Phoenicians and Kition." Pages 261–303 in *Beyond the Homeland: Markers in Phoenician Chronology*. Edited by Claudia Sagona. ANESS 28. Leuven: Peeters.
Smith, Jonathan Z. 1990. *Drudgery Divine: On the Comparison of Early Christianities and the Religions of Late Antiquity*. Chicago: University of Chicago Press.
———. 1995. "Aniconic." Page 51 in *The HarperCollins Dictionary of Religion*. Edited by Jonathan Z. Smith et al. San Francisco: HarperSanFrancisco.
———. 2004. "Trading Places." Pages 215–29 in *Relating Religion: Essays in the Study of Religion*. Chicago: University of Chicago Press.

Smith, Mark S. 1998. "The Death of 'Dying and Rising Gods' in the Biblical World: An Update, with Special Reference to Baal in the Baal Cycle." *SJOT* 12:257–313.

———. 2001. *The Origins of Biblical Monotheism: Israel's Polytheistic Background and the Ugaritic Texts*. Oxford: Oxford University Press.

———. 2014. "Ugaritic Anthropomorphism, Theomorphism, Theriomorphism." Pages 117–40 in *Göttliche Körper—Göttliche Gefühle: Was leisten anthropomorphe und anthropopathische Götterkonzepte im Alten Orient und im Alten Testament?* Edited by Andreas Wagner. OBO 270. Fribourg: Academic Press; Göttingen: Vandenhoeck & Ruprecht.

Smith, Patricia, Gal Avishai, Joseph A. Greene, and Lawrence E. Stager. 2011. "Aging Cremated Infants: The Problem of Sacrifice at the Tophet of Carthage." *Antiquity* 85:859–74.

———. 2013. "Age Estimations Attest to Infant Sacrifice at the Carthage Tophet." *Antiquity* 87:1191–98.

Smith, William Robertson. 1894. *Lectures on the Religion of the Semites: First Series, The Fundamental Institutions*. 2nd ed. London: Black. Unabridged facsimile by Elibron Classics series, 2005.

Sommer, Benjamin D. 2009. *The Bodies of God and the World of Ancient Israel*. Cambridge: Cambridge University Press.

Sommer, Michael. 2008. "The Challenge of Aniconism: Elagabalus and Roman Historiography." *MA* 11: 581–90.

Soyez, Brigitte. 1972. "Le betyle dans le culte de l'Astarté phénicienne." *MUSJ* 47:149–69.

Stager, Lawrence E. 1980. "The Rite of Child Sacrifice at Carthage." Pages 1–11 in *New Light on Ancient Carthage*. Edited by John Griffiths Pedley. Ann Arbor: University of Michigan Press.

———. 1982. "Carthage: A View from the Tophet." Pags 155–66 in *Phönizier im Westen: die Beiträge des internationalen Symposium über "Die phönizische Expansion im westlichen Mittelmeerraum" in Köln vom 24 bis 27 April 1979*. Edited by Hans-George Niemeyer. MB 88. Mainz: von Zabern.

———. 2006. "The House of the Silver Calf of Ashkelon." Pages 403–10 *Timelines: Studies in Honour of Manfred Bietak*. Vol. 2. Edited by Ernst Czerny et al. Leuven: Peeters.

———. 2014. "Rites of Spring in the Carthaginian Tophet: The Eighth BABESCH Byvanck Lecture." Leiden: The BABESCH Foundation.

Stager, Lawrence E., and Samuel R. Wolf. 1984. "Child Sacrifice at Carthage: Religious Rite or Population Control?" *BAR* 10:30–51.

Stavrakopoulou, Francesca. 2004. *King Manasseh and Child Sacrifice: Biblical Distortions of Historical Realities*. BZAW 338. Berlin: de Gruyter.

Steel, Louise. 2013. "The Social World of Early–Middle Bronze Age Cyprus: Rethinking the Vounous Bowl." *JMA* 26:51–73.

Steele, Philippa M. 2013. *A Linguistic History of Ancient Cyprus: The Non-Greek*

Languages, and Their Relations with Greek, c. 1600–300 BC. Cambridge: Cambridge University Press.

Steiner, Margaret L., and Anne E. Killebrew, eds. 2013. *The Oxford Handbook of the Archaeology of the Levant: C. 8000–332 BCE.* Oxford: Oxford University Press.

Stern, Ephraim. 2006. "Goddesses and Cults at Tel Dor." Pages 177–80 in *Confronting the Past: Archaeological and Historical Essays on Ancient Israel in Honor of William G. Dever*. Edited by Seymour Gitin, J. Edward Wright, and J. P. Dessel. Winona Lake, IN: Eisenbrauns.

Stewart, Peter. 2008. "Baetyls as Statues? Cult Images in the Roman Near East." Pages 297–314 in *The Sculptural Environment of the Roman Near East: Reflections on Culture, Ideology, and Power*. Edited by Yaron Z. Eliav, Elise A. Frieland, and Sharon Herbert. ISACR 9. Leuven: Peeters.

Stewart, Susan. 1984. *On Longing, Narratives of the Miniature, the Gigantic, the Souvenir, the Collection*. Baltimore: Johns Hopkins University Press.

Stieglitz, Robert R. 1990. "The Geopolitics of the Phoenician Littoral in the Early Iron Age." *BASOR* 279:9–12.

Stockton, Eugene. 1974–1975. "Phoenician Cult Stones." *AJBA* 2.2:1–27.

Struble, Eudora J., and Virginia Rimmer Herrmann. 2009. "An Eternal Feast at Sam'al: The New Iron Age Mortuary Stele from Zincirli in Context." *BASOR* 356:15–49.

Stucky, Rolf A. 1993. *Die Skulpturen aus dem Eschmun-Heiligtum bei Sidon: Griechische, Römische, Kyprische und Phönizische Statuen und Reliefs vom 6. Jahrhundert vor Chr. bis zum 3. Jahrhundert n. Chr.* AK 17. Basel: Vereinigung der Freunde Antiker Kunst.

Suriano, Matthew J. 2014. "Breaking Bread with the Dead: Katumuwa's Stele, Hosea 9:4, and the Early History of the Soul." *JAOS* 134:385–405.

Suter, Claudia E. 2010. "Luxury Goods in Ancient Israel: Questions of Consumption and Production." Pages 993–1002 in *6 ICAANE: Proceedings of the 6th International Congress of the Archaeology of the Ancient Near East; 5 May–10 May 2009, "Sapienza," Universita Di Roma*. Vol. 1. Edited by Paolo Matthiae and Licia Romano. Wiesbaden: Harrassowitz.

———. 2014. "Human, Divine, or Both? The Uruk Vase and the Problem of Ambiguity in Early Mesopotamian Visual Arts." Pages 545–68 in *Critical Approaches to Ancient Near Eastern Art*. Edited by Brian A. Brown and Marian H. Feldman. Berlin: de Gruyter.

Swearer, Donald K. 2003. "Aniconism versus Iconism in Thai Buddhism." Pages 9–25 in *Buddhism in the Modern World: Adaptions of an Ancient Tradition*. Edited by Steven Heine and Charles S. Prebish. Oxford: Oxford University Press.

Taylor, J. Glen. 1993. *Yahweh and the Sun: Evidence for Sun Worship in Ancient Israel*. JSOTSup 111. Sheffield: JSOT Press.

Treumann, Brigitte. 2009. "Lumbermen and Shipwrights: Phoenicians on the

Mediterranean Coast of Southern Spain." Pages 169–90 in *Colonial Encounters in Ancient Iberia: Phoenician, Greek, and Indigenous Relations*. Edited by Michael Dietler and Carolina López-Ruiz. Chicago: University of Chicago Press.

Turcan, Robert. 1985. *Héliogabale et le Sacre du Soleil*. Paris: Michel.

Turner, Victor, and Edith Turner. 1978. *Image and Pilgrimage in Christian Culture: Anthropological Perspectives*. Oxford: Blackwell.

Tylor, Edward B. 1871. *Primitive Culture: Researches into the Development of Mythology, Philosophy, Religion, Art, and Custom*. Vol. 1. London: Murray.

———. 1920. *Primitive Culture: Researches into the Development of Mythology, Philosophy, Religion, Art, and Custom*. Vol. 2. London: Murray; New York: Putnam's Sons.

Uberti, Maria Luisa. 1988. "Ivory and Bone Carving." Pages 404–21 in *The Phoenicians: Under the Scientific Direction of Sabatino Moscati*. Edited by Sabatino Moscati. New York: Abbeville.

———. 1992. "Stèles." *DCPP* 422–27.

Uehlinger, Christoph. 1996. "Israelite Aniconism in Context." *Biblica* 77:540–49.

———, ed. 2000. *Images as Media: Sources for the Cultural History of the Near East and the Eastern Mediterranean (First Millennium BCE)*. OBO 175. Fribourg: Academic Press; Göttingen: Vandenhoeck & Ruprecht.

———. 2006. "Arad, Qiṭmīt: Judahite Aniconism vs. Edomite Iconic Cult? Questioning the Evidence." Pages 80–112 in *Text, Artifact, and Image: Revealing Ancient Israelite Religion*. Edited by Gary M. Beckman and Theodore J. Lewis. BJS 346. Providence: Brown Judaic Studies.

Vance, Donald R. 1994. "Literary Sources for the History of Palestine and Syria: The Phoenician Inscriptions." *BA* 57:2–19.

van der Toorn, Karel, ed. 1997a. *The Image and the Book: Iconic Cults, Aniconism, and the Rise of Book Religion in Israel and the Ancient Near East*. Leuven: Peters.

———. 1997b. "The Iconic Book: Analogies between the Babylonian Cult of Images and the Veneration of the Torah." Pages 229–48 in *The Image and the Book: Iconic Cults, Aniconism, and the Rise of Book Religion in Israel and the Ancient Near East*. Edited by Karel van der Toorn. Leuven: Peters.

Van Seters, John. 1997. *In Search of History: Historiography in the Ancient World and the Origins of Biblical History*. New Haven: Yale University Press. Reprint, Winona Lake, IN: Eisenbrauns.

Veh, Otto, and Gerhard Wirth, eds. and trans. 2005. *Diodoros: Griechische Weltgeschichte; Buch XVIII–XX*. Introduction and commentary by Michael Rathmann. Stuttgart: Hiersemann.

Vella, Nicholas C. 2014. "The Invention of the Phoenicians: On Object Definition, Decontextualization and Display." Pages 24–41 in *The Punic Mediterranean: Identities and Identification from Phoenician Settlement to Roman*

> *Rule.* Edited by Josephine Crawley Quinn and Nicholas C. Vella. BSRS. Cambridge: Cambridge University Press.

Vernant, Jean-Pierre. 1990. *Mythe et religion et Grèce ancienne.* Paris: Seuil.

Wathelet, Paul. 1983. "Les Phéniciens et la Tradition Homerique." Pages 235–43 in *Redt Tyrus/Sauvons Tyr: Histoire phénicienne/Fenicische Geschiedenis.* Edited by Éric Gubel, Edward Lipiński, and Brigitte Servais-Soyez. SP 1. OLA 25. Leuven: Peeters.

Wagner, Andreas, ed. 2014. *Göttliche Körper—Göttliche Gefühle: Was leisten anthropomorphe und anthropopathische Götterkonzepte im Alten Orient und im Alten Testament?* OBO 270. Fribourg: Academic Press; Göttingen: Vandenhoeck & Ruprecht.

Walker, Christopher, and Michael B. Dick. 1999. "The Induction of the Cult Image in Ancient Mesopotamia: The Mesopotamian *mīs pî* Ritual." Pages 55–122 in *Born in Heaven, Made on Earth: The Making of the Cult Image in the Ancient Near East.* Edited by Michael B. Dick. Winona Lake, IN: Eisenbrauns.

Waterfield, Robin, trans. 2008. *Herodotus: The Histories.* With an introduction and notes by Carolyn Dewald. Oxford World's Classics. Oxford: Oxford University Press.

Welten, Ruud, and Johan Goud. 2009. "Aniconism as Quest for Aesthetic Lucidity: The Example of Emmanuel Levinas." Pages 79–97 in *Visual Arts and Religion.* Edited by Hans Alma, Marcel Barnard, and Volker Küster. Berlin: LIT.

White, Nicholas P., trans. 1997. *Plato: Sophist.* Pages 235–93 in *Plato: Complete Works.* Edited by Jonathan M. Cooper. Indianapolis: Hackett.

Whittaker, C. R., trans. 1969. *Herodian: History of the Empire; Volume I, Books 1–4.* LCL 454. Cambridge: Harvard University Press.

Wiggermann, F. A. M. 1995. "Theologies, Priests, and Worship in Ancient Mesopotamia." *CANE* 3:1857–70.

Winter, Irene J. 1982. "Art as Evidence for Interaction: Relations between the Neo-Assyrian Empire and North Syria as Seen from the Monuments." Pages 355–82 in *Mesopotamien und seine Nachbarn; XXVe Rencontre Assyriologique Internationale (Berlin, 2–7 July 1978).* Edited by H.-J. Nissen and J. Renger. Berlin: Reimer.

———. 1995. "Homer's Phoenicians: History, Ethnography or Literary Trope? (A Perspective on Early Orientalism)." Pages 247–71 in *The Ages of Homer: A Tribute to Emily Townsend Vermeule.* Edited by Jane B. Carter and Sarah P. Morris. Austin: University of Texas Press.

———. 2005. "Establishing Group Boundaries: Toward Methodological Refinement in the Determination of Sets as a Prior Condition to the Analysis of Cultural Contact and/or Innovation in First Millennium BCE Ivory Carving." Pages 24–42 in *Crafts and Images in Conflict: Studies on Eastern*

Mediterranean Art of the First Millennium BC. Edited by Claudia E. Suter and Christoph Uehlinger. Fribourg: Academic Press; Göttingen: Vandenhoeck & Ruprecht, 2005.

———. 2010a. "'Idols of the King': Royal Images as Recipients of Ritual Action in Ancient Mesopotamia." *OAANE* 2:167–95. First published in *JRtSt* 6 (1992): 13–42.

———. 2010b. "Is There a South Syrian Style of Ivory Carving in the Early First Millennium B.C.?" *OAANE* 1:225–333. First published in *Iraq* 43 (1981): 101–30.

———. 2010c. "Phoenician and North Syrian Ivory Carving in Historical Perspective: Questions of Style and Distribution." *OAANE* 1:187–224. First published in *Iraq* 28 (1976): 1–22.

Woods, Christopher E. 2004. "The Sun-God Tablet of Nabû-Apla-Iddina Revisited." *JCS* 56:23–103.

Woodward, Roger D. 1997. *Greek Writing from Knossos to Homer: A Linguistic Interpretation of the Origin of the Greek Alphabet and the Continuity of Ancient Greek Literacy*. Oxford: Oxford University Press.

Wunn, Ina. 2014. "Die Entstehung der Götter." Pages 31–50 in *Göttliche Körper— Göttliche Gefühle: Was leisten anthropomorphe und anthropopathische Götterkonzepte im Alten Orient und im Alten Testament?* Edited by Andreas Wagner. OBO 270. Fribourg: Academic Press; Göttingen: Vandenhoeck & Ruprecht.

Xella, Paolo. 1993. "Eschmun von Sidon: Der phönizische Askelpios." Pages 481–98 in *Mesoptamica—Ugaritica—Biblica*. Edited by Manfried Deitrich and Oswald Loretz. AOAT 232. Neukirchen-Vluyn: Neukirchener Verlag.

Xella, Paolo, Josephine Quinn, Valentina Mechiorri, and Peter van Dommelen. 2013. "Phoenician Bones of Contention." *Antiquity* 87:1199–1207.

Yasur-Landau, Assaf. 2015. "Fenestrated Axes between the Aegean and the Levant." *BASOR* 373:139–50.

Yon, Marguerite. 1991. "Stèles de pierre; Note sur la sculpture de pierre." Pages 273–353 in *Arts et Industries de la Pierre*. Edited by Marguerite Yon et al. RSO 6. Paris: Éditions Recherche sur les Civilisations.

Younger, K. Lawson. 2003. "The Azatiwada Inscription." *COS* 1:148–50.

Zevit, Ziony. 2001. *The Religions of Ancient Israel: A Synthesis of Parallactic Approaches*. London: Continuum.

Zobel, Hans-Jürgen. 1995. "*Kenaʿan; kenaʿanî*." *TDOT* 7:211–28.

Subject Index

Akhziv, 8, 96–97, 103–6, 108
Amathus (Cyprus), 12, 105–6
Anat(h), 17, 48, 57, 129
aniconism
  as primitive or advanced, 36–40
  definition of, 5, **27–36**
  Egyptian, 124–25. *See also* Egypt
  evolutionary theory of, 28, 37–38, 69–70, 82, 98, 101, 119, 141
  Greek, 132–34. *See also* Greece; Greeks
  Islamic, 1, 28, 33, 120, 135
  Israelite, 2–5, **125–32**. *See also* Israel
  Mesopotamian, 120–23
  Nabatean, 119–20,
  reasons for Phoenician, 134–39
ankh, 54, 63, 65–66, 86, 88, 89
anthropomorphism, 24, 28–29, 34, 39, **41–66**, 70–72, 77, 86, 95, 97 n. 23, 98–99, 101, 121, 135
Ambrosial Rocks, 68, 73–74, 86, 96
Arvad, 8, 14, 55
Assyria, Assyrians, 11, 14, 44, 46, 54, 76, 120–21, 136, 138–39
Astarte, 15, 17, 19, 45, 48, 51, 57, 61, 69, 75, 86, 105, 110, 112–15, 117–18, 129–30, 137, 139
astral symbolism, 11, 26, 31, 34, 43, 57, 63–64, 75–76, 78, 80–81, 86, 88, 101, 105, 111, 114–15, 119, 121–22, 124, 129, 130, 137. *See also* Sun
Baal deities, 15, 17–18, 36, 45, 47–48, 51, 55, 57, 59, 62–63, 64 n. 30, 69, 72, 92–93, 95, 101, 109, 115, 117, 126–27, 129, 137
Baal Hammon, 62–63, 64 n. 30, 72, 93, 95, 101, 109, 115, 117, 137
Baalat Gubal, 15, 17, 48, 57, 59
Bar Hadad Stele, **52–55**, 69, 72, 92–93, 95. *See also* Melqart
betyl, 28, 38, 48, 54, 70, **78–84**, 86, 88, 90, 92, 94–95, 97–99, 101, 103, 108, 112, 117, 119–20, 124, 142. *See also* Pillar; Stele
  definition of, 28, 79–81
bottle figure, 29–30, 89, 91–92, 95–96, **97–99**, 101, 105, 107
bowls, 10, 12, 41, 43–44, 52
Byblos, 4, 8, 14–15, 17, 52, 55, 57–58, 67, 70, 75, 138
Canaanites, 3, 8, 10, 13, 36, 48, 113, 132, 133
Carthage, 7–8, 13, 16–19, 29, 38, 47, 55, 59, 61, 63–64, 66–69, 71–72, 74, 86–91, 93, 95, 97, 99, 101, 107–9, 112–13, 115, 117, 135
child sacrifice, 17, 61 n. 28, 62–63, 71–72, 88, 97
Clement of Alexandria, 27–28
coins, 48, 50–51, 55, 57, 73–77, 80, 86, 101, 115, 117–19, 137, 142
Constantine (Algeria), 88 n. 18, 95
Cyprus, 12, 14, 16, 43–45, 47, 52, 54, 67, 75, 77, 93, 103, 105–7, 109
David (king), 10, 126–27
Dor, 8

175

Egypt, 11, 13, 14, 16, 18, 38, 41–44, 48, 54–55, 57, 63, 72, 74, 92, 119, **124–25**, 131
Elagabalus, 75
Emesa, 75
empty space, 21, 28, 30, 32, 34–35, 72, 101, 103, 105, 114–15, 128–30. See also Thrones; empty thrones
figural representation, 3, 28–30, 33–37, 39–40, 66, 69, 78, 84, 95, 98, 105, 107–8, 133–35
Gadir (Cádiz), 7, 17–19, 48, 52, 68, 72–75, 92, 138
Greece; Greeks, 5, 28, 31, 38, 59, 79 n. 10, **132–34**
Hadrumetum (Sousse), 63, 64, 95, 135
Hazor, 81–82
Herakles, 7, 17, 19, 51, 54–55, 74, 78, 93, 117. See also Melqart
Hiram, 10, 14, 17, 126–27
Hittites, 33, 45, 79 n. 10, 81 fig. 5.6, 82, 92
Ibiza, 48, 55, 59–61, 68
icon; iconism, **41–66**
idol; idolatry, 1–2, 22–24, 26–27, 32, 37, 69, 120, 131
images, 21–24
Israel, 2–5, 8, 10, 13, 21, 26–27, 32, 37–38, 48, 72, 79 n. 10, 83, 102, 119, **125–32**, 136, 138–39
Josephus, 17, 74, 126
Kulamuwa, 15, 116
Katumuwa, 83
Melqart, 7, 17–19, 44, 51, **52–55**, 57, 59, 68–69, 72–74, 79, **92–95**, 103, 113, 117, 139
Meteorites, 76, 114
Motya, 16, 29–30, 47, 86, 94–95, 97–98, 102, 112, 135
Nicosia (Cyprus), 105–6
Nora (Sardinia), 47, 70 n. 3, 86, 95, 97–98, 109
Overbeck, Johannes Adoph, 27–28

Paphos, Paphian Cone, 75–77
Persia, Persian period, 16, 18, 48, 50, 57, 92, 108, 117, 120, 139
Philo of Byblos, 14–15, 28, 73–74, 79 n. 11, 114, 117, 119, 137, 139
Phoenicia; Phoenicians
  art, style, 11, **41–46**
  etymology, 8, 10
  identity, **8–19**
  geographical boundaries, 8–10
  pottery, 11, 101, 126
Pillar, 33, 36–37, 48, 64, 70, 74, **78–84**, 95–97, 100–101, 106, 108–9, 112, 128. See also Stele; Betyl
pottery. See Phoenician; Phoenicians
Rothko, Mark, 39–40
Sardinia, 35, 47, 49, 55, 68, 70 n. 3, 95, 108
Sarepta, 8, 11, 47
Selinus, 47, 95
Shipitbaal, 15
shrines; stele-shrines, 29, 45, 47–49, 57, 59, 66–67, 70, 73, 81, 85, 90, 92, 95, 97–98, **101–9**, 111, 112, 120, 126, 128–31, 135, 137. See also Stele, Betyl.
  empty shrines, 70, **101–9**, 137. See also Thrones; empty thrones
Sidon, 4, 8, 10, 14–19, 47–48, 51, 60–61, 67, 69, 71–72, 84, 92, 108, 110–14, 117–18, 126, 135, 137–38
Solomon (king); Solomonic temple, 3, 10, 44, 126–29
sphinxes, 11–12, 43, 51, 55, 59 n. 26, 60, 62, 72, 86, 111–12, 117–18, 126, 130, 132, 142
stele, 47, 52–55, 57–59, 64–66, 68–70, 72, **79–97**, 98–101, 108, 112, 117, 128, 132, 134, 139. See also Betyl, Shrines; stele-shrines
stones; ovoid ritual objects, 28–29, 37–38, 70, 75–79, 80–82, 86, 88, 90, 92,

97–98, 100, 109, 112–15, 117–19, 133, 142
Sulcis (Sardinia), 47, 92, 95, 97 n. 23, 98, 108, 135
sun, 11, 26, 43, 57, 75–76, 78, 86, 88, 101, 105, 111, 115, 121–22, 124, 129–30, 137. *See also* Astral symbolism.
symbols; emblems (divine), 24, 26–27, 30, 32–34, 37, 63–67, 70–72, 76, 86, 88, 95, 97, 107, 109, **115–19**, 120–24, 136
Tanit, 59, **61–66**, 69, 72, 86, 88, 92, 95, 97 n. 23, 101, 113, 117, 119
Tharros (Sardinia), 35, 55, 95
thrones; empty thrones, 19, 30, 34, 51, 57, 59, 60, 62, 69, 72–73, 76–78, 80, 86, 89–92, 101, 103, **109–15**, 117–18, 121, 124, 127, 132–34, 137, 139. *See also* Shrines; stele-shrines
Tyre, 4, 8, 10–11, 13–15, 17–19, 44, 46–47, 52, 54, 61, 65–75, 78–79, 83–86, 89, 92–93, 96–97, 100–101, 104–05, 107–08, 113–14, 120, 126, 135, 138–39, 143
Ugarit, 13, 18, 48, 51, 54, 80–81, 84, 108–09, 138
Winckelmann, Johann Joachim, 37–38
Yehawmilk; Yehawmilk Stele, 15, **57–59**
Zeus, 75–76, 133–34

Ancient Sources

Hebrew Bible/ Old Testament

Genesis
- 10:15–19 — 126 n. 31
- 49:13 — 126 n. 31

Exodus
- 20:2–5 — 1–2, 131
- 23:24 — 128
- 34:13 — 128

Leviticus
- 26:1 — 128

Deuteronomy
- 4:15–20 — 132 n. 34
- 5:6–9 — 131
- 7:5 — 128
- 12:3 — 128
- 16:22 — 128

1 Samuel
- 28 — 84

2 Samuel
- 5 — 126 n. 31
- 5:11–12 — 10, 127

1 Kings
- 5:1–12 — 127
- 6:23–36 — 126
- 7:13–14 — 10
- 9:11–12 — 10
- 16 — 10
- 17–19 — 126 n. 31
- 21 — 126 n. 31
- 22:39 — 126

2 Kings
- 9 — 126 n. 31
- 10 — 126

Isaiah
- 23 — 10, 126 n. 31
- 44:9 — 27
- 44:9–20 — 26

Jeremiah
- 10:1–16 — 26
- 10:2 — 27

Ezekiel
- 26–28 — 10, 126 n. 31, 138
- 26:11 — 78
- 28:2 — 18, 138
- 28:16 — 78

Amos
- 1:9–10 — 126 n. 31
- 3:15 — 126
- 6:4 — 126

Ancient Near Eastern Texts

- Ashurbanipal Annals — 46
- Azatiwada Inscription — 15
- Carthage inscriptions — 62–63
- Eshmunazar Inscription — 137
- Karatepe Inscription — 45–46
- Kulamuwa Inscription — 15, 116
- Pyrgi Inscription — 17, 45
- Shipitbaal Inscription — 15
- Sippar tablet — 121
- Yehawmilk Inscription — 15

Ancient Jewish Writers

Josephus
Against Apion
1.116–120   126
1.117–118   74–75

Jewish Antiquities
8.146–148   17

Philo of Byblos, *Phoenician History*
14–15

Greco-Roman Literature

Diodorus Siculus, *Library of History*
20.14.5–7   47, 71–72 n. 5

Herodian, *History of the Empire*
3.4–5   75–76

Herodotus, *Histories*
2.66   78

Homer, *Odyssey*
14.300   10
15.388–484   10

Lucian of Samosota, *De Dea Syria*
Paragraphs 33–35   76–77

Nonnus, *Dionysiaca*
40.311–505   73–74

Silius Italicus, *Punica*
3.30–31   7, 74
5.5   74

Modern Authors

Álvarez Martí-Aguilar, Manuel, 17, 67–69, 73, 137
Amadasi Guzzo, Maria Giulia, 62, 64 n. 40, 68
Anderson, William P., 11
Assmann, Jan, 124, 132
Aubet, María Eugenia, 8, 10–11, 13–14, 16–18, 48, 59, 65, 73, 90, 103, 120
Azize, Joseph, 78, 124, 137
Bahrani, Zainab, 22–25
Bardill, Jonathan, 75
Bartoloni, Piero, 29, 61, 89, 92, 95, 97–98, 108, 112–13
Bénichou-Safar, Hélène, 29–30, 61, 89 n. 19, 90–91, 99, 108
Berlejung, Anjelika, 26–27, 33
Bertrandy, François, 63, 97 n. 22
Betlyon, John W., 51, 57
Bijovski, Gabriella, 73
Bikai, Patricia M., 11, 13–14
Bisi, Anna M., 42 n. 17, 47–48, 62, 68, 70 n. 3, 83 n. 15, 84, 95, 97 n. 23, 99, 102, 108–09
Blakolmer, Fritz, 31, 133
Bloch-Smith, Elizabeth, 17, 57, 83, 128
Boardman, John, 6, 42 n. 18, 48, 51, 55, 117
Bonnet, Corinne, 16–17, 52, 54–55, 57 n. 25, 68, 73 n. 7, 74, 78, 93, 136
Brentschneider, Joachim, 101, 108
Briquel-Chatonnet, François, 18, 127
Brown, Shelby, 42–43, 61–65, 89 n. 19, 93, 95, 97–98, 107, 117
Camille, Michael, 22–23

Cancik, Hubert, 31
Chiarenza, Nicola, 60–62
Chipiez, Charles, 41
Ciafaloni, D., 42 n. 17, 57 n. 25
Clifford, Richard J., 16, 46
Collins, Billie Jean, 24–25, 33, 79 n. 10, 81–82
Cornelius, Izak, 39, 57, 123–24
Crawford, Cory D., 23 n. 4, 24
Culican, William, 40, 48, 51–52, 54–55, 57, 63, 70, 72, 93, 97, 101 n. 24, 103–05, 108–9, 111, 112 n. 25, 126
D'Andrea, Bruno, 61 n. 28, 86, 102
Darby, Erin, 48, 127, 129
Dayagi-Mendels, Michael, 101 n. 24, 103–5
de Hulster, Izaak J., 79 n. 10, 127
Deleuze, Gilles, 23
Dick, Michael B., 25–27
Dietler, Michael, 16, 133, 137
Doak, Brian R., 84, 88, 129, 133
Döllinger, J. J. I., 69, 141
D'Orazio, Massimo, 75–76, 114 n. 28
Doumet-Serhal, Claude, 14, 18–19
Dunand, Maurice, 19, 52 n. 22, 54, 112, 118
Elayi, Josette, and Alain Gérard Elayi, 16, 50, 137
Elkins, James, 21–22
Evans, Carl D., 125 n. 30, 132
Feder, Yitzhaq, 132
Feldman, Marian H., 42–43
Fletcher, Richard N., 120
Frankfort, Henri, 41, 124

180

Frankenstein, Susan, 120
Frazer, James G., 36
Freedberg, David, 23, 29, 31, 69 n. 2, 135
Gaifman, Milette, 4, 27–28, 31 n. 12, 32–34, 36–38, 76–77, 79–80, 99–100, 132–34
Gal, Susan, 100
Garbati, Giuseppe, 69
Garfinkel, Yosef, 103, 128, 129, 130
Gladigow, Burkhard, 30–32, 34
Goodrich, Peter, 39
Gordon, Richard, 31, 98
Goud, Johan, 39
Green, Alberto R. W., 127
Gubel, Eric, 13–14, 42–44, 47–55, 57, 60, 93 n. 21, 97, 101 n. 24, 105, 111–12, 114, 126
Gunter, Ann C., 16, 43
Hackett, Jo Ann, 11, 13
Hallo, William W., 45–46
Hendel, Ronald S., 125 n. 30, 127, 132, 139
Herring, Stephen L., 23 n. 5, 24
Hirt, Alfred, 73
Irvine, Judith, 100
Jacobsen, Thorkild, 25–26
Karageorghis, Vassos, 47, 71, 105–6
Katz, Maya B., 37
Keel, Othmar, 55, 102, 125 n. 30, 127–31, 136
Khalifeh, Issam Ali, 14, 19
Kletter, Raz, 48, 127
Knapp, A. Bernard, 16
Krings, Véronique, 15–16, 42 n. 17
Kristensen, Troels M., 31
Lambert, Wilfred G., 25, 115
LaRocca-Pitts, Elizabeth, 82, 128
Lévi-Strauss, Claude, 102
Lewis, Theodore J., 39, 45, 81, 125 n. 30, 127–28, 132 n. 34
Lipiński, Edward, 13, 18, 52 n. 22, 71, 85, 103, 116, 139

Liverani, Mario, 127
López-Ruiz, Carolina, 8 n. 1, 10, 14–16, 62 n. 29, 82, 133,
Machinist, Peter, 24, 121, 136
Marín Ceballos, María Cruz Marin, 59, 68–69, 74
Marion, Jean-Luc, 24
Markoe, Glenn E., 11, 14, 16, 42–44, 47, 55, 57, 71, 124, 126
Massa, Aldo, 38
May, Natalie Naomi, 31–32, 124
Mazar, Amihai, 126
McCarter, P. Kyle, 13, 133
Mettinger, Tryggve N. D., 4, 26, 32–34, 36 n. 15, 45–47, 67, 71–76, 78–79, 82, 92, 101 n. 24, 113–14, 117, 119, 120, 122, 124–25, 128, 131–32, 136, 142
Metzger, Martin, 101 n. 24, 104–8, 111
Metzler, Dieter, 31
Michel, Patrick, 79 n. 10, 82
Mitchell, W. J. T., 22–23, 37
Moscati, Sabatino, 42–43, 47, 62, 70, 83 n. 15, 84, 88, 93, 95, 97, 135
Nam, Roger, 126
Naster, Paul, 73
Negbi, Ora, 48, 113
Niehr, Herbert, 115, 138
Núñez Calvo, Francisco Jesús, 11
Nunn, Astrid, 24, 48, 71, 99, 112–13, 122
Onnis, Francesca, 43
Ornan, Tallay, 24, 57, 105, 115–17, 120–23, 136, 138–39
Pappa, Eleftheria, 16, 89 n. 19, 120
Pardee, Dennis, 83, 138
Patrich, Joseph, 79 n. 10, 95, 112 n. 26, 119–20
Peckham, Brian, 13, 18, 38, 126 n. 31, 127
Perrot, Georges, 41
Picard, Colette, 97 n. 23, 117
Popko, Maciej, 82

Porter, Anne, 24–25, 82
Prag, Jonathan R., 8
Pritchard, James B., 11
Quinn, Josephine Crawley, 13, 61–62, 67, 81, 89 n. 19, 90, 95–97, 112, 137
Rawlinson, George, 69
Redford, Donald B., 124
Reyes, A. T., 16, 105
Ribichini, Sergio, 16–17, 46, 92
Röllig, Wolfgang, 13, 45–46
Rollston, Christopher, 11, 13, 116
Sader, Hélène, 11, 63, 65–66, 68, 79 n. 10, 83–89, 95, 101 n. 24, 108, 112, 119
San Nicolas, María Pilar, 59
Sanders, Seth L., 83
Sass, Benjamin, 125 n. 30, 136
Saur, Markus, 78
Schmidt, Brian B., 31, 84, 125 n. 30, 127
Schreiber, Nicola, 11
Seidl, Ursula, 122–23
Seyrig, Henri, 114, 117, 142
Slanksi, Kathryn E., 122
Smith, Jonathan Z., 18, 31, 36, 102
Smith, Mark S., 18, 24, 27
Smith, William Robertson, 36–37, 82, 97, 141
Sommer, Benjamin D., 79, 125 n. 30, 128
Sommer, Michael, 76,
Soyez, Brigette (Servais-), 12, 80, 86, 112 n. 26, 117–18

Stager, Lawrence E., 62, 64, 108
Steele, Philippa M., 16, 44
Stewart, Peter, 33, 75, 79
Stewart, Susan, 102
Stieglitz, Robert R., 13
Stockton, Eugene, 38, 70, 101 n. 24, 108, 112 n. 26
Stucky, Rolf A., 112 n. 25
Suriano, Matthew J., 83
Suter, Claudia E., 47, 126
Taylor, J. Glen, 129, 137
Turcan, Robert, 75
Tylor, Edward B., 36
Uberti, Maria Luisa, 42 n. 17, 83 n. 15
Uehlinger, Christoph, 55, 102, 125 n. 30, 127–31, 136
van der Toorn, Karel, 128
van Dommelen, Peter, 59, 62, 67
Van Seters, John, 74 n. 8
Vella, Nicholas, 13, 67
Walker, Christopher, 26–27
Welten, Ruud, 39
Winter, Irene J., 10–11, 43, 54 124, 139
Woods, Christopher E., 26, 121–22
Wunn, Ina, 24
Xella, Paolo, 19, 62
Yasur-Landau, Assaf, 54 n. 23
Yon, Marguerite, 109
Younger, K. Lawson, 45–46
Zevit, Ziony, 70 n. 10, 101 n. 24, 102–4, 125 n. 30, 128